THE ROUGH GUIDE to

CULT FOOTBALL

Credits

Editors: Andrew Lockett and Tom Cabot
Layout: Tom Cabot
Picture research: Andrew Lockett and Tom Cabot
Proofreading: Jason Freeman
Production: Rebecca Short

Rough Guides Reference
Editors: Kate Berens, Peter Buckley, Tom Cabot, Tracy Hopkins, Matthew Milton, Joe Staines, Ruth Tidball
Director: Andrew Lockett

Publishing Information

This edition published September 2010 by
Rough Guides Ltd, 80 Strand, London WC2R 0RL
345 Hudson St, 4th Floor, New York 10014, USA
Email: mail@roughguides.com

First edition published 2003 edited by Paul Simpson, Robert Jeffrey and Nick Moore of Haymarket Publishing for Rough Guides Ltd.

Distributed by the Penguin Group:
Penguin Books Ltd, 80 Strand, London WC2R 0RL
Penguin Putnam, Inc., 375 Hudson Street, NY 10014, USA
Penguin Group (Australia), 250 Camberwell Road, Camberwell, Victoria 3124, Australia
Penguin Books Canada Ltd, 10 Alcorn Avenue, Toronto, Ontario, Canada M4V 1E4
Penguin Group (New Zealand), Cnr Rosedale and Airborne Roads, Albany, Auckland, New Zealand

Printed in Singapore by Toppan Security Printing Pte. Ltd.

296 pages

A catalogue record for this book is available from the British Library
ISBN 13: 978-1-84836542-1

1 3 5 7 9 8 6 4 2

Picture Credits

The Publishers have made every effort to identify correctly the rights holders in respect of all images used for this book. If despite these efforts any attribution is absent or incorrect, the Publishers will correct this error once it has been brought to their attention in a subsequent reprint.

Colour Section: Mirrorpix – 1 (top & bottom), 2: Offside Photography – 3 (top & bottom), 5 (top & bottom), 6 (top & bottom), 7 (all), 8, 9 (top & bottom), 10, 11 (top & bottom) 12, 13 (top), 14 (top & bottom), 15, 16 (top): Press Association – 4, 13 (bottom), 16 (bottom).
Text: Mirrorpix – 130, 131, 167: Offside Photography – 45, 67, 96, 116, 120, 145, 245, 247: Press Association – 1, 11, 17, 25, 32, 38, 50, 59, 87, 92, 105, 113, 141, 156, 162, 222–3, 229, 234–5: Ronald Grant Archive – 179.
Cover: (outside) ActionImages; (inside front) Offside Photography; (inside back) Press Association.

THE ROUGH GUIDE to
CULT FOOTBALL

New edition
edited by Andy Mitten

With contributions by Joe Ganley, Ian Hawkey,
Graham Hunter, Louis Massarella, Sean Mahoney, Mark O'Brien,
David Parkinson, Ronald Reng, Craig Richard,
Martin Tarbuck, Joyce Woolridge

www.roughguides.com

About the Editor

Andy Mitten started the fanzine *United We Stand* (which he still edits) aged fifteen in 1989. A regular writer for *FourFourTwo*, his other credits include *The Independent*, *Sport*, *The National* (Abu Dhabi), *Manchester Evening News*, *The Guardian* and *GQ*. He has written or co-written ten books including the critically acclaimed *Glory Glory!* and *We're the Famous Man United*. Manchester born and red, Andy divides his time between M16 and Barcelona.

About the Contributors

Joe Ganley is a match-going Mancunian Manchester United fan who writes for United We Stand. **Ian Hawkey** is international football correspondent of *The Sunday Times* and author of *Feet of the Chameleon: The Story of African Football*, winner of the 2009 British Football Book The Year award. **Graham Hunter** is the former number one football writer at *The Daily Mail* and current Spanish football correspondent for Sky Sports. He also works for UEFA. **Sean Mahoney** is a freelance publisher and author who supports his local squad Red Bull New York, though the Addicks hold a special place in his heart. **Louis Massarella** is the features editor of *FourFourTwo* magazine. He has also contributed to *The Guardian*, *Spin* magazine and written four football books. **Mark O'Brien** is editor of the When Skies Are Grey website and author of *What's Our Name? Everton!* and *The Road to Rotterdam*. **David Parkinson** is a koppite and Subbuteo fanatic who can't resist awful footie films. **Ronald Reng** is the Spanish football correspondent for *Suddeutsche Zeitung* Germany's best newspaper. His book *The Keeper of Dreams* about Barnsley's German goalkeeper Lars Leese was described by Frank Keating in *The Guardian* as "by far the best soccer biography of the year". **Craig Richard** is a nom de plume of a football book fanatic and latter-day *PES* addict. **Martin Tarbuck** is the editor of Wigan Athletic's brilliant *Mudhutter Football Express*. The football writer **Joyce Woolridge** has a PhD in British football history and studies at the University of Old Trafford.

Acknowledgements

Andy Mitten would like to thank his family and his wife Ba for her love and support. The Publishers would like to thank Simon Kantor and Paul Simpson of Haymarket Publishing, for enabling this new edition, and all the original team. Thanks too to Mark Leech of Offside Photography for much assistance on pictures, and Dunstan Bentley, Kate Berens, Mark Ellingham, Jason Freeman, James Smart, Joe Staines, Phil Wickham, and the Wednesday bagel boys (you know who you are) and sundry others, for specialist advice on key topics and trivia such as which fat Maradona picture to include.

Contents

Foreword

The Italian coach was blocking us in. We couldn't move away from the stadium where Brazil had just played Italy in Barcelona. People still say it was the greatest ever game in a World Cup finals. I was the captain of Brazil, the favourites. We had an exhilarating side with players like Falcao, Eder and Zico – who remains the best I ever played with. We're still friends. I was at the carnival in São Paulo with him last night ... until nine o'clock this morning, actually. Junior was also with us – he's the best dancer.

Friends are important to me, money isn't. Poetry is important to me and I write my own, usually to read to the woman. I like women. I like to breed. I am 56 years old with six children and the youngest is three.

My younger brother Rai laughs at me. He was also the captain of Brazil, a World Cup winner in 1994. We were like the fathers of two hundred million Brazilians. Happy times, but fighting for democracy was just as important in my country. When I played for Corinthians, I started a democratic movement based on justice and fairness. We had a military government in Brazil in 1985. I was pleased when we won our fight for democracy.

But back to 1982. We had won our group games against Russia, Scotland and New Zealand.

We beat our old rivals Argentina 3–1. Pelé or Maradona, that's what people ask me. I played against the artist Maradona a few times and I was always on the winning side. Pelé, Cruyff, Maradona, Garrincha – they are the best ever. There are no players of that level now. I like your Paul Scholes, the boy with the red hair and the red shirt. He's good enough to play for Brazil, but he's not like Cruyff or the phenomenon Garrincha.

Italy were next and they'd beaten Argentina too. Whoever won went through to the semi-finals. We played in the Barcelona sun, not at giant Camp Nou, but the old Espanyol ground, with open stands so close to the pitch that we could smell the people. They were waiting for a big game, forty-four thousand souls crammed into the steep stands. People watched from nearby tower blocks.

Brazil v. Italy. I felt relaxed. I'd tried to stop smoking for the World Cup finals. I was a doctor – still am – and know that smoking is not good for anyone, not least a professional athlete. But I enjoyed it too much and still do. That's me.

Rossi scored for Italy. Five minutes. I equalized. Twelve minutes. He scored again, Rossi, 25 minutes. We were playing a man, not a country. We equalized, Falcao, 68 minutes. Rossi, yes him again, scored again after 74. We lost the game. Italy won the World Cup.

Some say that we were the greatest side never to win the World Cup. They tell us that to this day and talk more about us than my brother's side which won the tournament in 1994.

Our loss to Italy was not simple. It was like achieving the conquest of the most beautiful woman in the world, but then being unable to do what matters with her. Failing when it really matters. But it can happen, in life and in sport.

People remember our team because we lost, not won. Nobody tried to copy Italy, the pragmatic team which won the World Cup. The beautiful team, with the art and creativity, lost. The team with the perfect emotional, physical and technical balance lost.

And the Italian team coach blocked us in outside the tight stadium in Barcelona. All we wanted to do was go home. We had to wait for the celebrating Italians to board their bus in their own time. Our bus was quiet. And then a player shouted: "Don't worry everyone. It's all a dream. The game is actually tomorrow!" And part of me believed it. We wanted to believe it. Because people want to believe and to dream, especially in football.

Enjoy the book. It was an honour to be asked to do the foreword. Believe and dream.

The Brazilian Socrates,
São Paulo, February 2010

"Cop this": Vinnie Jones as Widow Twanky.

"Ref! I didn't even touch him!": Vinnie Jones hacks down the team mascot.

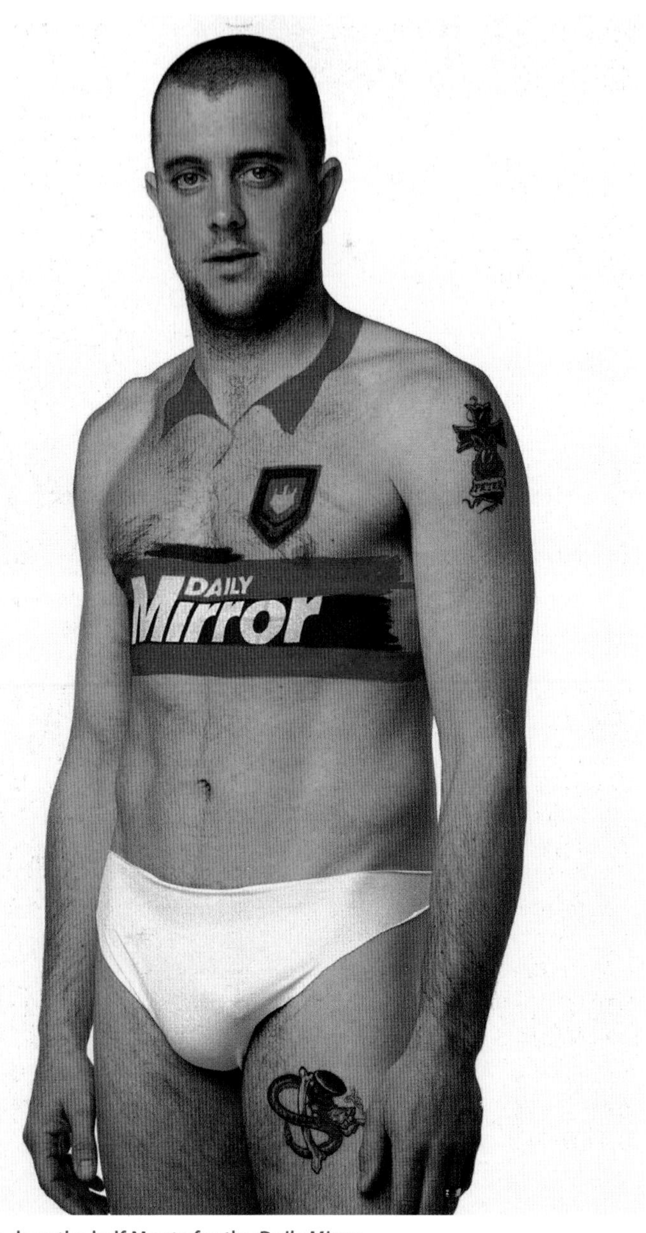

Julian Dicks does the half Monty for the *Daily Mirror*.

The acceptable face of fandom. A St John's ambulance man seems very pleased to see his hero Bobby Charlton up close and personal, October 1968.

Unimpressed. Teddy Sheringham's goal celebration is not to every Chelsea fan's liking in an FA Cup fixture of January 1998.

Guus Hiddink shows off some groovy dance moves with a cast member from the musical *Sister Act*.

Celebrating football the British way with beer and whisky at an "Old Firm" derby, 1961.

Continental artistry unveiled at a Real Madrid v. Real Mallorca tie, 2007.

FA Cup magic. The rooftops of Exeter loom over Xavier and Hutchinson of Everton as they take on underdogs Exeter City. Gary Alexander contests the header.

Old style facilities. Terraces at Colchester United's Layer Road ground in 2007. The team switched to the new Colchester Homes Community Stadium in 2008.

It could only be the 1990s! David Seaman, England v. Bulgaria, 1996.

Sponsor NOBO gets pride of place on Alan Gatting's 1991 Brighton shirt.

Stockport County celebrate a victory in the fashion stakes and in an FA Cup match against QPR. It was indeed 1994.

Hardman Ron "Chopper" Harris still does not look like someone to mess with, here waving to fans at a Chelsea home game in 2005.

Assistant referee Roy Burton appreciated by an affectionate Paolo Di Canio, in 2000.

Manchester United end up on top of Wolves as usual. Wayne Rooney and Paul Ince in 2006.

Chelsea fans prepare for the 1970 FA Cup final against Leeds. Not an oligarch in sight.

Team from another planet. Leeds United strike an artistic pose in 1975, not long after Brian Clough's controversial regime ended after 44 days on 12 September 1975.

European glamour. Behind the scenes at the Champions League, 2003. Players from AFC Ajax and AC Milan walk up the stairs to the pitch.

Premier league glamour. Alan Shearer leads his Newcastle team in 2001 on to the pitch as West Ham's Dr Martens stand remains a building site.

In the days before underpitch heating. Hamburger SV v. Bayern Munich in 1980. Jimmy Hartwig scores a goal past Hans Weiner in the snow.

Why would anyone want to consider a winter break? David Shipperly challenges Chris Simpkin with orange ball during Hull City v. Charlton Athletic, 1971.

Bolton v. Zenit St Petersberg, November 2005. Mexican Jared Borgetti and Russian Alexander Anyukov get a taste of English playing conditions.

Jimmy Bullard and Hull City team mates celebrate a 2009 goal, recreating manager Phil Brown's infamous team talk. Carlos Tevez of Manchester City looks on.

Spot the ball. Fourteen months before Sunderland's Darren Bent's infamous balloon goal against Liverpool, Andy Dawson hoofs a round object forward but which one?

Never the trimmest of figures, the "little fat chap" aka Hungarian football legend Ferenc Puskás in 1981.

Who Ate all the Pies? ... Paul Merson presumably. Ray Parlour shares in the punchline at an England v. Germany friendly in 2008.

Telenovella actress Andrea Del Boca can't quite take in the immensity of presence that is Argentinian legend Diego Maradona in 2004.

The Roots

How an English invention conquered the world …
and then the world conquered England

◀◀ Previous page: Preston North End, League and FA Cup winners 1888–89.

The Roots

"For as much as there is great noise in the city caused by hustling over large balls, from which many evils may arise, which God forbid, we command and forbid on behalf of the King, on pain of imprisonment, such games to be used"

Edward II bans football in London in 1314

ZUQIU FEVER AND OTHER FALSE STARTS

When England hosted the European Championship finals in 1996, the Football Association claimed that Britain had "given football to the world". This is at best an exaggeration; at worst, a lie. True, moustachioed young Victorian graduates may have exported the game to many corners of the Empire, but often all they did was present the locals with an organized set of rules for what had hitherto been a random kickaround.

Many races have strong claims to being the first to put boot to leather, yet none is definitive. The earliest is probably the Chinese: ancient documents dated at around 2500 BC allude to kicking or handling a spherical object through holes in a net stretched between two poles. The game was used to keep soldiers fit between battles. By 350 BC, this had become *zuqiu*, still the Chinese word for football. Four hundred years later, *zuqiu* had become **tsu chu**, with a leather ball filled with feathers and hair being hoofed between bamboo poles.

But the Italians can also lay claim to the game. **Harpastum**, practised by the Roman armies of around AD 200, bore certain similarities to the modern game in its rules (the field of play, the shape of the ball), but the action was a hybrid of rugby and American football with scrums and crude lineouts when players were tackled. Still, *harpastum* may have influenced football, as records show soldiers undertaking an official world tour, whipping conquered nations in a manner the English would fail to repeat in modern times. History doesn't record, however, if the Romans also popularized the sweeper system, the theatrical dive and the Alice band.

"Football is all very well as a game for rough girls, but it is hardly suitable for delicate boys."
Oscar Wilde

Across the globe, the **Aztecs** were crossing football with the Eton Wall game, forcing the ball through makeshift portholes. Their major contribution to football history was to

> **"... I debarre all rough and violent exercises as the foot-ball, meeter for lameing than making able the users thereof."**
> James I of Scotland

tie the leather together with laces, a practice which lasted well into the twentieth century. Some form of the game is also recorded before the Middle Ages in Egypt, Greece, Japan, Scandinavia and Central America.

It would be nice, at this point, to imagine the English developing the game around a common set of rules over a civilized cup of tea. Sadly, that didn't happen until the 1800s, and for most of the previous seven hundred years football was synonymous with riot, mayhem and official disapproval.

Entire towns chased balls – probably imported by the Romans or the Vikings – through streets, people's homes and across fields with little or no ultimate aim. What took place was more steeplechase than football match, with staying power and brute force emphazised over individual skill and proper teams. Matches in the City of London became popular, while games held in Derbyshire, Nottinghamshire and Surrey are still celebrated and re-enacted today.

It was such abandon that first brought "futeball" into confrontation with the authorities. Deaths were not uncommon, and the widespread disorder triggered when hundreds of young men rampaged through urban areas earned the wrath of the Church – clashes were often staged on the Sabbath. In 1314, **Edward II** became the first monarch to ban the game officially, citing "great uproar in the city [London], caused by hustling over large balls ... from which many evils perchance may arise." Edward III ordered footballers to take up archery. In Scotland (where games between married and unmarried women took place in several towns) James I proclaimed in 1424: "From this court I debarre all rough and violent exercises, as the foot-ball, meeter [better] for lameing than making able the users thereof." Other monarchs issued stricter edicts against the game (although **Charles II** – if not a convert – did attend a match in 1681). Local councils also banned it in almost every significant town in Britain. Football would be little more than a historical footnote had public schools not popularized it – though they did it for their own gain, not out of altruism.

The likes of Harrow, Eton, Rugby and Blackheath quickly recognized that football fostered team spirit, promoted physical fitness and was remarkably popular among the pupils. But the lack of a unifying code made inter-school competitions impossible and allowed blatant foul play to go unpunished. Even "gentlemen" footballers deemed it acceptable to hack at ankles, punch off the ball or shove viciously, while scorelines were often forgotten amid mass brawls.

Gradually two factions developed: those who favoured handling the ball and those who championed dribbling. Then, in the 1840s, a pair of Cambridge housemasters defined rules for use within the university, cutting down on hacking and handling. As graduates weaned on the game spread into positions of influence across the country, new clubs were formed playing a more unified code.

In 1863, a group of Cambridge graduates who were now masters at some of the top public schools met to decide matters once and for all. They drew up what were known colloquially as the Cambridge Rules, and in October that year, representatives of various schools and clubs in the London area endorsed the rules and formed the Football Association – the basis of the modern-day body.

The Cambridge Rules were still some way from the spectacle we enjoy today. Handling was still allowed in certain circumstances (it was soon banned, though many players had to wear gloves to remind them not to handle). Offside laws were rudimentary, and there was no set pitch size. Hacking, however, was finally consigned to the dustbin, and further refinements over the next twenty years would regulate kit, referees and numbers of players. **Blackheath**, a founding member of the FA was the notable dissenter in the whole debate and left the Association within months to embrace a handling code which later became rugby. Though egg-chasers claim the game evolved directly from a pupil at Rugby School picking up the ball and running during a match, this is almost certainly Victorian romanticism.

The organization of the game of the masses had very little to do with the

Where It All Began

Some of the world's most famous clubs started in very humble circumstances.

Everton (1878) Formed by Methodist churchgoers with the blessing of their Reverend.

Liverpool (1892) When the Everton side moved to a new ground, their old landlord decided to start his own team.

Manchester United (1878) Railway workers founded Newton Heath; the name changed in 1902.

Arsenal (1886) A works team for employees of a munitions factory; began in south London but soon moved north.

West Ham United (1895) Known as the Irons, as they began life at an ironworks

AC Milan (1899) Started by expat Alfred Edwards, who insisted on the English spelling of the city.

Inter Milan (1908) An Italian breakaway from Milan: Inter players wanted more free-flowing, less rigid play.

Benfica (1904) Essentially an import business, the Portuguese giants shipped in Africans to work in local factories and play football.

Dynamo Moscow (1887) An entrepreneur's ad in *The Times* asked for engineers who could also play the game to emigrate.

River Plate (1901) English residents in Buenos Aires founded this most Argentinian of clubs.

masses at this point. The strong sense of civic responsibility felt by young do-gooding public-school toffs left them feeling compelled to share the game with the less fortunate when they became clergymen, industrialists or teachers.

The 1850 Factory Act, meanwhile, meant that most workers now had Saturday afternoons off, and given the state of urban housing at the time, they were probably happier kicking a ball around than sitting at home. The government was happy, too. Despite its unruly history, football was seen as less harmful to the social order than drinking, voting or joining a trade union. Early organized competitions were still dominated by the southern schools or teams of former public schoolboys, but the game's popularity spread in northern industrial areas and in Scotland. Disgruntled, many public schools turned their back on their creation and returned to rugby.

Many of the best-known British clubs can be traced back to various good causes of the 1860s and 1870s, such as churches, factories, social welfare projects and even cricket teams. Notts County, generally regarded as the oldest club still playing professionally, were formed in 1862, although Sheffield, who began life in 1860, were the first northern, working-class side affiliated to the FA and still play in the lower echelons of non-league today. In 1871, player and journalist **Charles**

They Rewrote the Rules

Sam Chedgzoy In 1924 the Everton star dribbled all the way from the corner flag to score, upsetting the Spurs defence and prompting the FA to decree that a player taking a corner could only touch the ball once before another player touched it.

Bill McCracken The Newcastle defender's extraordinary success at managing the offside trap led to thirty free kicks in one match and a pitch invasion. In 1925, the law was changed to favour strikers who would, henceforth, be onside if there were two opponents between them and the goal.

William Gunn So adept was Notts County and England footballer – and England cricketer – William Gunn at the one-handed throw that, after Scottish protests over a match in 1882 where both sides threw the ball in whatever manner they liked, the rules were changed to ban single-handed throwing.

Hendry The partially monikered Notts County defender stuck his hand out to stop Stoke equalizing in a game in 1891. Notts County massed on the line to block the free-kick and the FA felt it had no option but to follow Ireland's example and introduce the penalty-kick.

Leigh Richmond Roose The legendarily eccentric keeper ruined the game for goalies, who had been allowed to handle the ball outside the eighteen-yard-box – until Roose carried the ball in his hands to the other end of the field.

Alcock persuaded fifteen English teams, and the leading Scottish side, Queen's Park, to take part in the first FA Cup, won at Kennington Oval in London by The Wanderers, who beat the Royal Engineers 1–0.

Such competition and the arrival, in the form of railways, of cheap mass transportation, increased interest in the game and turned it into a spectator sport, defining geographical allegiances and favoured players. Although only two thousand saw the first final of football's oldest competition, by the turn of the century all manner of matches were attracting six-figure crowds.

Media interest was piqued by the first official international fixture between England and Scotland at the West of Scotland cricket ground in Glasgow a year later. It was a goalless draw, but the event soon became an annual one. The Scots were briefly dominant against their neighbours as they realized the English dribbling game was fundamentally flawed and intuitively sensed they might make headway if they actually passed the ball occasionally.

By 1888, there were twelve clubs of sufficient size and stature to form the world's first league, won by Preston North End, who also took the FA Cup in the same year to complete the first Double. Professionalism was by now widespread, after the FA sanctioned the payment of "expenses" to key players. Cash transfers followed, and there was a furore when **Alf Common** left Sunderland for Middlesbrough in 1905 for £1000, the first-ever four-figure fee.

FOOTBALL GOES GLOBAL

Meanwhile, the game was being exported successfully by British traders, the armed forces and colonials. Australia and the US preferred their own handling-based derivatives of the game but by the 1920s, football was known in every country on the planet and played enthusiastically in most. The fact that the British were so zealous in foisting their creation on the rest of the world would, of course, come back to haunt them.

But the early pioneers knew only the joy of introducing the natives to the first organized, enjoyable and – crucially – cheap team game they had been able to take part in. All over the globe, locals set up clubs, formed leagues and introduced a degree of professionalism along British lines.

Europe was conquered first. In the 1890s, football spread through Scandinavia, Holland, Germany and beyond. Italy dropped its foot-based game, *calcio*, when introduced to football, and Brits helped form the great Turin side, Juventus, in 1897. Barcelona, meanwhile, began life after a game against the Royal Navy.

Argentina had been hooked on football since the British built railways there in the 1860s. The large expat community soon spread the word across the continent, notably to the first world champions Uruguay and, later, Brazil, where the first recorded match also involved the British Navy (tours by teams like **Chelsea** and, er, **Exeter City** helped popularize the beautiful game in Rio and Saõ Paolo). Africa and Asia boasted pockets of footballing activity in the nineteenth century but development proved slower.

In 1904 FIFA was formed in Paris as an overall regulatory body for the many international sides and matches that had by now sprung up. England resisted joining for a year and was still stubbornly refusing to play ball by the time the first World Cup was staged in Uruguay in 1930. Romania's King Carol II picked his own World Cup squad and the hosts paid the travelling expenses of the twelve nations involved, but the lengthy sea voyages did for most of the visitors. Uruguay triumphed with a 4–2 victory over Argentina.

The fourth World Cup in Brazil in 1950 was England's first and led to one of the greatest international shocks of all-time when the USA beat a team containing the likes of **Tom Finney** and **Billy Wright** 1–0. The result was treated as a fluke back home, but three years later the humiliation deepened when Hungary's "Magical Magyars" arrived at Wembley. Led by **Ferenc Puskás**, Hungary demolished their hosts 6–3, the Magyars' mastery so complete their play seemed, to the marooned British defence, like a form of sorcery. The result, England's first home defeat to a

Star Players

King Charles II Given a demonstration of the Italian football hybrid, *calcio*, at his court and thus gave his blessing to the game, becoming the first monarch for centuries not to immediately ban football.

Oliver Cromwell Was said to have been a "boisterous" player at university, but didn't approve of the working classes indulging in the game, flogging boys caught playing in the street. Ironically, after his (posthumous) execution, his head is said to have been used for a kickaround in Westminster Hall.

Pope John Paul II An accomplished goalkeeper during his youth, yet as a childhood friend recalled: "A couple of minutes before four o'clock, he would just leave the field. Everyone would be angry, but he would just say: 'I'm sorry, but I promised my father I would be home.'"

Julio Iglesias A goalkeeper in Real Madrid's youth team, he was forced to give up football in 1963 after a car crash. While in hospital, a nurse lent him a guitar, thus sparking a musical career.

Albert Camus His time between the sticks for the Algiers University team gave the legendary philosopher and novelist plenty of time to contemplate the nature of existence. "Everything I know about morality, I owe to football", he once wrote.

Rod Stewart Likes to boast of his time on Brentford's books, but his talent must be in question if he couldn't make the grade at Griffin Park.

Sylvester Stallone World champion boxer, celebrated war hero and – without even trying – the greatest goalkeeper in the world during *Escape to Victory*.

side from outside the British Isles (Ireland had beaten England in 1948 at Goodison Park), symbolized football's rapid development overseas. Television had brought a new audience of armchair spectators in European nations and with it a greater desire for foreign competition.

> **"At that time we had forwards and defenders doing separate jobs, but he did everything."**
> Matt Busby on Alfredo di Stéfano

Top players had begun to move not just between clubs but also countries, and the rise of the "star player" was imminent. **George Best** is usually credited as the first footballing icon, a claim which ignores the fame of Denis "Brylcreem Boy" Compton but, in the 1950s, **Alfredo di Stéfano** of Spain and his Real team-mate Puskás were the real revolutionaries. Ability had been stifled by rigid tactics and shibboleths about the role of team-work – players like di Stéfano defied such categorization, forcing coaches to change their tactics.

Such talent was showcased with the advent of European competition in 1955. After Wolverhampton Wanderers had beaten Honved of Hungary in a floodlit friendly match in 1954, their manager Stan Cullis proclaimed them champions of the world. Prompted by **Gabriel Hanot**, editor of *L'Equipe*, the new European

Alfredo di Stéfano of Espanyol (right) greeting Ferenc Puskás (left), playing for di Stéfano's former club Real Madrid, before a match between the two teams, 17 September 1964. Real Madrid won 2–1.

Tactics or Tictacs: The Great Formations

In the beginning was the **"WM"**. Defenders lined up on the points of a W, attackers on the point of an M. The tactical formation, in which the centre half was reinvented as a "stopper", was prompted by the 1925 offside law which said an attacker could not be offside if two opponents were between him and the goal-line.

Before World War II, tactical innovations in British football were about as rare as an unblinkered FA official. Yet abroad, exiled Scottish coach **Jimmy Hogan** was helping the Austrians perfect a short, passing game which would be known as the **Vienna School** and would give the Austrians the best team in Europe in the 1930s – despite Italy's two World Cup victories.

In the 1950s, Tottenham manager Arthur Rowe caused great excitement – in Britain – with the "push and run" school in which short passes and bursts of speed were used to attack; the Vienna School with go-faster stripes. All conventional wisdom about tactics would be overturned by the Hungarian side of the 1950s, who played a precursor of total football in which centre-forwards came so deep they almost ended up down the pit. The speed of their positional changes and passing bewildered slow-footed opponents but had as much to do with the genius of the personnel (and the fact that they played for club and country together) as any revolution in tactics. Yet the Hungarian side still ran off the ball with more imagination than most present-day players.

football association, UEFA, put the boast to the test. Wolves weren't invited (they weren't champions) but even the might of Manchester United was no match for Real Madrid, as the Spaniards – inspired by di Stéfano – swept all before them. Madrid won the first five European Cups; their 7–3 win over Eintracht Frankfurt in Glasgow in 1960 is regarded as the greatest match ever played.

On the world stage, the idea that football could achieve the grace and beauty of an art no longer seemed utterly preposterous. Italy and West Germany had taken the World Cup to Europe after Uruguay's initial victory, but between 1958 and 1970 Brazil took the title three times with breathtaking skill – England's 1966 triumph on home soil, which interrupted the run, was a rare highlight for industry.

The 1970 Brazil side was almost as good as the Hungary team of the 1950s and boasted, in **Pelé**, the most complete talent the game has ever seen. Having finished top scorer in the 1958 tournament in Sweden aged just seventeen, he had blossomed into a footballing artist who seemed to embody his nation's sporting ethos – to play for sheer enjoyment (although he was not averse to the odd foul). Brazilian coaches prized attacking invention, forcing European tactics and techniques to play catch-up and, perhaps, provoking total football. Team-mates such

Brazil won the 1958 World Cup with a flowing **4–2–4** formation which should have ushered in a golden age of attacking football. As the Italians switched to *catenaccio* (the word means doorbolt), the **4–3–3** became a sterile defensive formation, although its pioneer, Helenio Herrera, always insisted it was an attractive system – if only the left backs could be bothered to join the attack in what today we might call overlapping full back mode. Still, *catenaccio* gave us the sweeper, the *libero*, which, to the English, still conjures up images of men with flat caps and cigarettes surgically attached to their lower lips trying to keep the roads clean. England won the 1966 World Cup with a wingless 4–3–3 formation but this soon fell into disrepute as the Germans and the Dutch dominated the 1970s with **total football**, which meant that any player could play anywhere; not a style you could play if your defenders were as mobile as **Steve Foster**.

Total football, like tank tops, fell out of fashion and the world fell back on **4–4–2** and 3–5–2 (4–3–2–1, **Terry Venables**' Christmas tree formation, lasted as long as a real Christmas tree does). Variations on the theme include the pressing game – Milan coach **Arrigo Saachi's** 4–4–2 but with added bite in the tackle further up the pitch, split strikers (or the striker in the hole – i.e. just behind the centre-forward), and **10–0–0**, the approved formation whenever a team gets a player sent off. If the term wing half can make a comeback, there's still hope for the revival of the **inside forward**, as rare these days as a good word for football agents. We haven't mentioned the **long ball game** for obvious reasons.

as **Didi**, **Rivelino** and **Garrincha** were sometimes unjustly overshadowed by Pelé's stardom but still take their place in the pantheon of greats.

By the time the next true superstar, **Diego Maradona**, was stealing the show as Argentina won the 1986 World Cup, the game had changed. Defenders resorted to ever more cynical fouls and the pressure to perform would tell on Maradona, who, by the time Italia '90 came around, would have a waistline to match that of Luciano Pavarotti, singer of the tournament theme. Maradona's fate mirrored the game's malaise, as off-the-field violence and hooliganism reached its nadir with the loss of 39 lives in the Heysel disaster of 1985.

UEFA's resulting indefinite ban on English clubs participating in European competitions should have been a turning point for the English game. Sadly it took the Hillsborough disaster and the subsequent Taylor report to shift the game to a more family-friendly footing with all-seated stadia in the top divisions and a range of anti-hooligan measures. As football in the UK welcomed more gentrified punters to fixtures, the women's game received a big boost with the staging of the first World Championship as amateur participation levels for girls began to climb. These were developments long overdue.

THE WOMEN'S GAME

Big Ron probably wouldn't last too long if he was thrown to the Millwall Lionesses, but he isn't alone in deriding women's football. The idea of the fairer sex playing it has long sparked curiosity, schoolboy sniggers and outright disgust.

Even in staid Victorian times, pioneers were getting girls into the game – and themselves into trouble. Nettie Honeyball took it upon herself to organize both a British Ladies' side and a North versus South exhibition game in London in 1894, "with the fixed resolve of proving to the world that women are not the 'ornamental and useless' creatures men have pictured." The 1890s saw something of a mini-boom for the ladies' game, but the large crowds were mostly flocking to see a "freak show". Meanwhile, doctors were encouraged to explain how football could harm the delicate female physique and even render players infertile.

In the 1920s, the Dick Kerr ladies' team came to national prominence – formed at a Preston factory of the same name as a means of raising money for charity, the team made a virtue of male distaste through aggressive poster campaigns and became something of success. A series of challenge matches against male sides culminated in over fifty thousand packing into Everton's Goodison Park to see them play, and they later undertook a US tour.

The FA didn't see the funny side – even though one player performed cartwheels when she scored – and in December 1921, ruled: "The Council feel impelled to express their strong opinion that the game of football is quite unsuitable for females. The Council request the clubs belonging to the Association to refuse the use of their grounds for such matches." Since almost every club, professional or amateur, has to belong to the FA or use FA-affiliated facilities, this edict starved the women's game of resources. As a direct result, however, the English Ladies FA was formed, matches were played on rugby pitches, and the women's game developed its own ethos and ideals. The Women's FA was formed in 1962, and had nearly two hundred member clubs by the time the FA finally deigned to recognize them in 1973.

Other European nations had embraced the game in the 1960s, with Italy boasting the world's first, short-lived, professional league and Scandinavian countries actively encouraging the game. Yet an unofficial World Cup held in Mexico in 1971 illustrated the difficulties still facing female players at the time – many players found themselves shooting at pink goals and being asked to wear hot pants and blouses.

> **"Women should be in the kitchen, the discotheque and the boutique, but not in football."**
> Ron Atkinson

FIFA woke up to the need for parity in the 1990s, staging the first official World Championship in 1991 and women's football became an Olympic sport in 1996. (England, incidentally, are just as consistently disappointing as their male counterparts, though in 2009 they won their first international

Marta – Best Player in the World. No Contest.

Debate if you will the merits of Lionel Messi, Cristiano Ronaldo or Wayne Rooney, the only uncontestable "best player in the world" accolade has to go to Brazilian Marta Vieira da Silva. At 5 feet 4 inches the ponytailed Marta is no Peter Crouch but her skills on the "deck" mean the long high ball would always be superfluous. Lazily labelled the female Pelé, her dribbling prowess and high technical level are actually much closer to that of compatriot Ronaldinho or fellow left-footer, Messi. Having won FIFA best player of the year every year from 2006 to 2009, she topped it off with a golden boot and best player of the tournament award at the 2007 women's World Cup. At club level she has played in Brazil, Sweden (a hotbed of the women's game) and the US (its commercial centre). A simultaneous move from Umeå IK to Los Angeles Sol along with clubmate Johanna Frisk triggered that staple speculation of female sports reporting, the rumoured lesbian relationship. Both players have denied it.

If Marta's looks matched her footballing talent she would be on every advertising billboard from Auckland to Alaska. As it is, you might better scrutinize her mesmerizing dribbles on YouTube – the Marseille turn is a particular favourite – and admire a technician at the top of her craft: the undisputed best player in the world.

trophy, the Cyprus Women's Cup.) Fulham became the first British club to run a full-time professional women's side, but when cost-cutting was needed, the idea was rapidly abandoned. Arsenal, the most consistently successful women's side in England, with a staggering 32 major trophies by 2009, are semi-professional. The best hope for the future lies in the US, where girls have picked up on the game faster than boys (without the inbuilt prejudices of the public school system, for example, it is not seen as a "male" sport) and the national team enjoys enthusiastic support. A 2008 survey demonstrated that the women's game continues to expand, with 26 million women and girls worldwide playing football, 4.1 million of them in affiliated clubs. New competitions attest to this popularity. 2010 sees the first FIFA Women's Club World Cup competition. Even so, the days when the sexes compete on a level playing field remain the stuff of sub-standard ITV drama series …

TROPHY BITTER: THE CUPS THAT TIME FORGOT

The ubiquity of football after Heysel and Hillsborough wasn't confined to the women's game. The opening up of television sports accelerated a trend seemingly unique to the UK of over-playing, still the best suspect for why injury-decimated English teams so often fail to perform in June World Cups after yet another match-crammed season. Too many fixtures, too many tournaments. This feature of the UK game is though as deeply rooted as the 4–4–2 and started much earlier, with some of the biggest crimes committed in respect of the lower leagues where rare trophies could be prized without fear of the big boys always spoiling the party.

In 1969 Swindon Town won the **League Cup** but, due to some obscure footballing bylaw, because they were in Division Three they weren't allowed to play in Europe. To prevent a mob of torch-wielding Wiltshiremen bearing down on Lancaster Gate and ritually sacrificing Bert Millichip, the FA hurriedly invented the **Anglo-Italian Cup** as a consolation prize – and in the process unleashed a barrage of extraneous football tournaments on the fans.

In the inaugural Anglo-Italian final, the Robins beat Roma 5–2 on aggregate, not a result we expect to see repeated any time soon. That said, Swindon returned to the final a year later and beat Napoli 3–0. Italian fans, enraged, started hurling their seats in the direction of John Trollope and his Swindon colleagues.

Newcastle and Blackpool were the only other clubs to bring the cup back to Blighty before it was left to swim with the fishes in 1975. It was, though, revived in the 1990s when, after another four seasons of games watched by minuscule crowds, Notts County added their name to the Anglo-Italian roll of honour.

> **"I just opened the trophy cabinet. Two Japanese soldiers fell out."**
> Tommy Docherty

By now, however, a mania for meaningless competitions had set in. In 1970 the **Watney Cup**, a pre-season festival of fun for the two top-scoring clubs from each division, was introduced. Innovations included – gasp! – penalty shoot-outs and an offside rule only applicable in the penalty box. Derby County thrashed Manchester United 4–1 in the first final, each player presumably receiving a commemorative Party Seven with their medal. The barrel was finally drained after four seasons, with Stoke City the last winners.

Texaco clambered on the bandwagon in 1971, gathering together teams from England, Scotland and Ireland who weren't otherwise heading for Europe. Wolves defeated Hibs to become the first winners of the **Texaco Cup**, taking home a set of tumblers, a *Motoring Atlas of Great Britain* and a hundredweight of Green Shield stamps. The Irish clubs then pulled out due to the Troubles and, in 1976, it was replaced by the **Anglo-Scottish Cup**. Like its forerunner, it never managed to get itself taken very seriously, though Newcastle were once kicked out for scandalously fielding a weakened team against Ayr United. It lasted five seasons before the Scots took their ball home in a huff at the declining status of the English teams – they probably had a point: the ultimate final was a mouthwatering affair that saw Chesterfield beat Notts County.

The competition lumbered on as a contest for lower-division English clubs as the **Football League Group Cup** (1981–82) and then the **Football League**

Trophy (1982–83) – heady days for Grimsby and Wimbledon, the two winners. Then, semi-interestingly, it was relaunched again as the **Associate Members' Cup**, a competition still very much with us, despite having undergone more makeovers in the 1980s and 1990s than Madonna – incarnations include the **Freight Rover Trophy**, the **Sherpa Van Trophy**, the **Leyland DAF Cup**, the **Autoglass Trophy**, the **Auto Windscreens Shield** and now the **LDV Vans Trophy**. Do we detect a theme here? Perhaps the most pointless tournament of the lot (though maybe not to Chester City fans) was the **Debenhams Cup**, involving the two lower-division teams who had gone furthest in the FA Cup. Chester won it in 1977 and it remained their sole honour until the club was dissolved in 2010. A year later, Blyth Spartans extracted some kind of revenge on their fifth-round FA Cup conquerors Wrexham by beating them in the Debenhams.

Trying to fill the void left by the post-Heysel European ban in 1985, the **Screen Sport Super Cup** provided the six English teams who might otherwise have been heading for the Bernabéu or San Siro with the consolation of a jaunt to Carrow Road. Liverpool beat Everton in the first final – played more than twelve months after the tournament began.

That season also saw the launch of the **Full Members' Cup**, devised by then Crystal Palace chairman Ron Noades on the notion that a crunch Southern Area group match against Reading would lure back all those missing punters. Ignored by the big clubs, terrestrial television and most sane fans, it was won twice by Chelsea and Nottingham Forest, and sponsored by Simod and Zenith Data Systems. The high point was a titanic 6–6 draw involving Tranmere and Newcastle in 1991–92, which saw hat-tricks from moustachioed Scouse poachers **John Aldridge** and **Mick Quinn**, a penalty for each team in the first minute of extra time, Newcastle coming from 5–3 down to 6–5 up, and Tranmere winning the shoot-out. The tournament was still axed at the end of the season.

In 1988, the Football League marked its hundredth birthday with a whole banquet of meaningless events. These kicked off with the **Mercantile Credit Centenary Classic**, an all-star friendly match at Wembley – what better way to celebrate than bringing together Diego Maradona and **Steve Ogrizovic**? This was followed by the **Centenary Festival**, a surreal two-day knockout event at Wembley involving ten-minute games featuring sixteen teams from all divisions – the kind of "innovation" for which we have known and loved Jimmy Hill for decades. Nottingham Forest, acquiring a worrying taste for this sort of thing, won, although Cloughie didn't turn up. The **Centenary Trophy**, which rounded off the celebrations, saw Arsenal defeat Manchester United at a semi-deserted Villa Park.

Just to prove England doesn't have a monopoly on this kind of thing, the 2000 **FIFA World Club Championship** in Brazil, Sepp Blatter's attempt to launch a global alternative to UEFA's Champions League, was initially held to be as spectacularly pointless as, say, the Watneys Cup. Manchester United famously pulled out of the FA Cup to play against the likes of Real Madrid, Al-Nassr and South Melbourne, but the 2001 event, slated to include Hearts of Oak, Woollongong

Wolves and Los Angeles Galaxy, was cancelled for assorted reasons, none of which was lack of interest. Its relaunch in 2005 as the Club World Cup has seen Blatter's idea grow in credibility, though not in England, where the FA refused to allow Manchester United to wear a 2008 winners' badge on their shirts.

A KICK IN THE GRASS: THE NASL REMEMBERED

Despite the success of USA '94, a creditable performance by the US team in the 2002 World Cup, and the recent strengthening of Major League Soccer, the US view of "soccer" is still best encapsulated by an episode of *The Simpsons*. In it, Homer and family are enticed by a TV commercial ("It's all here – fast-kicking, low-scoring … and ties? You bet!") to watch a football match so boring it sparks a riot. But it could have all been so different. In the 1970s the North American Soccer League (NASL) had it all – big names, full houses and super-sized helpings of razzmatazz from sea to shining sea. Alas, the NASL over-reached itself and had collapsed by 1984 – but it left behind a legacy of ridiculous club names, audacious rule changes and memories of an era when **Tommy Smith** could grace the same Astroturf as **Teofilo Cubillas** …

THE TEN MOST MEMORABLE NASL CLUB NAMES

1. New York Cosmos (1971–84) Pelé, Franz Beckenbauer and Shep Messing; the Cosmos were the NASL's superpower. Inspired by Carl Sagan's blockbusting 1970s intergalactic space opus. Or not.

2. Team Hawaii (1977) The most glamorous away trip in history. Statistics don't record whether they ever won 5–0, or indeed if fans advised referees to "book him, Danno!"

3. The Caribous of Colorado (1978) Never Colorado Caribous, oh no. Named themselves after a type of stag, and wore a brown kit with Wild West-style fringing on the chest. Yes, really.

4. Chicago Sting (1975–1984) In no way related to the box office hit of the time (part one). But no doubt teams ran out to a rousing selection of Scott Joplin rags.

5. San Diego Jaws (1976) In no way related to the box office hit of the time (part two). Just when you thought it was safe to go back to the soccer stadium …

6. Las Vegas Quicksilver (1977) If there's a lesson from this list, it's that the teams with the best names lasted the shortest. Cashed in their chips after finishing bottom, below Team Hawaii.

7. New England/Jacksonville Tea Men (1978–80) Let soccer flood out! Okay, so New England has a solid connection with tea, but Florida? The team was owned by the Lipton Tea Company, amazingly.

8. Detroit Express (1978–80) Sounded a bit like a 1970s soul group and were the product of a transatlantic "Motown" link-up with Coventry City as part of Jimmy Hill's brief foray into the NASL.

The New York Cosmos team line up before the match, 28 August 1977: featuring Pelé (10), Jomo Sono (22), Giorgio Chinaglia (9), Franz Beckenbauer (6) and Carlos Alberto (25).

9. Tampa Bay Rowdies (1975–84) Once the summertime home of Frank Worthington and Rodney Marsh. Still can't work out why they called themselves rowdy, mind …

10. Washington Diplomats (1974–81) They used to be the Diplomats; now they're down the laundromat. Easily the dreariest name in NASL history. Probably carried their boots in briefcases.

THOSE NASL RULE CHANGES IN FULL

The Offside Line

In 1972 the nascent NASL introduced a rule seemingly nicked from Subbuteo which stated that players could only be offside beyond a line marked 35 yards from the goal-line. Intended to generate more goals, the change's major impact was to bring the NASL into conflict with FIFA, and it was eventually dropped.

The Shoot-out

Because it was assumed that Joe American couldn't cope with draws, the NASL simply scrapped them. If a match was drawn it went into "overtime", before being settled by a shoot-out – but not from the penalty spot. Instead, five players from each team were given five seconds to run from the 35-yard line and score by either dribbling round, chipping over, or blasting the ball past, the outrushing keeper.

Six US Soccer Moments

1) **Brigham Young v. New Mexico, 2009:** University of New Mexico defender Elizabeth Lambert made national highlight reels for her mixed martial-art playing style. In defence of Lambert, seen punching one opponent in the back and wrestling another to the ground by her ponytail, she didn't start either confrontation, the latter offence in retaliation for what appears to be an attempted frontal female version of a wedgie. The booking came later, for kicking a prone opponent in the head.
2) **San José v. LA Galaxy, 2003 (5–4 aggregate):** The Earthquakes were 2–0 down coming into the home leg of their MLS cup tie. That quickly turned to 4–0 before they answered with five straight, the last an extra-time golden goal off the foot of Brazilian striker Rodrigo Faria.
3) **MLS All-Stars v. Chelsea, 2006 (1–0):** The annual "best of" game pitted fans' selections against a pre-season Chelsea squad helmed by "Special One" José Mourinho. Long grass slowed the Londoners' attack, and Canadian Dwayne De Rosario scored a seventieth-minute stunner that sent the Blues packing.
4) **Real Salt Lake v. LA Galaxy, 2008:** Real's Fabián Espíndola put in a glancing header and followed it with his trademark backflip celebration. But the goal was ruled offside and Fabián hobbled off the field after breaking his leg during his finishing flourish.
5) **USA v. Mexico, 2002:** North America's greatest football rivalry showed its ugly side when "El Tri" defenceman Rafael Márquez's flying head-butt on US striker and all-time caps leader Cobi Jones earned him a straight red and a four-match ban. The animosity between these teams remains strong.
6) **Alexi Lalas v. Popular Music, 1998:** Having moved to New York's MetroStars following two years of service at Serie A relegation side Padova, the carrot-topped US defender released a pop-rock album entitled, appropriately, *Ginger*. Fans and critics were unanimous in their complete lack of interest.

The Mini-game

In the two-legged play-offs, ties weren't settled on aggregate score. If both teams had won one match each, the outcome was settled by a thirty-minute mini-game played straight after the second leg. In 1979, Vancouver Whitecaps beat New York Cosmos in their first meeting, but the second match was tied at ninety minutes. Americans don't do tied games, remember, so it was on to overtime which still couldn't separate the teams. New York won the shoot-out, so after two hours of football in eighty-degree heat, the teams now faced a thirty-minute mini-game... which was drawn. Cue another shoot-out – which Vancouver won to take them into the Soccer Bowl where, fully rested, they beat Tampa Bay.

The Points

The NASL continually fiddled around with the points system, awarding bonus points for goals to encourage attacking play. During the League's glory years, teams were awarded six points for a win, one point for a shoot-out win, and up to three more points if they scored three goals …

"BECKENBAUER … PELÉ … HECTOR!": SIX UNLIKELY NASL PAIRINGS

1. Gerd Müller and Keith Weller (Fort Lauderdale Strikers, 1980–81)
Der Bomber is best remembered for netting fourteen goals in the World Cup. Keith Weller is best remembered for wearing tights one chilly afternoon at Filbert Street.
2. Carlos Alberto and Charlie Cooke (California Surf, 1981)
The 1970 legends of the Copacabana and the Kings Road briefly teamed up for a creaky Indian summer in sunny Anaheim.
3. Franz Beckenbauer and Dennis Tueart (New York Cosmos, 1978–79)
Der Kaiser and, erm, Der Dennis were both delegates at the Cosmos' United Nations of soccer in the late 1970s. And Tueart scored two in the 1978 Soccer Bowl.
4. Roberto Bettega and Phil Parkes (Toronto Blizzard, 1983)
Roberto Bettega was a sort of goalscoring Don Corleone, while Phil Parkes was a sort of goalkeeping Donkey Kong.
5. Johan Cruyff and Bobby Stokes (Washington Diplomats, 1980)
Yes, Johan might have pulled off the odd Cruyff turn in his time, but he never ran a greasy spoon "caff" like the late Bobby Stokes.
6. Ruud Krol and Kevin Hector (Vancouver Whitecaps, 1980)
In the shadow of the Rocky mountains, Ruud supplied the total football while a great, big, goalscoring old Hector from Derby added the finishing touches.

MAJOR LEAGUE SOCCER – THE US TODAY

The glamorous but short-lived North American Soccer League (NASL) briefly captured the American imagination with its outlandish razzmatazz and flamboyant team names. Big name European players hardly complained as they crossed the Atlantic for a final payday, and for a while it seemed like soccer had finally moved into the mainstream.

But a league comprised of ageing greats alongside untrained upstarts made for a poor foundation. Despite fireworks, skydivers and miniskirt-clad cheerleaders, attendance dwindled, teams bled money – and in 1984, after just fourteen seasons, the whole soccer experiment collapsed in on itself.

Determined not to repeat the same mistakes, Major League Soccer (MLS) was founded in 1996 as an outgrowth of the US-hosted 1994 World Cup finals. A new set of fancy names appeared: MetroStars, Columbus Crew, Colorado Rapids (who now play at the gloriously named Dick's Sporting Goods Park), LA Galaxy and Kansas City Wiz, although it was the more conservatively named DC United who

Where Are the Profits?

With all the money in the game a big issue remains: where are the profits? Author Simon Kuper and economist Stefan Szymanski, in their book titled *Soccernomics* in US and *Why England Lose* in the UK, reckon that at most levels the business of soccer – certainly if you compare it with really big business like oil or banking – is a hopeless case (see pp. 203). Clubs can't "appropriate" (convert to cash) more than a small fraction of their fans' interest, loyalty and passion. And when they bring in grizzled captains of industry, such as Alan Sugar, to run them on a proper commercial basis then, as Spurs fans will recall, neither entertainment nor trophies necessarily follow. Most of the money disappears in the direction of players and there always seems to be an oligarch or rich owner who will want to pay more to get the best. This is not mere madness. One of Kuper and Szymanski's other conclusions is that there is a strong correlation between player wage bills and success. Note, not transfer spend – though expensive players command high wages. It's just that it is the wage bill that really counts. And neither does league success follow the moment this season's new high earners touch down at Heathrow with their agent in tow. If there is a solution – and one might wonder if fans and owners really want one – it is for clubs to accept they are like museums: "public-spirited organizations that aim to serve the community whilst remaining reasonably solvent". Don't hold your breath!

bagged three of the first four league cups. While long-in-the-tooth superstars like Lothar Matthäus and Roberto Donadoni were part of the initial mix, youth development was always to the fore and budgets were reined in.

Still, MLS lost millions between its founding year and 2004, though the future looks promising. A successful 2002 World Cup campaign for the US team and the plaudits won by former MLS players abroad raised domestic interest, and average crowds began to creep upwards, alongside increased airtime on sports networks. US women's soccer also drew attention after strong World Cup showings, and a women's league was formed in the early 2000s, but lasted only briefly – a new league, the unsubtly named Women's Professional Soccer, launched in 2009 with closer ties to MLS and their marketing resources.

As MLS league expanded, struggling clubs were jettisoned and new teams were welcomed into the league from traditional soccer hotbeds. Canadian side Toronto FC joined in 2007 while Seattle Sounders, formerly one of the best-supported teams in the NASL, joined in 2009 and were all watched by huge crowds. And while the majority of teams played on shared American football fields for their first years, most teams now play in newly built stadiums constructed for association football with capacities around the twenty-five thousand mark – the most impressive being the Red Bull Arena just outside New York City. With the addition of MLS teams to the (Confederation of North, Central American and Caribbean

Association Football) CONCACAF Champions League, top US sides are expanding their reach and have done well even in hostile Central American stadiums, though the strongest competition and biggest draws come from clashes with neighbouring Mexico's first division clubs.

Not forgetting the impact of that most low-profile of English footballers David Beckham, when he joined LA Galaxy in 2007 concordant with an easement of salary caps, which helped bring some top stars to teams otherwise shackled by a small and sensible pay structure. You might have heard about it. Suddenly the MLS was big international news, even if Americans were initially unimpressed and Harrison Ford referred to the new star as "David Beckenham".

SILLY MONEY

Money would save football just as it shaped it in the first place. Industry – and in particular television – woke up to the commercial possibilities of the people's game. Safer stadiums were funded by huge TV revenues, sometimes with satellite broadcasters, and merchandizing deals. Twin powers, Italy's Serie A and Spain's La Liga, emerged, attracting talent from all corners of the globe. Soaring income from TV deals meant that England's Premiership would later join them.

Players – previously more tradesmen than celebrity entertainers – reaped the rewards. Transfer records rocketed – from £3 million for Maradona in 1982 to £45 million for **Zinedine Zidane** nineteen years later, although Cristiano Ronaldo's 2009 fee of £81 million dwarfed this – and so did wages. The potential merchandising profits drove Western clubs into Asia and the US. FIFA has staged the World Cup in the US (1994) and Japan and South Korea (2002) to exploit these opportunities, while Africa staged its first World Cup in 2010 – although few expected Pelé's famous prediction that the continent would produce the tournament's winners to come true any time soon.

Football's future, sadly, has come under threat from financial speculators, internal corruption and commercialization. The US Glazer family's takeover of Manchester United, bought with £540 million of borrowed money, has loaded £700 million of debt on to what was, prior to 2005, the world's richest club. Italy's 2006 *calciopoli* match-rigging scandal implicated amongst others Juventus and AC Milan. Rising ticket prices and the increasing commercial global exploitation of football saw the alienation of local communities from clubs. Football still stands on its own two feet, but it is beset by problems of its own-making.

TWENTY-FIRST-CENTURY CLUB OWNERS

Football clubs used to be owned by the local butcher "done good", or the steel merchant who wanted a bit of profile for his profits, a seat in the director's lounge and his name in the local rag.

Then serious money flowed into football and the butcher was increasingly replaced by wealthy foreign owners. Manchester United and Liverpool were both taken over by Americans, who borrowed heavily to fund the purchases. Another American, Randy Lerner, proved far more popular with his plans for Aston Villa, chiefly because he used his own money. Roman Abramovich, a Russian oligarch, bought Chelsea and his millions helped turn them into champions. Oil money funded the purchase of Manchester City by an Abu Dhabi-based group from the disgraced former prime minister of Thailand; a Hong Kong-based consortium bought Birmingham City; while an Icelander briefly owned West Ham, before selling the club to the former owners of Birmingham.

Continuing the ownership merry-go-round, Portsmouth Football Club was sold four times in 2009–10, with mystery surrounding every purchaser – before entering administration and having nine points deducted by the Premier League in March 2010. At a lower level, Notts County made a mockery of the Football Association's "fit and proper persons test" when they were briefly owned by, well, nobody really knows. Whoever they were didn't have the money they purported to have, and the expensively acquired coach Sven-Göran Eriksson's surprising sojourn by the Trent lasted only a few months.

Things are very different in Germany, where the law ensures that fans have significant power and representation. Cheap admission prices and safe standing areas mean that the Bundesliga boasts the highest average attendances in Europe. Huge clubs like SV Hamburg and Schalke 04 are more than 51 percent owned by supporters, while large corporations like Volkswagen and Bayer fund Vfb Wolfsburg and Bayer Leverkusen respectively. And even Germany's low Champion's League profile ended in 2010 when once again Bayern Munich reached the final.

FAN-OWNED CLUBS

As more and more English clubs go into administration, the trend for fan ownership of clubs continues. In the top flight, ambitious Manchester United and Liverpool fans – disgruntled after American takeovers plunged them hundreds of millions of pounds into the red – aim to replicate the supporter-owned democracy on show at FC Barcelona.

A group of disenfranchized United fans went further and formed the breakaway club FC United of Manchester following the Glazer takeover of 2005 based on the model of AFC Wimbledon, which was set up when Wimbledon were moved against fans' wishes to Milton Keynes. FCUM has been a success, rising up the non-league pyramid with average home gates in excess of 2,000 at Bury's Gigg Lane (as they look towards building their own home in Manchester).

Exeter City have successfully been fan owned since 2004, with gate receipts of £653,511 from an FA Cup tie at Old Trafford helping them clear their debts, while Ebbsfleet United were bought by a consortium of 27,000 online fans in 2007, each paying £35, in the belief that team selection would be put to a vote. The scheme started brightly and Ebbsfleet won the FA Trophy in 2008 – though the manager still picked the team. A dip in interest the following season saw them face cutbacks. Maybe someone should have told the investors that a football team should be for life … not just a season.

EASTERN PROMISE

Jordi Cruyff didn't initially enjoy his time in England. Forced out of Barcelona where his dad had been manager, as far as the willowy striker was concerned there was no bigger club in the world than the Catalans. Then he went on a pre-season tour of the Far East with his new club Manchester United.

"Twenty-five thousand fans watched the team train arrive in Bangkok", said Cruyff. "Not even Barça could pull in those crowds. Five thousand people were waiting for us at airports at 6.00am and I said to myself, 'Jordi, wake up. You're at an incredible club.'"

Although Spain's Primera Liga is more admired in Latin America, the English Premiership has conquered much of the planet, nowhere more evidently than in Asia. Premier League games are broadcast to over 600 million homes in 202 countries worldwide and are particularly popular in Asia and the Middle East.

British clubs like United, Liverpool and Chelsea have made regular pre-season tours of Asia since the 1990s, usually to the richer economies of China, Japan, Thailand and Malaysia, rather than the less affluent Vietnam, Laos or Burma.

A 2008 survey commissioned by United's American owners, the Glazer family, claimed United had 333 million fans – one in twenty of the planet's inhabitants. It further suggested that seventy percent of the fans lived in Asia – yet while United have talked up the size of their eastern support, its measurable financial value is limited, accounting for less than one percent of the club's £245 million turnover that year.

English clubs have tried to replicate their domestic merchandizing success abroad, but rampant counterfeiting within lower-wage economies remains a serious obstacle to their pursuit of the Asian dollar. Why, for instance, would a Thai fan of any big English club buy an official shirt for the equivalent of £40 when they could pick up a convincing replica (of a replica) for £4?

The one area where British clubs have had success is in selling TV rights, though even here they could be accused of killing the goose that laid the golden egg. In 2001, the Premier League made £1 billion from the sale of domestic TV rights and £178 million from overseas sales. By 2007, three-year domestic rights were costed at £1.7 billion while the foreign rights had increased to £625 million – the biggest overseas deal for sport in the world. Showtime Arabia paid £60 million for the Middle-Eastern and North-African market, NowTV shelled out £100 million to secure the rights for Hong Kong, while WinTV spent £50 million at auction to show games in China.

The Chinese deal saw raised eyebrows as WinTV was a little-known subscription operator who, like BSkyB in the UK in 1992, hoped to build up its subscription base on the back of Premier League football. The Premier League's smaller clubs, with no interest in the Chinese market, were happy to take the deal which offered the most money upfront. However, by 2010 WinTV had built up subscriptions to just thirty thousand in a country of 1.3 billion with viewing figures so low they could barely be registered – exploding the myth that hundreds of millions of Chinese are glued to the Premier League. That the leading clubs began privately to voice their concern was understandable. In 2003, over three hundred million Chinese fans watched Manchester City v. Everton on China Central Television, the major state broadcaster (the match's appeal admittedly boosted by the novel presence of a Chinese player in both sides). With the WinTV deal, suddenly less than one percent of that potential audience could access Premier League football.

Aware of the criticism, the Premier League sought a new terrestrial partner for their next television deal on mainland China. Like Formula 1, they want as many people as possible to see their brand – even in countries where it has proved difficult to earn money from reputedly vast support. They see sponsorship and advertising as the way forward … rather than selling Darren Fletcher key rings or subscription fees to watch Bolton v. Blackburn.

The Legends

An unashamed celebration of the men who made the game what it is, from George Best to Pongo Waring

◀◀ Gianni Rivera of Italy, November 1965.

The Legends

"In my private life I do what I like. The night is my friend. If I don't go out, I don't score."

Romario explains to Valencia's coach why he won't stop disco dancing

What makes a footballing legend? The highest levels of achievement in the game are a useful pre-requisite, but not the only criteria: equally important, if not more so, are *charisma*, style and the common touch. Not everyone in this selection has made it at the highest level. Many never even came close. Yet they all endeared themselves to the sporting public by standing out from the crowd. Some, like **Tony Adams**, are celebrated for their ordinariness despite being quietly remarkable; others, like **Garrincha** or **George Best**, took the game to a new level.

SALAH ASSAD

Creator of "The Elastic"

At outside left, he was dazzling: quick feet, fierce shooting and distinctive frizzy, slightly auburn hair which had grown so long by the early 1980s that the style could almost be described as an Afro. By the middle of 1982, Salah Assad had gained a reputation that extended well beyond his native Algeria. He was part of an attacking quartet, along with Rabah Madjer, Lakdar Belloumi and Mustapha Dahleb, that captured the imagination of the audience at the World Cup finals in Spain. Assad had been electric in the sensational, opening round defeat of West Germany, in the course of which he destroyed the heralded German full back, Manfred Kaltz. Behind the scenes, he was feisty, too.

Algerian FA regulations at the time prevented players leaving the country to play elsewhere before the age of 28. With a queue of European clubs lining up to sign Assad during and after the World Cup, he was motivated to take on the Algerian authorities, and led a series of players' protests against these draconian local rules that seemed to so unfairly restrict their career development.

The players won the day, and the newly free Assad signed to Paris Saint-Germain soon after Algeria's World Cup fixture against Chile where his two first-half goals had inspired a 3–2 victory.

He had his moments at the next World Cup in Mexico, too, despite Algeria's early departure after finishing last in their group. He is remembered, too, as the inventor of the so-called "Elastic" manoeuvre, a dribbling trick revived more recently and most famously by Ronaldinho. But knee injuries cut short his career.

Returning home to Algeria, he became disenchanted with the footballing and political establishments and progressively became associated with the rapidly emerging Islamic movement within the country – the Front Islamique du Salut (FIS). The FIS became outlawed as a political party in March 1992 and there were mass arrests of party members and supporters – including Assad. He was never formally charged but was kept in prison for four years, some of those in the remote Sahara desert. And he was tortured: "They just wanted to make an example of me because I had a profile", he says now, "just because I had a strong faith. I never did anything wrong and have always believed in peace."

MOACIR BARBOSA

"The man that made all of Brazil cry"

Football folklore has long told us that some goalkeepers are different, but in the days before gaffes were caught on video and instantly whizzed around the Internet to millions of potential armchair viewers, you would be correct in assuming that those barmy glove-men of yore might have got away with the odd hasty flap at a cross, or the occasional skewed clearance.

Unfortunately for Barbosa, Brazil's goalie at the 1950 World Cup, one unconvincing grope at his near-post changed the course of his life. Caught out during the competition's dying moments, Barbosa instantly morphed from the most admired keeper at the Finals into football-crazy Brazil's equivalent of Lee Harvey Oswald – the man who sabotaged a nation's dreams.

The burly but agile keeper was almost thirty and in the form of his life. Having won a host of honours with Vasco de Gama and helped the national team to victory in the 1949 Copa América tournament, Barbosa and his fellow team-mates were on the verge of being anointed national heroes.

As hosts, the Finals were Brazil's chance to confirm their emergence as a modern, upcoming country. The buoyant post-war government approved plans for a new national stadium, the Estádio do Maracanã, that could hold up to two hundred thousand spectators. Fantastic, if you're selling booze and seared beef to punters outside; not quite as reassuring if the entire nation's morale depends on you not spilling a bobbling ball delivered by a wily Uruguayan winger.

The hosts needed only a draw in their final game, against Uruguay, to become world champions because of the competition's unusual structure – there were two group stages and no knockout. Seemingly in control at 1–1 with twenty minutes to go, the apocalyptic moment arrived. With eleven minutes to run, Alcides Ghiggia jammed a shot from the right through Barbosa and sealed Brazil's fate. Eminent playwright Nelson Rodrigues would go on to describe the defeat as Brazil's "Hiroshima". Subsequently, Barbosa, along with the other black members of the squad, was pilloried in the press.

In an attempt to exorcize his demons, Barbosa was alleged to have used the goal posts from that fateful day to fire up an especially lively barbecue. An apocryphal tale, but his descent into goalkeeping hell was under way. Decades after the match, an unknown woman famously stopped the veteran while he was out shopping, only to lambast him as "the man that made all of Brazil cry".

Ostracized by the national squad and the nation, Barbosa died impoverished and estranged – proof eternal of the risks that face those that crouch and suffer between the sticks.

GEORGE BEST

"One day people might say I was another Ryan Giggs"

George Best was watching his own ghost, in a rerun of a 1971 League game against Southampton when he grabbed a hat-trick. On the screen in his hotel suite, he watched as he beats John McGrath – the Saints defender who had told him before kick-off: "If you put the ball through my legs I will kill you" – waits for McGrath to catch up, and then beats him again. Even Best was elated by this reminder of his prowess. Jumping from the sofa, he mumbled hoarsely: "God, I was f***ing quick. I'd forgotten I was that f***ing quick."

> **"It was getting embarrassing. I didn't want to score any more, so I spent the last twenty minutes at left-back."**
> George Best

It was easy to forget that, before he ended up on the nation's front pages whenever he took a drink, that before the "where did it all go wrong, George?" talk, Best was a footballer of outrageous natural talent. This was a player who, having scored six in an 8–2 thrashing of Northampton Town, decided to give his marker a break: "It was getting embarrassing. I didn't want to score any more, so I spent the last twenty minutes at left-back."

Best was called the fifth Beatle, on a par with the Fab Four for his dark Celtic beauty, Beatle-ish haircut (later he sported a fetching Ché Guevara beard) and the kind of unbridled hedonism celebrated in actors or musicians, but frowned upon in athletes, Best was as much a rebel of his time as John Lennon. **Denis Law** may have been as vital to United, but he never bedded Miss World(s) or ran a boutique; **Kevin Keegan** might have bossed a European Cup run, but he never went to prison, didn't appear on the TV news besieged by the media whilst holed up in Sinéad Cusack's flat … didn't make your parents shake their heads in disapproval.

Tony Adams – Donkey Man

To call Tony Adams a cult – yes, Spurs fans, that says "cult" – seems, at first glance, somewhat ridiculous. After all, he wasn't some little-known midfielder with a disgraceful barnet or a suspect goal celebration. He was one of the most reliable English centre backs of modern times, the greatest captain Arsenal have ever had (twice winning the Double) and one of England's most rousing skippers. But this most effective and inspirational defender was also a donkey, and for that he was all the more loved by the Highbury crowd.

It was always reciprocated irony, too. When Adams' name was announced over the tannoy, twenty thousand fans would bray in unison and the "ass" himself would beam delightedly from the centre circle, pumping his fist in the air in time, then giving a double thumbs-up to each of the ground's four stands. To the outside world Adams was the archetypal, resolute George Graham player, getting the job done in a manner that valued efficiency over elegance. True enough, he used to turn like an oil tanker and run with the ball like a Keystone Cop. But while he might have been a donkey, to Arsenal fans he was their donkey. For a brief period, cardboard donkey ears were even worn at matches in a slightly surreal show of solidarity.

The whole donkey business stemmed from the 1988–89 season when, after an undistinguished European Championship for England in West Germany,

After The Beatles split, "El Beatle" (as Best had been dubbed by the Portuguese press after United's victory over Benfica in the 1965 European Cup quarter final) was almost more of an icon than Lennon and McCartney.

Best stood out by being more interesting than anyone else in the game. He was a man of many faces, from the eight-stone Belfast boy dancing round hospital tackles from gnarled defenders, to the drunken loon embarrassing himself on *Wogan*. A player with the finesse, speed, vision, control and ability to score from impossible angles, who tragically, because of his alcohol addiction, died yellowed and gaunt, when his transplanted liver finally failed.

Best remembered himself above all as the European Player of the Year and European Cup winner, hailed "the best in the world" by **Pelé**. He also pointed out that his career lasted longer than many assume. He was called up to play for his country at 35, and left Manchester United – where he was top scorer for five seasons in a row (between 1965 and 1969 he only missed two league games) – because he was tired of carrying an ageing, substandard side. He departed Old Trafford the same season as Bobby Charlton and Law.

Ultimately, it seems that professional football cannot cope with stars like Best. Sadly, it also appeared that George Best could not cope with his own demons.

Adams began to take regular flak for lack of pace and mobility. Opposing fans began making donkey noises whenever he got the ball and, following a 1–1 draw at Old Trafford, in which he scored both goals, a waggish sports editor at the *Daily Mirror* had donkey ears drawn on his picture.

After that it wasn't uncommon for him to get pelted with carrots, but after a particularly veg-tastic ninety minutes at Middlesbrough the Arsenal fans stepped in and took control of the hee-hawing rights. With the insult thus muted, Adams' swift collusion turned it into an in-joke love-fest as he orchestrated the braying.

For the Arsenal crowd to latch on to it this way had far more resonance than simply being a bit of a laugh. The constant criticism in the press, which he felt was undeserved, was starting to sting and though any stick from opposing fans tended to spur him on, the donkey noises and carrots were getting through. Especially the carrots. To have it spontaneously turned around to cement the bond between the fans and their captain – who had never played for another club – did a huge amount for Adams' sense of self-worth.

There was no question that it was enormously appreciated – and was a big part of what made his time at Highbury so special – but it did have a downside.

As he revealed after Arsenal's 1997–98 Double win, it could be a bit of a pain when over-refreshed Gooners sustained the mantra across restaurants – restaurants where, you could bet, the new-model sober, Old Vic-attending, art gallery-visiting, piano-playing, degree-doing, Shakespeare-studying, Sunday paper columnist donkey was eating anything but carrots.

LUTHER BLISSETT

Now we are one

It's just as well **Luther Blissett** isn't of a particularly nervous disposition, or he might begin to feel someone is out to get him. Blissett was a reasonably gifted striker who simply found himself out of his depth when he went to play Italian club football in 1983. When Blissett left Vicarage Road, Watford, for AC Milan, the common perception was that the Italians, in true **John Motson** style, had got their black players mixed up and had meant to sign **John Barnes**. Either way, a somewhat deflated Blissett was back in Hertfordshire just a year later having scored only five goals for the Italian team. But, little did he know that his time at Milan would some years later give rise to a cult in his name that shows little sign of abating.

In 1998, four Italians were arrested for fare-dodging on a train and all four of them gave their names in court as Luther Blissett – their "collective identity". It seems that they had chosen our hero because he was "just a nice guy who had problems with the Italian way of playing football" and may have suffered because of his skin colour. Fellow anarchists picked up the Blissett ball and ran with it, publishing books as a collective on the Renaissance and papal history and a highly acclaimed novel, *Q*, about sixteenth-century Lutherans.

Apparently, "the 'Luther Blissetts' don't exist, only Luther Blissett exists". The Internet has allowed the idea to spread across Europe and South America. "Blissett" has even become a byword for anarchism in several countries, with Blissett manifestos and philosophies cropping up, particularly in Germany. There are those who believe the author Umberto Eco to be behind it all. Blissett himself, having initially described the occurrences as "strange", now prefers not to discuss them.

PAUL BREITNER

Be here Mao

Only three men have scored in two separate World Cup finals: Brazil legends **Vava** and **Pelé**, and a big-haired Maoist German defender called **Paul Breitner**. Nicknamed "Der Afro" for his extraordinary barnet (still celebrated on certain websites), Breitner was a classic 1970s German defender, seemingly involved in every great side of the era. By the age of 22, the fearsome left back, noted for his raids down the wing and his powerful shot, had won all the biggest prizes in football.

World Cup 1974 – FIFA Farewell Dinner, Munich. World Champions Gerd Müller (left) and Paul Breitner smile and smoke cigars.

Breitner took the European Championship with West Germany in 1972, starred in the legendary European Cup-winning Bayern Munich side of 1974 (also scooping four Bundesliga titles), and a few months later bagged the World Cup. It was no ordinary performance: Breitner coolly slipped home a penalty in the final, putting Germany level after they'd gone a goal down against the Cruyff-inspired Dutch without touching the ball. Breitner then went to Real Madrid, winning La Liga four times, and resurfacing in the German international side of 1982 as a midfielder, scoring a consolation goal in their 3–1 loss to Italy.

A millionaire with extreme left-wing views and an unfashionable (for a Bavarian millionaire) admiration of Mao, Breitner was unusually outspoken for a German, clashing regularly with team-mates and coaches. Like **Eric Cantona**, he used his striking physical presence to good effect as an actor as well as a player, starring in "action crime" films like *Kunyonga*, and switching from midfield general to army sergeant for a role in the 1976 flick *Montana Trap* – a German "comedy Western" (now there is a thought).

Breitner is now established as a German football pundit, and is not exactly reticent in this arena either. "I am actually sorry for my mate Berti", he said when his former colleague Vogts struggled as Scotland's new coach, "because the way his players are punishing the ball will give him a gastric ulcer. Those Scots had nothing to do with the British football that we've feared for decades. There is no technical quality at all … [they are] footballing dwarves." Don't beat about the bush, Paul – tell us what you really think.

STEVE BULL

The boy from the Black Country

Wolves fans will never forget the enormous contributions of Stephen George Bull, MBE, to their club. The striker scored 250 league goals (306 if you include all competitions) in 561 appearances over a 13-year-spell at Molineux, where a stand bears his name alongside those of fellow legends **Billy Wright** and **Stan Cullis**.

The Wolves Bull joined in 1986 was very different to the club of today. The glories of the 1950s were a distant memory and three sides of the ground had been condemned as unsafe – average attendances were down to four thousand.

Bull almost single-handedly lifted Wolves out of the doldrums of the Fourth Division to the brink of the top flight. Bull scored over fifty times in successive seasons, making it impossible for Bobby Robson to leave him out of his 1990 England World Cup squad.

Born in the Black Country town of Tipton, Bull was raised on a sprawling council estate known as "The Lost City", where residents have an accent impenetrable to outsiders. Bull never lost his and needed a locally born journalist to act as his unofficial interpreter to translate his thoughts to a baffled national press.

That didn't matter to Bull who was loved for his rough-and-ready style, down-to-earth rapport with the supporters and total loyalty to their cause. They sang "Wooly Bully, Wooly Bully, Wooly Bully, Wooly Bully ..." *ad infinitum* to the 1965 hit tune of that name by Sam the Sham and the Pharaohs. That he came from local rivals West Bromwich Albion for just £65,000 made it even sweeter. He'd played four games for the Baggies in 1986, including one as a substitute in what would be his only ever appearance in the English top flight.

Detractors say that Bull never did it at the top level – but he scored four goals for England from thirteen appearances.

ERIC CANTONA

No seagulls or trawlers please

"I am happy to be crazy", **Eric Cantona** once said. "The world in which we live is boring. If you're different, you are considered crazy." Anyone with the vaguest interest in English football over the past twenty years cannot have escaped Eric Cantona's craziness: he was one of the finest players in the Premiership and probably its maddest. His antics at Manchester United are well documented – the kung-fu attack on a Crystal Palace fan, the seagulls-following-the-trawler "explanation" and the inspirational play that led the Red Devils to the Double.

Less well known is what came before, and has followed since. Before his move to Leeds United, Cantona played for six French clubs, and the way he is admired in England (recently being voted Manchester United's player of the century) is greeted with a Gallic shrug on the other side of the Channel. His reputation in his homeland is that of a maniac and agitator. Looking at his behaviour during his French domestic football years, it's easy to see why: controversy followed Cantona at every stop along the way from Auxerre Martigues and Marseille, to Bordeaux, Montpellier and Nîmes.

At Auxerre he punched team-mate **Bruno Martini**, and when he was challenged by seven angry opponents after an ill-tempered reserve match, he put four of them in hospital. Montpellier colleague **Jean-Claude Lemoult** had Cantona's boots thrown in his face after a perceived indiscretion, while France manager **Henri Michel** was once dismissed as "a shitbag", earning the fiery forward a year's ban from the national side.

At Marseille he threw his team shirt on the ground in disgust, and while at Nîmes he chucked the ball at a referee. After being suspended for two months, Cantona dramatically announced his retirement. He was back within weeks.

Cantona eventually decided that France did not suit his skills, came to England, and the rest is history. Since returning home, as well as becoming first a player in, then manager of the French beach soccer team, he has entered a profession the French take as seriously as the British take football: cinema. It was a typically awkward choice for Cantona, but he has since won great acclaim for his performances.

British cinemagoers first saw him on the big screen sporting dubious period facial hair in the movie *Elizabeth* (1998) with **Cate Blanchett**. More recently, in Ken Loach's *Looking for Eric* (2009), he showed he was unafraid to send up himself and his legend.

"... a shitbag ..."
Eric Cantona, describing France manager Henri Michel

In France he has had some critical success: his screen debut, *Le bonheur est dans le pré* (1995), won him rave reviews for the relatively sedate role of a rugby-playing duck farmer named Lionel, although the film suffered somewhat from shameless and unlikely product placement by his sponsor, Nike.

However, a degree of typecasting has since shown how the French people might really see him ... in three films he's played a violent maniac. In *Les enfants du marais* (1999), he had a major role as a moody boxer; in *Question d'honneur* (1997) as a moody boxing promoter; and in the comedy *Mookie* (1998), as a moody boxer who befriends a chimp. In *L'outremangeur* (*The Overeater*, 2003), Cantona played a greedy cop, wearing a 160-pound fat-suit. It's ironic that the French couldn't understand this most Gallic of men's singular football gifts. It may be that his role on the screen could finally persuade them to take the crazy genius of Cantona seriously. Then again, maybe not.

JOSÉ CHILAVERT

A life outside the box

Build from the back, say the game's experts. Quite what José Chilavert, Paraguay's most famous goalkeeper, thought of this theorem, we may never know. His answer would probably include a range of expletives, delivered as he sped up the field past his long-suffering defensive colleagues to take another free kick on the edge of the opponent's box, leaving his own net as naked as a centrefold.

The man Paraguay paid to keep out shots managed to put 62 goals past the opposition during his career, including 8 for his country. While his box-to-box antics amused and enthralled, Chilavert was actually an excellent keeper, who enjoyed a long and consistent career in front of his own goal.

Yet, Chilavert's successes – including those at Argentinian side Vélez Sarsfield, where he helped them to four championships and the prestigious Copa Libertadores – seem lost amid a catalogue of episodic buffoonery.

In the popular imagination, Chilavert will always be remembered for his free kicks and frequently bizarre personality. After bursting onto the public stage at the 1998 World Cup, where crowds lapped up the spectacle of his forays upfield to take set pieces with a mixture of bemusement and delight, he crashed back down to earth at the same competition four years later. After missing the first three games of the event thanks to a ban for spitting on Brazilian left back

Roberto Carlos, Chilavert boasted that not only would he keep a clean sheet, but also that he would score against his estimable Spanish counterpart, Iker Casillas … twice. Unfortunately, Chilavert failed to convert his free kicks and made a lamentable keeping error that gifted Spain one of their three goals.

Nevertheless, it is unlikely Chilavert's unique blend of bustle and brio could ever be surpassed. This is a man who has brawled with Faustino Asprilla, donned goalkeeping jerseys that would make Madonna blush, and backed out of tournaments because he felt the prize money would be better spent on the ailing education systems of South America.

Chilavert retired in 2004, ending a career that endeared him to the hearts of all those who like their football quirky and quarrelsome. With a temper that roared like a forest fire, Chilavert likened one match against Brazil to war, alluding to the devastating War of the Triple Alliance (a conflict between Paraguay and an alliance of Brazil, Argentina and Urauguay, that lasted six years from 1864 and resulted in over three hundred thousand Paraguayan deaths!).

He finished his career as the highest scoring goalkeeper in the game's history. There is "thinking outside the box" and then there is José Chilavert, removing himself completely, resulting in years of entertainment and recklessness.

LAURIE CUNNINGHAM

The Black Pearl

Genius is an easy word to bandy about where favourite footballers are concerned, but Laurie Cunningham really was one man worthy of such an accolade – albeit in a flawed kind of way.

Ron Atkinson once said that Cunningham could run through snow and leave no footprints, such was his balletic grace, and he was certainly one of the most underrated players ever to grace the English – and later Spanish – game. Cunningham, a winger, was the first black player to wear the Three Lions in a competitive international match (for England's under-21s) and he was arguably the most skilful footballer of his generation. Quite simply, few players in England could match Cunningham's physical grace, attacking instinct or creative invention.

"There was so much at stake for an individual who was desperate to prove so much, but he took the hardest option of all."

Ron Atkinson on an unfit Laurie Cunningham counting himself out of the 1983 FA Cup final

The shy, slim (he weighed less than eleven stone) Londoner began his career as an apprentice at Leyton Orient during the mid-1970s. Within months of his debut, his displays had prompted **Johnny Giles** to sign him for **West Bromwich Albion** (for

£110,000 in 1977) and he quickly became one of the hottest properties in football. Giles was soon on his way but the gung-ho, all-attack style of his successor – Ron Atkinson – suited him perfectly, and he narrowly missed out on League Championship success in 1979. But against Valencia in the UEFA Cup that year he put in a performance that marked him out as a world-class talent, running ragged a side including such luminaries as **Rainer Bonhof** and **Mario Kempes**. **Real Madrid** were quickly alerted, and a bid of £995,000 secured his move to Spain. (Folklore has it that he travelled to Madrid during the summer of 1979 to demand a move to the Bernabéu.)

The "Black Pearl" scored on his debut, but his dream move soon turned into a nightmare as he was subjected to relentless and cynical tackling. Injuries inevitably set in and, before too long, Cunningham had been reduced to a journeyman. He tried his luck briefly at a number of clubs – Manchester United, Marseille, Sporting Gijon and Leicester City among them – before joining Wimbledon in March 1988. He promptly picked up an FA Cup winners' medal as the Crazy Gang registered their famous Wembley win over Liverpool, and it earned him another crack at the Spanish League, this time with Rayo Vallecano. But just as his career looked to be getting back on track he was killed in a car crash near Madrid, aged just 33.

Cunningham's contemporaries described him as one of the most athletic figures in the game, a world-class talent who could ghost past players with his sublime skill and pace. But there was a darker side to his story. One of the first black players in England, Cunningham was subjected to racist abuse from opponents and the terraces, but while Albion team-mates Cyrille Regis and Brendon Batson simply rammed the ignorance back down their throats, Cunningham felt the injustice keenly.

In May 1979, an all-black team was put together to play the Baggies in a testimonial match for Len Cantello. Cunningham featured alongside the likes of Regis, Garth Crooks and big Bob Hazell, but felt that an important point could be made by keeping the side together to tour England. "We have the basis of a very good squad and it would be ideal to be kept together", he said. "I am sure more people would want to see our side."

Just how big a person Cunningham could be is revealed by the fact that during a loan spell at Manchester United, he found himself in the frame for a place in the 1983 Cup final but was unhappy with his lack of fitness. He knew that the Cup final could be his big chance to revive his career but confessed to United boss Ron Atkinson that he felt he would "let the lads down" if he played. It was a display of professionalism that made a big impression on Big Ron. "There was so much at stake for an individual who was desperate to prove so much, but he took the hardest option of all", remembers Atkinson. "That was why five years later I was delighted to see him make the Cup final with Wimbledon."

Few would want to argue with that.

WILLIAM RALPH "DIXIE" DEAN

Football's very own Shakespeare

At most football clubs, especially those with long, illustrious histories, there will always be a certain amount of debate about who represents their greatest ever player. Though not at Everton, where one name is universally accepted as the "number one", the "governor", the "grandaddy of them all." That name is Dixie Dean, and the sheer weight of goals he scored during his 433 appearances for the Blues, starting in March 1925, contemptuously crushes the claims of any of the other outstanding players to turn out for the Toffees in the last 130 years.

The 383 goals he scored in 433 appearances, including 37 hat-tricks, is unsurprisingly a club record by some distance, but it's actually another goalscoring feat for which Dean is more famous: scoring an unassailable 60 league goals during the course of the 1927–28 campaign.

Needing seven goals from the last two matches of the season to beat the record set the year before by Middlesbrough's George Camsell, Dean duly notched four at Burnley's Turf Moor before facing Arsenal at Goodison Park on the final day of the season. Incredibly, he grabbed a brace in the first three minutes of the match – but then his team-mates spent over an hour desperately trying to tee him up for the

Everton's Dixie Dean climbs high as the ball is crossed into the box, Arsenal v. Everton, 29 August 1936.

record-breaking sixtieth goal. With nerves beginning to fray, the moment eventually arrived as Dean rose in trademark fashion to head home an Alec Troup corner in the eightieth minute, eliciting a monumental noise from the Goodison faithful who were reportedly more interested in Dixie reaching his milestone than the possibility of Everton being crowned champions.

It might have been very different, however, as Dean was involved in a motorcycle crash in 1926. Popular legend has it that not only did he make an astounding recovery from his serious injuries, but that a metal plate was inserted into his head, which was the secret of his immensely powerful heading.

Quotes abound concerning Dean, but perhaps it is one from Liverpool's Bill Shankly that has endured best. He said: "Those of us privileged to see Dean play talk of him in the way people talk about Beethoven, Shakespeare or Mozart – he was that good." Dixie played for Everton until 1938, before moving on to Notts County. He died in 1980, after suffering a heart attack while watching a Merseyside derby at his beloved Goodison Park.

PAULO DI CANIO

His dark materials

"I have always felt a special affinity towards the weak, the disadvantaged, the unloved", explains Paulo Di Canio of his love of Lazio. "And I loved their symbol, the Lazio eagle."

A member of predominantly fascist Lazio supporters group the Irriducibili, Di Canio once sprayed "Roma is shit and their curva stinks" on a wall in his neighbourhood. While a player in Lazio's youth teams, he would play on a Saturday and then travel overnight to attend first-team away matches with the Irriducibili, by then Italy's biggest Ultra group.

"I kept the club in the dark about my travels. If they had known that I spent my Sundays with the Irriducibili, visiting far-flung corners of Italy, they would probably have kicked me out of the youth academy", he says. He was spotted by the Lazio physio at one away game at Atalanta and warned to stay away, a warning he didn't heed. On one occasion, Di Canio was only five yards away when the head of Bergamo's police was stabbed.

By 1988, a teenage Di Canio was in Lazio's first team and although he didn't last long, playing fifty-four games and scoring four goals in his first spell at the club – before playing for Juventus, Napoli, Milan, Celtic, Sheffield Wednesday and West Ham – he did score in a derby. The ball in the net, he ran straight towards the Curva Sud, where the Roma fans were stood, later claiming that "the roar at my back, from Lazio's Curva Nord, was spurring me on. I ran under the fans, finger raised, face contorted in a mixture of ecstasy, relief and fury." At Celtic and West Ham, he was similarly idolized by hardcore fans, always wearing his heart on his sleeve and scoring audacious goals.

JULIAN DICKS

"I ended up smashing loads of my clubs"

Julian Dicks was one of British football's last true hard men. Or, as actor, West Ham fan and professional Cockney, Danny Dyer, puts it, "Dicks was an animal. I remember him having a go at Vinnie Jones once and Vinnie's arsehole fell out. When he kissed that West Ham badge, he meant it."

A no-nonsense left back with not inconsiderable ability and a shot like a rocket, "The Terminator" was actually a Bristolian who played for Birmingham City for three years before arriving in East London in 1988. Yet Dicks will always be considered West Ham through and through, even questioning the right of some current players to wear the Claret and Blue. "Certain players think they've got a God-given right, but they haven't", he once said. "They've got to earn that right to play at West Ham."

The Hard Men – From pin-prickers to Leg-biters

In January 1971, George Best was fined £250 for accruing three yellow cards in twelve months, a disciplinary record the tabloids described as "appalling". Today, such misdemeanours would be the work of three weeks to the average defender. However, to look back on yesteryear as a golden age of flair would be inaccurate. Put simply, as long as there have been eleven men and a ball, there have been players willing to bend the rules to get their own way. For some, be it through bad luck, repeatedly bad timing or simply an absence of any other creative talent of their own, the ability to foul and cheat has become a defining characteristic.

This can be traced back to 1920s' legend, ex-blacksmith Frank Barson, who associated with criminals off the pitch and whose "Barson Bruiser" shoulder-charge was infamous. In 1919, Villa broke the transfer record to capture his valuable services. 1930s' legend Wilf Copping, though a fine player, is most fondly remembered for his chiselled jaw (he never shaved before a match, to intimidate the opposition) and crunching two-footed tackles. George Allison rebuilt Herbert Chapman's great Arsenal side around Copping, a former miner from Barnsley who learned his trade at Leeds, where he was known as "The Iron Man".

It worked. The Gunners took the league twice during Copping's five-year tenure – and he also starred in the 1934 "Battle of Highbury" between England and Italy in 1934. Bill Shankly, who blamed a Copping tackle for his different-sized ankles, recalled: "He didn't need to be playing at home to kick you – he would have kicked you in your own back yard or in your own chair … He had no fear at all."

The legend of the hard man was born, but it was in the 1960s and 1970s that such players became venerated by a media hungry for headlines and

Becoming captain aged just 23 in 1991, Dicks was stripped of the armband the following season despite leading West Ham to promotion and winning two England-B caps, after he was shown the red card three times. He then joined Liverpool for a season (1993–94), scoring the last goal in front of the old Kop before returning to Upton Park considerably heavier than when he'd departed. When re-signing Dicks, West Ham manager **Harry Redknapp** was told by his chairman he was "off his rocker", but Dicks helped keep the Hammers in the Premier League season after season, even top-scoring in 1995–96 as the club finished tenth.

But years of full-blooded challenges – not all of them fair – had taken their toll and Dicks retired in 1999 following a succession of knee injuries, with 64 goals in 315 games for the Hammers. He then took up professional golf, but the fire remained. "Golf's meant to be a gentleman's sport but I tended to lose my rag when I fluffed a shot. I ended up smashing loads of my clubs." In 2001 he made a brief return to football after signing for non-league Canvey Island, but played only four matches. He went on to run the Shepherd & Dog public house in Essex, before moving to Spain.

controversy. Ron "Chopper" Harris of Chelsea, Liverpool's Tommy Smith, Norman Hunter of Leeds and the omnipresent Nobby Stiles were full-blooded but generally deemed fair. Stiles became a national hero after his 1966 World Cup performances. Billy Bremner – and the entire Leeds team he played in – was less palatable, though his value to the team was celebrated.

However, it was the players who didn't necessarily seek trouble but didn't run from it who were the hardest. Dave Mackay bossed the Spurs midfield so ruthlessly he inspired them to the Double. Graeme Souness, generally accepted to be one of the hardest players ever himself, George Graham and Alex Ferguson would become Championship-winning managers by building their teams around hard men and defending them to the hilt.

Man-marking, meanwhile, was largely a Continental invention – Italy's Claudio Gentile's shocking handling of Diego Maradona during the 1982 World Cup was its most brutal example – but Argentina's Carlos Bilardo was reputedly even more unjust, pricking opponents with a drawing pin before running away.

Then there are the hotheads; Roy McDonough holds the record for red cards (fifteen in all, not counting "friendlies") in a career of thuggery that took in Southend, Colchester and Cambridge. Mark Dennis wasted his talent with woeful challenges and a hatred of referees while at Southampton. Vinnie Jones, for all the cartoon posturing, was genuinely fearsome (ask Liverpool). Referees are now far less tolerant of the tackles from behind and the two-footed lunges which were the staple of the hard man defender. And the flying elbows of the burly striker bulldozing his way into the box are given short shrift. But the hard man still remains a nostalgic cult figure with many fans: from Sydney "Skinner" Normanton (Barnsley, 1947–53) to "Big" Billy Whitehurst (Hull City, 1980–85).

JOSEBA ETXEBERRIA

Free folk hero

It wasn't quite what UEFA's Michel Platini had in mind when he suggested a salary cap, but when, at the start of the 2009–10 season, Athletic Bilbao's Joseba Etxeberria announced that he wanted to play for free for the club he had represented since 1995, it was seen as a selfless gesture, the antithesis of the greed that enveloped football.

Capped 53 times by Spain, the distinguished winger started out at Athletic's Basque neighbours Real Sociedad in 1995; his rapid £3-million transfer to Athletic (then a record for an under-18 player in Spain) was controversial.

Sociedad were outraged that their great young hope was joining their chief rivals and felt that a gentlemen's agreement not to poach each others' junior players had been broken. The two clubs even broke off formal relations for two years.

Etxeberria failed to appear at La Real's home in San Sebastian the following season, so he missed the giant peseta notes that his old fans had made for him, accusing him of being a mercenary. He would return later and in 2001 scored twice, when the abuse was so bad that Sociedad were fined by the Spanish Federation for the conduct of their fans.

Etxeberria was never a mercenary. He'd supported Athletic as a kid and once there, never moved again as the Basque club turned down several bids for the player. When he offered his services gratis, he had played over five hundred games for Athletic and spurned a final lucrative contract: "I wanted to do this gesture as a thank you to the behaviour of the club towards me and the love I have received from so many people."

His decision made Athletic's cult hero even more popular and freed up money to be spent developing other home-grown talents.

DUNCAN FERGUSON

Hard Toffee

"Fergie", "Big Dunc", the "Birdman of Barlinnie", or even "that big lazy bastard", Duncan Ferguson is a man of many names and indeed many faces. His cult status at Goodison Park was assured well before he finished his career in the final game of the 2005–06 season, with an almost symbolically scruffy late goal against West Brom, but there will always be those who agree with Joe Royle's assertion that the Scottish centre-forward became a legend at Everton before he even became a player there. It's true that in another era, Ferguson, who scored 72 goals in 191 games in two spells at Everton, may not have become such a folk hero on the blue half of Merseyside. The Everton he joined from Glasgow Rangers in 1994 was no longer the Everton of Kendall, Harvey and Ball, or Bracewell, Sheedy and Reid. For much of the 1990s, it was a club characterized more by Mark Pembridge, Mitch Ward and Marc Hottiger … with so little for the supporters to cheer in terms of quality, the six-foot-three Scottish international stood literally head and shoulders above the rest.

He came down South with a reputation for trouble and a court case pending as a result of head-butting Raith Rovers' John McStay. The sense of injustice at his eventual jail sentence only cemented his place in the hearts of his new fans though, already overjoyed after seeing him score his first Everton goal. It came in the best way possible: in a 2–0 win over Liverpool, opponents who, along with Manchester United, would bring the best out of him for years to come.

Fergie's larger-than-life off-the-field persona was a constant delight to all but the most uptight Evertonians, and he lived up to it when his celebrations following that first derby win ended with an arrest for drink driving. He was tempestuous on the field too, and eventually became as well known for his outrageous temper as for his goalscoring prowess. Indeed, he holds the Premier League record for the most red cards in one season – an impressive total of eight. He's also the only footballer to have beaten up burglars at his home on not one … but two occasions.

A couple of famous images endure of Ferguson's time at Everton, and they encapsulate what made him such an enigmatic icon. The first is of him running the length of the Goodison pitch, twirling his shirt above his head after crashing a header past Peter Schmeichel. The second is of him attempting to throttle the life out of Leicester City's Stefan Freund.

WILLIAM FOULKE

Room for one more?

In Edwardian England, if you were of a mind to go to Blackpool on a sunny summer's day, you might find yourself playing "Beat the Goalie" on the golden sands. And the goalie you were trying to beat in the penalty shoot-out would have been none other than former England and Chelsea keeper **William Henry Foulke**. He was known to his friends as "Fatty".

It was an odd, slightly sad end to a career which had seen Foulke blaze a glorious trail as a *bon viveur*, persecutor of centre-forwards and referees, and general man-mountain. It's often said that goalkeepers fill the goal. Weighing in at 24 stone, Foulke genuinely did. Born in 1874, he enjoyed a league career which took him to Sheffield United, Chelsea and Bradford … wherever there was a good breakfast, really. At Chelsea he popped into the club canteen one match day before the rest of the team and ate all eleven breakfasts – and those of the

> **"You can call me anything, but don't call me late for dinner."**
> William "Fatty" Foulke

opposition too. When his understandably outraged team-mates took him to task, Foulke told them: "You can call me anything but don't call me late for dinner". This was more than slightly disingenuous in that nobody had ever had to call Foulke to dinner in his life. He would always be there at the head of the queue hoping that someone wouldn't turn up so he could have their serving too.

But Fatty wasn't simply famous for being fat. He once kept goal for England and won two FA Cup finals with Sheffield United, so he must have been halfway decent at his job. Of course he would have been even more at home in the modern game where he would have had one hell of an advantage in all those penalty shoot-outs which now seem to loom large in every team's season.

But it was Foulke's attitude towards referees and centre forwards – whom he regarded with the same single-mindedness as a square meal – that looms large in his reputation. After his beloved Blades had lost the 1901 FA Cup final to non-league Tottenham, an enraged Foulke chased the referee **Tony Kirkham** into a boot cupboard. He was only prevented from causing the referee actual bodily harm by the presence of the FA secretary. Apparently Foulke sat in the team bath after the game plotting his revenge on the referee. (History doesn't record how many team-mates managed to squeeze into the bath with him.)

Centre forwards were frightened of him for several very good reasons. He was not the kind of keeper you would relish competing with for a cross and he had been known, when riled, to take the law into his own hands. One time, when Liverpool striker **George Allan** was deemed by Foulke to be going about his work with undue enthusiasm, the keeper strode towards him, picked him up and stuck the amazed forward, head first, in the mud. The Reds got a penalty out of it but the lesson was not lost on other strikers … or on referees. Against Port Vale, in 1905, Foulke picked up an opposing forward and threw him into the net; the referee pointed to the spot and later noted: "I kept a reasonable distance from Foulke for the rest of the game." When he wasn't turning strikers into sticks in the mud, he was snapping crossbars (imagine 24 stone of flesh dangling from a slender beam of Douglas fir) and breaking stretchers (once when he was injured, six men had to carry him off because the stretcher couldn't bear the load).

Foulke wasn't really the kind of man who worried what anyone thought about him, as long as they thought to bring him some food. All of this made his end as the custodian of a novelty goal on Blackpool beach that much sadder. He caught a chill on the beach one day and died of pneumonia in 1916, but he left behind an enduring legend.

He was the first goalkeeper really to convince the rest of the world that you had to be crazy to do the job. It's hard to see him fitting into today's game. While an industrial crane could always be on hand to pull him off the pitch if he got injured (thus sparing his team-mates the burden), he'd never get used to eating just chicken and pasta. Still, you'd always know where to find him on the morning of a match – at the nearest purveyor of cholesterol-based food.

ROBIN FRIDAY

Thank God it's Friday

Everybody knows about football's disastrous underachievers: the Gascoignes, Bests and Worthingtons who should have produced so much more than they did. Few have heard of **Robin Friday**, because his underachievement was so spectacular, and ultimately tragic, that he never fulfilled anything close to his potential. His ludicrous antics – drugs, booze, women, fights, prison and even being impaled on a spike – meant he never had a chance. But find a Reading or Cardiff City fan who saw Friday play in the mid-1970s and they'll soon be trying to convince you he was Acton's very own answer to Pelé.

Born in 1952, Friday spent a chaotic London youth in and out of borstal. But his talent for football was God-given and, despite a disdain for training, he soon stood out as the best forward in the capital's non-league game. He was signed by Reading aged 21, became a cult hero at Elm Park within weeks, and had journalists enthusing over the "sheer magic" which turned an average Royals team into an awesome one. His skill and vision were beyond doubt. He could beat players with ease and his

Cardiff City's Robin Friday gives a two-finger salute to Luton goalkeeper Milija Aleksic after scoring his second goal at Ninian Park, 16 April 1977.

53 goals are widely considered among the best Reading have ever seen. Even experienced referee Clive Thomas was reduced to applauding one strike in 1976, telling the player that "even up against Pelé or Cruyff, it rates as the best goal I've ever seen."

As Friday fired Reading to promotion in 1976, managers like **Bertie Mee** and **Bob Paisley** queued up to court the mercurial talent. But just as his star was rising, Friday's hellraising was beginning to get him in serious trouble. A notorious boozer, he was soon barred from virtually every pub in Reading for fighting, often while naked. The list of his misdemeanours is endless. He terrorized his elderly neighbours with loud heavy metal at 3am. He stole shirts from markets, posed as a guard on trains to get free tickets and removed statues from graveyards. He consumed prodigious quantities of dope and LSD – on one away day he was caught naked on a hotel snooker table flinging balls around the room; on another, he paraded around a team meeting with a swan under his arm, procured from a nearby lake.

Friday wasn't much better on the pitch. He drank before games, kissed policemen after scoring, kicked players in the face and grabbed them by the testicles. His disciplinary record was appalling, and only his stellar performances ensured that his managers kept patience. By 1977, though, his career was already on a downward spiral and, after a mysterious bout of dysentery, he was transferred to Cardiff City.

There he produced a number of performances that can still make Bluebirds fans misty-eyed, but he would go missing for days at a time and the club finally lost faith in him. He returned to London to work as an asphalter, but never managed to turn his life around. Divorced twice in acrimonious circumstances, he reportedly lived in squalor out of plastic bags until he died in 1990, aged just 38.

Ultimately, it's hard to gauge how much Friday deserves to be put up on a pedestal. His story seems to grow with each telling, and in many ways it's sad that such a tragic figure has been painted as a hero for the *Loaded* generation (his story inspired the Super Furry Animals' top-twenty hit, "The Man Don't Give a F***"). But it sure makes for a better yarn than an anodyne **Michael Owen** autobiography.

Reading coach Maurice Evans once told the forward: "If you'd just settle down for three or four years, you could play for England." The reply: "Yeah, but I've had a far better time than you've ever had", is a fair summation of Robin Friday's life.

WALTER FROSCH

"My biggest rival was always the bar"

He came off the pitch after a Bundesliga game with Kaiserslautern in the 1970s, when a television reporter detected a strange bulge in Frosch's sock.

"Ehm, sorry, Walter, but what's that there in your sock?"

"Ah, just a pack of cigarettes."

"What? You had a fag during the game?"

"No, no, I thought I could have a nice and quiet smoke on the substitute's bench, but then I had to come on, because a team-mate did get injured, it went all so fast that I did not know where to put my cigarettes, so, you know, I just panicked and put them in my sock."

> **"I did not know where to put my cigarettes, so, you know, I just panicked and put them in my sock."**
> Walter Frosch

In his own words, Walter Frosch preferred "a good fag, even to shagging."

A hard defender with Kaiserslautern and St. Pauli, one season he was booked 27 times in 37 games. The next season the German Football Federation introduced a new rule to suspend players after five consecutive yellow cards, claiming they could not allow "people like Frosch" to get away with such extreme behaviour. The fans, though, celebrated his tackles – even his fouls – like goals. Being tough was sexy in football in the 1970s. And who in Germany was tougher than Frosch?

Once he turned up with bloodshot eyes two hours before a game. "Conjunctivitis", he explained. In fact he had been out drinking until 3.00am the night before, the lager-session only interrupted by a wager with his drinking pals – who would win a four-hundred-metre race, right then, at the nearby track. Frosch won the contest and collected the prize: ten more beers. "My biggest rival was always the bar", he said. At the testimonial of his mate Klaus Thomforde at St Pauli, he finally managed to smoke during a game.

Although he understandably gave up cigarettes after five cancer operations, he continues to reside in his natural element – he runs the club bar at amateur side VfL Hamburg.

SAINT-JOSEPH GADJI CELI

"Allez les Elephants"

Saint-Joseph Gadji Celi was blessed with twin skills as a young boy growing up in Ivory Coast just after the country's independence from France in 1960. He could play football and sing. He had nimble feet, and was fast – he also had a beautiful singing voice, a wonderful sense of rhythm. He liked to perform too, which served him well in both his professions, and his great set of lungs were handy for a hard-working midfield player – useful for a *chanteur* too.

In the dressing rooms at ASEC Mimosas of Abidjan, Ivory Coast's leading club, Gadji Celi announced himself as a leader of men at an early age. Partly he did so through song. "And God Created ASEC" was the first composition he wrote and performed to motivate his team-mates ahead of crunch domestic engagements against the likes of Africa Sports, or before testing African Cup away games against

Egypt or Nigeria. But the song became a nationwide hit. More followed. Ahead of every expedition by the Ivorian national team, Gadji Celi would produce a track, embellished with the distinctive twanging of guitar strings and his inimitable voice.

"Allez les Elephants" geed up the Elephants, as the Ivorian national team are nicknamed, in the 1980s. Gadji Celi captained them to their first and only triumph at the 1992 African Nations Cup. Retiring, he devoted himself fully to his music, broadening his compositional range to encompass love ballads and powerful "message" lyrics calling for peace and social responsibility. Sales of his discs rose yet higher, and he assumed the powerful position, in a nation that loves its music, as the head of the national union of recording artists. He remains a popular figure among the next generation of players, too, often invited into the dressing rooms now occupied by such luminaries as Didier Drogba and Kolo Touré, where they all know his tunes off by heart.

GARRINCHA (MANUEL FRANCISCO DOS SANTOS)

The ultimate "malandro"

Popular opinion has determined that Pelé is the greatest footballer of all time. Ask a Brazilian, however, and they'll tell you Garrincha was the daddy of them all (often literally, as well as figuratively). Yet while Pelé's indiscretions never prevented him becoming an ambassador for Brazil, sport and Viagra (something Garrincha never needed), his older, more entertaining team-mate is best known for dying in poverty, aged just 49, having squandered his money and spurned advice from former team-mates and the fans who worshipped him. Given the nature of the man it couldn't have happened any other way. Pelé grabbed the glory because he scored the goals and came out with the snappy one-liners; Garrincha was intellectually not his equal, but put a ball at his feet and he could beat any defender in the world. Most of Pelé's greatest goals were supplied from Garrincha crosses and he has acknowledged that he could not have won three World Cups without him; the pair lost only one of sixty matches (in the 1966 World Cup) while on the same side.

Garrincha had first graced the world stage when a player revolt led to his inclusion in the 1958 squad. In 1962, with Pelé injured, he stepped out of the shadow of his friend to win the ultimate prize in Chile almost single-handed. Sadly, the 1966 World Cup proved to be his international swansong. As a man Manuel Francisco dos Santos (1933–83) or "Little Bird" (as his name translated), was a mess. He walked out on his wife and eight children to live with a samba singer, and fathered innumerable offspring through brief dalliances, including one that led to a son, Ulf, conceived after sneaking out of training camp at the 1958 World Cup in Sweden.

He also drank to distraction, a problem exacerbated by an early retirement from the game. In truth, however, he had always known the end would be premature – he'd been unable to walk as a child and only an operation as a six-year-old had given

1962 and All That ...

Maradona excepted, perhaps no other player has dominated a World Cup finals as Garrincha did in 1962. Against England in the quarter-finals he scored with a header and a "banana ball" into the corner of the net. In the semi-final he was sent off for kneeing a Chilean defender in the behind after being continually fouled, but was allowed to return for the final – which he played in despite suffering from a severe fever. Botafogo's second championship in a row followed later in the year but by 1963 he was scarcely able to play consecutive matches because of his damaged knee. After an operation in 1964 his glory days were well and truly over.

him mobility, though his legs were permanently curved. His other main nickname, "angel with bent legs", was a tribute to the extraordinary curvature of his legs, said to be one factor why defenders found it so hard to follow his bamboozling runs on the wing.

There have been other dashing wingers but maybe no one in the history of the game has been such a prodigious dribbler. Garrincha did it for fun, returning to beat a player once twice, three times – even spurning an open net for another dribble. He was once even threatened with a sending off by a referee for dribbling around a defender too often. His coach at Botafogo tried to get him to dribble less in favour of crossing, though he was expert at that too. Brazil's continuing obsession with Garrincha – thousands lobbied the authorities and threatened boycotts when his statue was moved from a public area of the Maracanã Stadium to a VIP enclosure – can be explained by his status as the ultimate "Malandro", a kind of mystical slave folk hero. The Malandro breaks free from his masters and lives a life full of joy and style yet lacking in any discipline. Some would say Garrincha took the concept too far; to Brazilians, who still well up at the mere mention of his name, he got it just right.

CHARLIE GEORGE

King George

For Arsenal fans, Charlie George really was like the "Second Coming". Born in Islington, the wispy forward grew up watching his beloved Gunners from the terraces, so when he made his debut at the start of the 1969–70 season, the Highbury faithful were always going to treat him like one of their own. But George was much, much more than just a local lad; he was the man who, at just twenty, scored the goal – a long-range stunner deep into extra-time against Liverpool in the 1971 FA Cup final – that secured Arsenal only the second "Double" of the twentieth

Arsenal's winning goalscorer Charlie George (left) and captain Frank McLintock (right) parade the FA Cup after their 1971 extra-time victory against Liverpool.

century. His "Jesus Christ-type celebration" – lying on his back on the Wembley turf with his arms outstretched – helped spawn a famous chant the following season: "Charlie George, superstar, how many goals have you scored so far?" "The musical had just gone to Broadway and was being played everywhere", George explained.

While opposition fans had a slightly different view – "walks like a woman and he wears a bra" – George continued to be the darling of Highbury, with his long hair, rebellious streak and penchant for the spectacular. George was disciplined by Arsenal after head-butting Liverpool's Kevin Keegan in the 1971–72 season, and again for flicking "V"s at Derby County fans after scoring at the Baseball Ground. He later joined The Rams, winning the league title in 1975 and his solitary England cap a year later, when he unsurprisingly fell out with disciplinarian manager Don Revie, after being played out of position, then substituted after an hour.

George is now back at Arsenal, hosting tours of the stadium, where he's still regarded as something of a deity by some supporters. "A few older Arsenal fans still do the 'Charlie, Charlie, Born is the King of Highbury' song." Amen.

JIMMY GLASS

"If I could write scripts like that"

"I believe in alien beings. I believe in Frankenstein. I believe in God", said eccentric Carlisle United chairman Michael Knighton, the man who promised fans that the club would compete in one of the best stadiums in Europe. "And most of all, I believe in on-loan goalkeepers who can score goals in the 91st minute."

Journeyman lower-division goalkeeper Jimmy Glass had just completed the fairytale to end all football fairy tales, a story even Carlisle-supporting literati like Hunter Davies and Melvyn Bragg would struggle to pen. In 1999, at home to Plymouth Argyle, the Cumbrians needed a goal to stop them slipping out of the Football League when Glass was desperately urged to go forward in the dying minutes.

> **"The referee has been swamped ... they're bouncing on the crossbar."**
> BBC commentator

A corner was parried out by the visiting keeper, which fell towards Glass who lashed home a volley. Carlisle stayed up and Scarborough – whose game had finished and whose fans were already celebrating, assuming they were safe – were relegated back to non-league football.

Carlisle fans invaded the pitch in celebration, leading to the BBC commentator to say: "The referee has been swamped … they're bouncing on the crossbar!" They were used to late reprieves, but nothing as dramatic as this.

"If I could write scripts like that", concluded Carlisle manager Nigel Pearson, "I wouldn't be in football. I would have a very good publishing contract."

Glass, who only joined Carlisle because regular first-team goalkeeper Tony Craig had been sold by Knighton to Blackpool on transfer day, only ever played three games for Carlisle. He moved on after his fifteen minutes of fame; Knighton and Pearson followed too.

The amiable Glass isn't remembered as being anything like the best goalkeeper to play in the Border City, but his popularity endures and he is regularly invited to be guest of honour among Carlisle fans. He fits such duties around running a taxi firm in Dorset.

"MÁGICO" GONZÁLEZ

The nightcrawling wizard

Known as "the wizard" by fans who adored him, Jorge Alberto González Barillas was an El Salvadorian striker who attracted Spanish sides Cádiz and Atlético Madrid.

In an age before international scouting networks, he had come to their attention in 1982 after being the star player in an El Salvador side which had qualified for only their second World Cup finals in their history. Of his two suitors, one was an established European giant, the other a provincial club with fans who celebrated drinking beer rather than winning.

Given his love of nocturnal attractions, it was perhaps no surprise that González chose Cádiz. At the age of 24, his outrageous skills had finally provided his passage out of the deprived Luz barrio of San Salvador.

He embraced his new life in Europe with such a vigour that it didn't enhance his career, keeping the Cádiz publicans and party girls busy. Cádiz fans overlooked and even celebrated his indiscretions and they loved it when he stayed with the club after relegation to the second division in 1984, despite offers from Paris Saint-Germain, Sampdoria and Fiorentina. The club management could tolerate his lifestyle no longer. They were fed up with trawling the local discos to find him at 4.00am and so he left for Valladolid in 1984. There, his contract stipulated that he was to be paid $700 for every game he played and nothing for the ones he missed. He lasted nine games.

Free from the distraction of football, the wizard's partying continued until a new Cádiz coach tempted him back. This time, Mágico stayed for five years, cementing his legend. He still loved discos, but by this time had learnt to avoid any search parties from his club by hiding in the DJ booth – where he later admitted sleeping on many occasions. He slept in and missed the start of one game against Barcelona, but with Cádiz losing 1–0 at half-time, the wizard was reluctantly released onto the field. He scored twice as Cádiz won the game.

Back in El Salvador, he has been awarded the highest civilian honour and the national stadium now bears his name.

PERRY GROVES

The future's orange

Even **Perry Groves**' song had a whiff of hallucinogenics about it. To the tune of "Yellow Submarine" and with cheerful disregard for poetic structure, the crowd would croon: "We all live in a Perry Groves world, a Perry Groves world, a Perry Groves world." This normally happened while Groves was warming up in front of Highbury's East Stand, something he seemed to do regularly (if not actually best) as a perennial bench-warmer for Arsenal for the second half of the 1980s and early 1990s. Manager **George Graham**'s logic seemed to be, "Twenty minutes to go – get the ginger kid on to run at their knackered defence." The thing was, it often worked, too.

Whereas many cult heroes have their status established by a single act or event, Perry Groves had just so much to endear him to the amiably sardonic section of the Arsenal faithful. Most of it was as trippy as his song. He was George Graham's first signing (£75,000 from Colchester United in 1986), a winger in a midfield where silky skills were the least of anybody's worries. He was the nephew of 1950s Arsenal legend **Vic Groves**. He once scored against Spurs (as did Uncle Vic). He had hair so orange it could surely be seen from space, and his approach to styling owed more to dramatic licence than sound judgement. And he frequently bamboozled himself in his mazy dribbles.

Groves spent so much time sprinting up and down the cinder track he must have got to know most of the residents of the East Stand Lower by name. Yet it's widely recognized that Groves' energetic appearance as substitute in the 1987 League Cup final was Arsenal's turning point against the strongly fancied Liverpool – with the scores at 1–1, it was his run and cross that set up **Charlie Nicholas**' deciding goal. And remarkably, for a player of such unremarkable talents, Groves has more Championship winners' medals than Paul Gascoigne, Gary Lineker, Alan Shearer and Michael Owen have between them.

Groves left Arsenal in 1992 and retired in 1995. His cult status remains undiminished by his latest incarnation as a radio pundit.

RENÉ HIGUITA

Colourful scorpion king

The old Wembley stadium was one of England's most symbolic icons; players considered themselves lucky even just to play there once. In interviews, foreign professionals would wistfully recall watching the classic FA Cup finals of yore, and reveal what a dream it was to walk under those famous arches.

However, when Colombia visited in 1994, famously "loco" goalkeeper René Higuita appeared utterly nonplussed. Indeed, Higuita's antics indicated that this was a goalie that might, very literally, believe he was on a dance floor somewhere in Ibiza, not fretting about Alan Shearer's straying elbow.

In a tight, scoreless match, after Jamie Redknapp hit a wayward cross towards goal, Higuita planted his hands on the turf and thrust his feet back over his head, clearing the ball with a ridiculous act of showmanship. The crowd gasped incredulously, as thousands presumably wondered if they had dropped a few tabs of LSD and simply forgotten about it.

Higuita's idiosyncrasies were legendary in South America, where he spent most of his career with Medellin team Atlético Nacional and formed the last line of defence in their 1989 Copa Libertadores triumph.

Yet it was with the national team that the "scorpion" king made his name. Amazingly, in a country where some believe that defender Andrés Escobar, Higuita's club mate, was murdered by gangs for merely scoring an own goal, *el loco* was deeply admired.

During the 1990 World Cup, Higuita even attempted to dribble past Cameroonian striker Roger Milla while some forty yards from his unguarded net. Milla's hilarious tackle and subsequent goal sent Colombia home and sealed Higuita's reputation.

Even a cameo in a kidnapping plot involving drugs chieftain Pablo Escobar failed to puncture his popularity. An unhinged clown, René Higuita made millions of football fans simply glad to be alive.

The Men in Black – Eight Officials of Note

Ken Aston

One of the few referees who can claim to have changed the game as we know it. Ken Aston devised the system of yellow and red cards in the wake of the fiery England–Argentina match during the 1966 World Cup, when Bobby and Jack Charlton only learned the next day that they'd been cautioned. Aston was struck by the solution as he drove home in his MG: "the traffic light turned red", he later recalled. "I thought, 'Yellow, take it easy; red, stop, you're off.'"

Aston always retained a philosophical approach. "The game should be a two-act play with 22 players on stage and the referee as the director", he once said. "There is no script, no plot, you don't know the ending, but the idea is to provide enjoyment."

Tofik Bakhramov

Better known as "the Russian linesman" (even though he was from Azerbaijan) who decreed that Geoff Hurst's shot did cross the line to put England 3–2 up against West Germany in the 1966 World Cup final. Swiss referee Gottfried Dienst didn't see the incident and turned to Bakhramov, who as Kenneth Wolstenholme informed us, could only speak Russian and Turkish. "I still don't know if the shot was in or not", admitted Dienst not long before he died. "I have to say that I was standing in a poor position for that shot, exactly head-on instead of diagonal to the goal. I wouldn't have allowed the goal if Bakhramov hadn't pointed to the middle with his flag." Asked once to explain his infamous decision, Bakhramov simply replied, "Stalingrad".

Pierluigi Collina

A football icon not for his resemblance to Uncle Fester, but for his ability to officiate with firmness and fairness while missing very little – a combination that won him the respect of fans and players alike. (For the record, he lost his hair in the space of a fortnight after an attack of alopecia.) The Italian (a financial consultant by day), took up refereeing in his teens, following a brief playing career in which he failed to live up to the standards he set as an official. "For a defender, I don't think two red cards in five or six years is out of the ordinary. It can happen to anyone, can't it?"

Jack Taylor

A butcher from Wolverhampton who achieved World Cup immortality when he became the first referee to award a penalty in the final. The Germans hadn't even touched the ball in 1974 when Johan Cruyff broke straight up the field from kick-off and was tripped in the box by Uli Hoeness. "You are an Englishman", a perceptive Franz Beckenbauer hissed angrily at Taylor.

Impressively, he also once halted a pre-match pitch invasion at Stamford Bridge in the 1970s by marching into the centre circle and relaying a warning over the PA that he'd wait until midnight to start the game if he had to.

Clive Thomas

Known as "The Terror of Treorchy" and the source of deep-seated grudges from the Maracanã to the Mersey. In 1977, Everton were locked 2–2 with Liverpool in an FA Cup semi-final when a Duncan McKenzie header clipped Bryan Hamilton's hip on its way into the Liverpool net. Thomas ruled it out, despite there being no offside flag or handball. To this day, all he will say of the incident is: "there was an infringement" – it's still bitterly contested by Everton supporters.

One year later in the World Cup, as Brazil and Sweden were drawing 1–1 in Buenos Aires, Zico headed into the net in the dying seconds. Thomas ostentatiously disallowed it, claiming he'd blown for time while the ball was in mid-air. Brazil's appeal was unsuccessful but it was the end of Thomas's international career.

Tom "Tiny" Wharton

"The last time I saw you, you were in evening dress, and I must say you're better at the dancing than the football." It was this kind of remark (to Stranraer's flamboyant Freddie Laing) that helped to turn Tom "Tiny" Wharton into a landmark in Scottish football. Instantly recognizable at 6 feet 4 inches 4in tall, the Brylcreemed behemoth even seemed to tower over the likes of Billy McNeill. Football journalist Doug Baillie, a colourful centre half with Falkirk and Dunfermline in the 1960s and 1970s, noted on Wharton's retirement that it was almost a pleasure to be booked by the man: "I've warned you before about your tackling, Mr Baillie. I'm going to have to caution you this time, Mr Baillie. What is your name please, Mr Baillie?"

Arthur Ellis

Perhaps the first referee to achieve star status in Britain. Ellis's most celebrated ninety minutes came during the 1954 World Cup when he officiated at the "Battle of Berne" between Brazil and Hungary. He awarded two penalties, and sent off three players for fist-fighting – one of them a Hungarian MP. A Brazilian defender was hit by a bottle thrown from Hungary's bench, and the defeated Brazilians brawled with the Hungarians in their dressing room afterwards. Ellis sat drinking tea at the time. It was perfect training for his later role as umpire of *It's a Knockout*.

Graham Poll

A prime example of the sinister modern phenomenon of the "celebrity referee". Poll was once damned as a "village official" and "an English referee in every way" by a peeved Vieri and a bruised Francesco Totti after a 2002 World Cup game between Italy and Croatia. The only British ref to qualify for the 2006 World Cup, Poll was sent home after awarding three yellow cards to one player.

GLENN HODDLE

Le bon dieu

One comedian was only half joking when he said: "I hear Glenn Hoddle has found God. It must have been one hell of a pass." Long before he was sacked as England manager in 1998 for ill-judged remarks relating to his religious beliefs, the mercurial midfielder forged a reputation as one of the finest passers the game has ever seen, his vision and spectacular goals earning him ironically the nickname "Goddle" among Tottenham fans.

The eighteen-year-old marked his first start for Spurs in 1976 with a spectacular strike past England keeper Peter Shilton and Hoddle repeated the trick on his full England debut less than three years later. In the same season (1979–80), Hoddle was also named PFA Young Player of the Year and won *Match of the Day*'s goal of the season for a breathtaking volley against Manchester United.

"I hear Glenn Hoddle has found God. It must have been one hell of a pass."
Comedian Jasper Carrott

He confirmed his reputation as the most gifted English player of his generation by inspiring Spurs to FA Cup victories in 1981 and 1982 and the 1984 UEFA Cup. Hoddle would miss the '84 final through injury, but so outrageously good was his performance in the 6–2 aggregate win against Feyenoord in the second round that opposition captain Johan Cruyff went to the Spurs dressing room to offer Hoddle his shirt as a sign of respect.

After teaming up with Spurs and England team-mate Chris Waddle for top-20 hit "Diamond Lights" – complete with a buttock-clenchingly cringy performance on *Top of the Pops* – Hoddle left for France, where his talents were appreciated even more. **Michel Platini** said of his fellow playmaker, who won 53 caps for England, that had he been French "he would have won 150", or as Monaco captain Jean-Luc Ettori put it: "Glenn was *le bon dieu* … he was a god. There's nothing else to say."

VINCENT JULIUS

Anti-apartheid pioneer

South Africa in 1976 was a tinderbox. Apartheid by then was more reviled across the world than any other political system. But, inside South Africa, racial discrimination was being maintained with rising levels of state violence. In Soweto in 1976, schoolchildren rioted against the compulsory teaching of the Afrikaans language. Police fired on them – there were 23 fatalities.

And in 1976, one brave man took on the principle of segregation that governed sport and won. His name was Vincent Julius. He was well known as a versatile and talented player in what were then the various "Non-White" leagues of South

African football. So versatile was Julius he had established a good reputation as a goalkeeper even before he tried out as a centre forward. So good was Julius as a striker that it was he whom a leading club in the "White" league, Arcadia Shepherds, decided to sign and select in an open challenge to the laws that forbade black and white mixing on the sports field.

"You could have heard a pin drop," according to the Arcadia coach Kia Johaneson, when Julius took the field against Highlands Park at kick-off. The opposition protested his presence – the hitherto all-white National Football League, to their credit, resisted the subsequent pressure. Even the apartheid government took no action. Arcadia had warned them of their intentions and, rather than fight them and create another racist incident to be reported around the world, the government raised a cautious white flag. From then on, mixed teams began forming and started to thrive.

For Julius, one obstacle during his landmark debut remained: facing the taunts of the opposition players, one of whom called him "kaffir" (a horribly racist term) throughout. Julius scored for Arcadia, and running back past his abuser, asked politely and quietly: "So, what did you think of the goal the kaffir just scored, eh?"

ROY KEANE

"You can stick your World Cup up your arse"

Season after season during a trophy-laden twelve years spent at Manchester United from 1993 to 2005, the snarling Cork man was the team's best player. **David Beckham** may have occupied more magazine covers, Eric Cantona or Ryan Giggs have scored more spectacular goals and **Paul Scholes** have boasted more finesse and a purer style, but Roy Keane was the club's best-paid player for a reason.

Signed from Nottingham Forest for a £3.75 million British-record transfer fee in 1993, Keane had learned his trade under Brian Clough before he took over Bryan Robson's mantle as United's driving force, a box-to-box midfielder who ran hard and tackled harder. If he didn't, then he felt he was cheating himself. If team-mates didn't pull their weight, then they felt his wrath. **Jesper Blomqvist** claimed that Keane was still fuming with him six weeks after a foul he committed while stretching to pick up a poor delivery from Blomqvist led to a booking and thus his missing the 1999 Champions League final. Devastated not to play in the final, Keane can look back to the Juventus semi as his finest hour in red as he led United from 0–2 down to a 3–2 victory. Not one for hyperbole nor self-aggrandizement, he claims he did "alright".

Keane was a winner, the player Sir Alex Ferguson wanted to be on the field. Bright and brutally honest, his interviews were always engaging and his 2002 autobiography a controversy-filled bestseller. Keane is a complex, intense individual and his decision to leave the Republic of Ireland's training camp in Spain before the 2002 World Cup finals divided a nation. And still does.

A move into management has seen him lose little of his fire, but he's enjoyed mixed fortunes and has so far been unable to replicate his phenomenal success as a player.

JOHN KING

"Get 'em out. Come on, get 'em out!"

A bearded, toothless scaffolder from the Liverpool overspill estate of Kirkby, John King was a midfielder who looked like Brutus from *Popeye*. An Evertonian born and bred, he had been on Liverpool's books as a youngster: "Wearing that red shirt made me sick", recalled King. "I lasted four games before moving to Harry Catterick's Everton, but Harry thought I was a little too robust. At fifteen years old I weighed over thirteen stone. The doctor at my medical sized me up and said, 'You're a big lad, there's not much chance of you losing out in a tackle is there?' That was like loopy juice to me, I came out feeling invincible."

He signed for Altrincham, known as the "Manchester United of non-league football" in 1977. King's insatiable desire to succeed may have curtailed his Everton career, but it provided the edge Altrincham needed. "Kingy had problems on and off the field, but he was a winner", said a team-mate. "He used to kick the away team dressing room door and shout, 'Get 'em out. Come on, get 'em out … let's get this fucking game on.'" A rival Kettering Town manager later admitted that his players went white whenever they heard that thump.

In 1979, Altrincham drew a Tottenham side featuring new Argentinian signings **Osvaldo Ardiles** and **Ricardo Villa** away in the FA Cup third round. Captain King stoked up the atmosphere pre-match by pointing out that all foreigners were dirty divers. During the game, King didn't take long to make his mark. Fourteen seconds, in fact. The home crowd roared as they watched Ardiles sent sprawling.

"They kicked off, the ball went to him [Ardiles] and I just went for it", remembers King. "I wanted him to know that whilst he might have been a top-class player, I was going to shake him up and let him know that he had another 89 minutes of the same thing." But, surprisingly, King had met his match.

> Fifteen minutes later Ardiles came flying into me and there was a little altercation. The referee said, "Any more of that and you're both off." Ardiles started talking foreign, pretending that he didn't understand, but as we walked away, Ardiles turned to me and in perfect English said: "I saved us both a booking there." We shook hands and swapped shirts after the game. The Tottenham manager went mad at him for that, saying that his players had disgraced themselves by not beating Altrincham. Ardiles took me to one side in the players lounge for a photo with him and his partner. At the time I had long hair and the picture looked like three Argentinians."

King later took his legendary commitment into management taking Tranmere Rovers from the brink of relegation from the football league to Premier league contenders and, in 1990, Leyland DAF Cup victors – leading to cult status and a Prenton Park stand named in his honour.

RAYMOND KOPA

In the red corner

In May 1968 France came to a standstill for two weeks. Ten million workers downed tools, while in Paris nearly a million students and workers marched through the capital demanding the fall of de Gaulle's "police state", better salaries and more favourable working conditions. Alongside the protesters – and rioters – were a small group of French international footballers. They too had their grievances, and their leader was **Raymond Kopa**.

Kopa was a natural choice as rabble-rouser – a Polish immigrant, he was always something of an outsider to the French. Born Raymond Kopszewski, his name was shortened to Kopa to help his host nation pronounce it. Like most immigrants in his adopted hometown of Nœux-les-Mines, Kopa was destined for a life down the mines, not one of public prominence. As a child, he worked alongside his father quarrying coal for a living. A hand injury put an end to that career, but Kopa was about to start earning with his feet.

The creative inside forward was spotted playing for Nœux by Angers, who signed him up. Even his skills on the football pitch seemed somehow alien to

Atletico Madrid goalkeeper Pazos (left) makes a flying save from Real Madrid's Raymond Kopa (second right) in the 1959 European Cup semi-final, second leg.

France – he played more like a Brazilian, and was often scorned in his early days for dribbling the ball too much. He impressed for Angers, however, and eventually transferred to France's premier side Reims in 1950, helping them to dominate French football for the next six years. They even reached a European Cup final, where they faced the mighty Real Madrid. Kopa's sublime skills had already caught the attentions of the Spanish giants, and he took to the field knowing that his transfer to the Bernabéu was assured. Reims lost that game, but the man now known as "the Napoleon of Football" was not to lose many more.

From 1956 to 1959 Kopa played with Puskás and di Stéfano in one of the best teams the world had ever seen, winning the European Cup three times on the bounce. The last – by strange coincidence against Reims, to whom he transferred back the following season – was his greatest. Kopa was the undisputed star player at the World Cup in Sweden in 1958, laying on most of **Just Fontaine**'s record thirteen goals, and he wound up European Footballer of the Year.

He played 45 times for his country, and *France Football* placed only Platini and Zidane ahead of him in a recent list of great French players. But his career was to end amid controversy, as Kopa began to campaign for player power. French clubs held property rights over players until they were 34 years old – meaning they could only break free of contracts with their side's blessing or once they were washed up. Kopa became a thorn in the authorities' side, and played a huge part in getting players improved rights. He was a revolutionary on and off the pitch.

LADISLAO KUBALA

Franco's second-favourite footballer

When Barcelona celebrated their centenary in 1999, they held a vote for the greatest player of those one hundred glorious years. The winner wasn't a Catalan, or even Spanish. Slovakian **Ladislao Kubala** has a place in the hearts of the Nou Camp faithful that even **Johan Cruyff** would envy. This is nothing short of remarkable when you consider he was regarded as a traitor in his homeland, received a one-year ban from FIFA and was once followed by a private detective hired by his club to observe his drunken antics. Kubala was a player of such intelligence and elegance, he would be forgiven almost anything.

> **"I put him in a cold shower, gave him a massage with pure alcohol and made him drink a cup of black coffee before putting him to bed for a few hours."**
> Angel Mur

Born in Hungary in 1927 to Slovak parents, Kubala was a Czech international at the age of 17 but also went on to play for Hungary and Spain, winning 28 caps in all. He fled Communism in 1949, pitching up to play in Italy, but the Hungarian regime was furious and saw him successfully banned for twelve months. Kubala ended up in a refugee camp where he formed a team of exiles to tour Europe. His talent saw him courted by both Barça and Real Madrid; legend has it he signed for the former because their president got him so half-cut he no longer knew where he was or who he was joining. It has a ring of truth.

Soon, however, he was a legend, adored by the crowd whose love for him was christened *Kubilismo*. Like Real's Gento, he was a favourite of General Franco, who had him star in a popular anti-communist film. Though he was viewed with suspicion by non-Catalans, nobody could deny his ability and he fired Barcelona to three titles, two Spanish Cups and two Fairs Cups before he left in 1961. He trained longer and became fitter than his team-mates, a remarkable feat considering his fabled bouts of drunkenness. However, the club finally saw red and slapped a tail on him after he led the squad into a red-light district on the eve of a crucial European tie.

In Jimmy Burns' book on the club, *Barça: A People's Passion*, fellow player **Angel Mur** recalled nipping round to Kubala's place on the morning of a match to find the star paralytic: "I put him in a cold shower, gave him a massage with pure alcohol and made him drink a cup of black coffee before putting him to bed for a few hours. Later he got up and went and played as if nothing had happened."

MATT LE TISSIER

A big fish in a medium-sized pond

"I'll tell you who I used to love watching", says Xavi Hernandez, Barcelona's mercurial midfielder who can lay claim to being the best in the world. "Matt Le Tissier. He played for South-hamp-on, a small club with a small stadium. But he would never leave. He wasn't like a typical English player and he would have done well in Spain. He had offers all the time to leave, but he stayed where 'is heart is, where he is loved and with his family. I'm like Matt Le Tissier, but for Barça. I've had offers to leave but I'm here for as long as possible." Le Tissier didn't make it to Spain, he didn't even make it away from Southampton, where he made 444 appearances between 1986–2002, scoring 162 goals.

The Channel Islander has received many plaudits. **Michel Platini**, confused by the Guernsey-born Le Tissier's French surname, tried to recruit him for "Les Bleus". His home nation largely ignored his languid talents and he played for England just eight times – never finding the net. Critics, among them England manager Glenn Hoddle, termed him a "luxury player", others accused him of laziness. However, his lackadaisical, unexpected elegance often gave a misleading impression. A hefty, awkward-looking six-footer, who was allegedly rejected as a youth by **Oxford United** because he was overweight, he was capable of sublime moments of grace and spectacular, beautiful goals. "He gets the ball, he takes the piss", as they used to sing of "Le God" at The Dell. He was also an icy cool penalty-taker, converting 48 out of 49 attempts. Once memorably subbed for "Bambi on ice" hoaxer Ali Dia in 1996 – the "cousin" supposedly recommended by "George Weah" on the telephone – Le Tissier claims he never considered leaving Southampton. "I played the game the way I wanted to play it, and had I gone on to a bigger club, I probably wouldn't have been able to do that. I enjoyed being a big fish in a medium-sized pond."

WLODZIMIERZ LUBAŃSKI

Poles apart

What if **Paul Gascoigne** hadn't made that suicidal lunge at **Gary Charles**? What if **Diego Maradona**'s handball goal had been disallowed? And what if **Włodzimierz Lubański** had been fit for the 1974 World Cup? The last question is probably the biggest lingering imponderable in Polish football.

Poland came third in that World Cup – losing to West Germany in the semi-finals on a sodden pitch that suited the more physical host nation and disrupted the fluent passing game of the underdogs. Had Lubański played, however, many feel Poland might well have had enough to win their first World Cup. But while the Polish players were doing a lap of honour with their bronze medals, their nation's greatest-ever goalscorer was under the surgeon's knife, getting his knee mended.

Rewind nearly twelve months to 6 June 1973. The game in progress was Poland v. England and the host nation were cruising to a 2–0 win – Lubański having scored one of the goals – when a crunching challenge by England defender **Roy McFarland** ended the Polish striker's World Cup hopes. The damage was a serious knee injury and three years in the international wilderness.

"He was a revelation to play with... it would be hard to pick out any weaknesses."
Grzegorz Lato on Włodzimierz Lubański

It's worth pointing out here that Polish football in the 1970s was enjoying a golden age, boasting such fantastic players as Grzegorz Lato, **Kazimierz Deyna**, Jan Tomaszewski, Andrzej Szarmach, Jerzy Gorgon and **Zbigniew Boniek**. Apart from **Michel Platini**, Boniek was perhaps the greatest European player of the 1980s. Deyna enjoyed a glittering career, but of Lubański – one of a kind even among so many greats – little is remembered.

Having captained the Polish national team to the gold medal in the 1972 Olympic Games, he was pencilled in as a challenger for the Golden Boot two years later – little surprise given his staggering 40 goals in 52 internationals (in many of which he was also skipper). He was strong, quick and a terrific header of the ball. His goals for **Górnik Zabrze** helped them win League titles galore and he just missed out on a European Cup Winners' Cup medal – his team losing 2–1, to Manchester City, in the 1970 final – before he moved to **Lokeren** in Belgium.

In his first season (1975–76) he scored seventeen times, and helped the Belgian side to six top-four finishes in seven seasons, including the runners-up spot in 1980-81. That was Lokeren's best ever season: they also got to the quarter-final of the UEFA Cup and the final of the Belgian Cup.

Lubański's international career resumed in 1976 and he scored a further four goals in thirteen appearances. He played at the 1978 World Cup in Argentina and, in the eyes of team-mate **Lato** (who, in his absence, had won the 1974 Golden Boot), was quite simply the greatest goalscorer of his time. "He was a revelation to play with", said the little Pole. "He knew exactly where you would be and we had almost a telepathic relationship. He was quick, technically excellent and knew where the goal was.

"As a person he was terrific to have around. He had the respect of the team – as every great captain should – and was unique in terms of being a superb all-rounder. It would be hard to pick out any weaknesses."

CRISTIANO LUCARELLI

"Avanti popolo"

When **Cristiano Lucarelli** first played for Italy's Under-21s in March 1997, he celebrated a goal by peeling back his jersey to reveal a Che Guevara T-shirt. Italy's junior coaches never picked him again, but in his home city of Livorno, the gesture would not be forgotten.

Lucarelli – raised in the so-called "Shanghai" quarter of the Tuscan port city – was a lifelong club supporter who became a celebrated Livorno player and icon and took every opportunity to celebrate the city's fame as the birthplace of the Italian Communist party. He even had the tune of "The Red Flag" as his mobile phone ringtone.

In the summer of 2003 Lucarelli gave up potential deals worth a rumoured one billion lire more, for the chance to join the club he loved – exchanging life as a better-paid, wandering goalscorer in middle-ranking Serie A teams to drop a division and devote his goals to the reddest club in Italy. He was 28 at the time, and had been playing for Torino, the latest stop on a career that had included spells at Perugia, Cosenza, Padua, Valencia (in Spain) and Lecce.

Money be damned, Lucarelli declared: his beloved Livorno had just been promoted to Serie B and he wanted to be part of the adventure. Twenty-five goals later, he had hoisted them into the top flight. Sadly he left Livorno somewhat under a cloud in 2007. However, in 2009, comfortably into his thirties, he rejoined the club on loan to oversee another promotion to Serie A.

His mouthy, revolutionary spirit may have curtailed his international career, but his zeal was seldom tamed. Taking part in a primetime Italian TV debate with the infamously right-wing Lazio player Paolo Di Canio he was asked if he would feel offended to be called a communist. "No, I wouldn't be offended", he replied. Che Guevara, he added, was "the symbol of proletarian revolution."

RODNEY MARSH AND STAN BOWLES

Super hoops

Lots of fans go misty-eyed for the 1970s, the supposed "golden era" of English football, but few more so than supporters of **Queens Park Rangers**. The west Londoners can look back to a brief period spent as the best club in the capital, inspired by two flash players who made the rest of the league envious: **Rodney Marsh** and **Stan Bowles**.

The English forwards shared curious parallels beyond wearing the famous QPR number ten shirt. One was a Mancunian who ended up in London; the other was a Cockney who eventually escaped to Manchester. Marsh and Bowles were both flamboyant entertainers on the pitch and boozed-up rascals off it; they both had run-ins with their managers; neither won as many England caps or trophies as their talents merited; and they both became controversial pundits.

Alf Ramsey: "If you don't work harder I'll pull you off at half time." Rodney Marsh: "Crikey, Alf, at Manchester City all we get is an orange and a cup of tea."

Exchange between Marsh and the England manager. He was never picked again.

Both started out with immense promise. Eastender Marsh played as an amateur with West Ham United before finding his feet at Loftus Road. He was a rare English creative magician, and knew it: when asked what he thought of being called "the white Pelé", he answered: "Nah, Pelé's the black Rodney Marsh." His career highlight came in 1967, when he scored the winner for QPR in the League Cup final against West Bromwich Albion before one hundred thousand fans. [fact-checking - winner or equaliser]

It was an amazing feat for a Third Division club, and Marsh was instrumental in taking the Hoops up to the top flight – scoring every other game. Marsh soon found out he was very famous, recalling: "I went to a restaurant and the owner walked up to me and cut off my tie. Apparently it was the custom of the house for celebrities, but nobody asked me."

Unfortunately, his move to Manchester City in 1972 was the start of his downfall. Although still a magnificent player recognized with nine England caps, Marsh did not blend in well with City's direct style, and many fans blamed him for their failure to win the league in 1972. "I slowed down their pattern of play", he admitted. Marsh's difficulties led to alcoholism and depression, and by the time he signed for Tampa Bay in 1976, he was drinking a bottle of vodka a day. And teaming up with George Best at Fulham twelve months later didn't help.

On the pitch, Fulham's "showbiz eleven" entertained the crowd by mucking about tackling each other: off it, Marsh and Best terrorized the fashionable Kings Road in Chelsea. Marsh finally got the wake-up call he needed when his doctor told him that his liver was almost twice the size it should have been.

QPR fans may have worried that they couldn't replace Rod, but then they didn't reckon on **Stan Bowles**, the forward with a left foot "as good as a hand" according to **Terry Venables**. Bowles was at the centre of QPR's best-ever team (1976–77) that made the quarter-finals of the UEFA Cup. But Mancunian Bowles had difficulties off the pitch, particularly with gambling. "If only Stan could pass a betting shop like he could pass a ball", his favourite manager, Ernie Tagg, famously lamented during his time at Carlisle. During his early days at Manchester City Bowles had fallen in with Mancunian crime syndicate the "Quality Street Gang", enraging his Manchester City assistant manager and noted bon viveur **Malcolm Allison**, who he ended up punching outside a nightclub.

He almost gave up the game after that, admitting: "I stopped training, except for running to the bookmaker's for the two o'clock race." He eventually started playing again, winding up at QPR. At Loftus Road, Bowles' dazzling artistry inspired Rangers even more than Marsh had, the highlight being their second-place league finish in 1976. He soon adapted to life in the capital too, losing huge sums playing big-money cards with notorious hoodlums (he was a terrible card player).

Unfortunately, it all eventually caught up with him. Bowles blew £250,000 gambling, became addicted to Valium and ended up getting arrested in a stolen van loaned to him by a dodgy mate. He even got drunk the night before appearing on *Superstars*, where he registered the lowest score in the show's history. He was sold to Nottingham Forest in 1979 where he fell out with **Brian Clough**, then went to Leyton Orient and Brentford before retiring in 1984.

Inevitably, like Marsh, Bowles ended up as a pundit, the two of them winding up the public on a regular basis, much as they did to opposition players years before. Marsh left Sky Sports after an on-air joke alluding to the 2004 Asian tsunami disaster. In a corner of west London, the pair will never be forgotten.

FRANK MCAVENNIE

Girls, goals and gumption

When Frank McAvennie called his 2003 autobiography *Scoring: An Expert's Guide* he wasn't just referring to his on-field exploits. Loved by fans for his maverick approach he never wore shinpads as much as his goalscoring prowess, the sex, drugs and rock'n'roll lifestyle that football fame afforded him would ultimately be the undoing of this flawed Glaswegian genius.

Told he'd never make it as a professional by his boyhood heroes Celtic, McAvennie's "bollocks to you" attitude took him to St Mirren, where he was sent off for fighting in his trial game against local rivals Morton. But convinced of his "bottle", the club signed the tearaway just before his 21st birthday and McAvennie was part of a Saints side that competed in the upper echelons of the Scottish Premier Division and even played in Europe.

Signed by West Ham for £340,000 in the summer of 1985, McAvennie was an instant hit at Upton Park, with his mixture of goals and gumption. After a flying start to the season and an appearance on *Wogan*, McAvennie was soon a regular at London's trendy Stringfellows "nightclub", rubbing shoulders with gangsters, popstars and Page-three girls, one of whom, Jenny Blyth, he later married.

Two years later, McAvennie fulfilled a lifelong dream, signing for Celtic and immediately endearing himself to the fans by getting sent off on his Old Firm debut. He shone briefly as The Hoops won the double, but was soon back at West Ham, where a broken leg was the beginning of the end. "That was when I started doing cocaine regularly and drinking too much", explained McAvennie, but his popularity endures. "I think the fans took to me because I was one of them. If I hadn't made it as a player I would have been there with them paying to watch the game."

ALLY MCCOIST

All-time cult hero

Player, manager, actor, presenter, prankster, heart-throb. Ally McCoist has done it all. But to Rangers fans, he will always be "Super Ally", the club's all-time record goalscorer with 355 in all competitions, each one celebrated with that cheeky chappy persona that made McCoist such a popular figure with fans of all clubs both sides of the border.

Professional football didn't always come so easily to McCoist, though. Rejected by St Mirren manager Alex Ferguson for being too small, McCoist failed to score in his first two seasons for his first professional club, St Johnstone, before grabbing 23 in his third, earning him a move to Sunderland in 1981. The goals again dried up and McCoist returned to Scotland after two seasons. The rest, as they say, is history. Nineteen major trophies including ten league titles and two European golden boots led to McCoist being named Rangers' all-time cult hero in 2005, polling a staggering sixty-three percent of the vote.

By then, McCoist was a respected television pundit and award-winning presenter, had been voted the 87th Sexiest Man of the Millennium by a leading women's magazine and starred in a Hollywood film alongside Academy Award-winning actor Robert Duvall. McCoist's legendary sense of humour and mischief also made him an ideal team captain on BBC TV's *A Question of Sport* for eleven years. On his farewell episode in 2007, the joke was on McCoist as in the "Mystery Guest" round he failed to recognize former Rangers boss Walter Smith – McCoist is now assistant manager to Smith at Ibrox!

In honour of their local hero, in January 2010 the £3.5 million Ally McCoist Sports Complex was opened by the man himself in South Lanarkshire. Not bad for a once misfiring striker who was deemed too small to be a professional footballer.

TED MCMINN

Tin winger

Affectionately nicknamed "The Tin Man", Scottish winger **Ted McMinn** became a legend as much for his inelegant running style as his love of lager. One former **Rangers** team-mate reckoned that he once ran down the wing at full speed, and having crossed the ball from the by-line was unable to stop so he jumped over the wall into the Copland Road stand, where he ran up the stairs and promptly disappeared into the stand.

McMinn broke into professional football aged twenty at his local club **Queen of the South**, realizing his boyhood ambition to play for them. He then played for clubs as diverse as **Glasgow Rangers**, **Sevilla**, **Derby County**, **Burnley** and **Slough Town**. At Rangers, where he played between 1984 and 1987, manager Graeme Souness said: "How can I tell Ted what to do when he doesn't know what he's going to do?"

Admitting that he stepped out of line too often at Ibrox under Souness, he joined former manager **Jock Wallace** in Andalusia. In a single season at Sevilla, he broke his leg early, but recovered in time to play 22 times and see the fans protest when he announced he was returning to Britain. His name was above Diego Maradona's on Sevilla's centenary strip.

Injury would scar McMinn's career – and his life after his career – and yet, despite the short spells he stayed at clubs, the ebullient winger always ended up being a fans' favourite.

In 2008, an infection in a cut became so bad that half of his foot had to be removed, before a surgeon told him that he was better having his leg taken off below the knee. It was a shock, but despite the pain he goes through every day, McMinn continued to play golf and accepted an invitation to play in the British Open for amputees.

VALENTINO MAZZOLA

Tragic Italian hero

As the leader of arguably the greatest Italian club side in history, and with the rugged good looks of a classic Hollywood actor, **Valentino Mazzola** was one of football's first superstars. A dazzling inside forward adept in all areas of the pitch, Mazzola was the fulcrum of a **Torino** side that won five consecutive league titles in the 1940s before being wiped out in a tragic air crash at Superga on 4 May 1949.

Even after the Superga disaster, in which Mazzola and seventeen fellow Torino players perished, the team's legacy held sway over both Torino and Italian football in general. At the centre of this legacy was the man known simply as "Captain Valentino", a redoubtable leader blessed with extraordinary playing ability.

Italy v. Portugal, Genoa, 27 February 1949, some two months before the Superga tragedy. Captain Valentino Mazzola (second right) shakes hands with the Portuguese captain.

Mazzola began his career with a team at the sprawling Alfa-Romeo factory in Milan. Snapped up by Torino president Ferruccio Novo in 1943, Mazzola quickly galvanized the club. It was not long before the whole of Italy began to laud Torino's magnificence.

When talking of Mazzola's influence, centre half and fellow team-mate Mario Rigamonti claimed that "he alone is half the squad". Heroic enough, but this was within a group of players so overflowing with talent that in 1947 Torino provided ten of the eleven names that constituted Italy's team for an international fixture against Hungary.

Yet in the company of these many exemplars of footballing skill and style, Mazzola was the chief. Playing in an advanced midfield role, he managed to score 29 goals in one season alone, during the days when strikers were expected to convert the bulk of the chances.

Alongside a roaring shot and a deceptively strong physique, Mazzola would also direct the team's play. On occasions when Torino were struggling, the Filadelfia stadium's in-house trumpeter would summon a storm, the iconic Mazzola would roll his sleeves up, and Torino would swarm all over the opposition. The ritual rarely failed; in five years of dominance, Torino scored almost five hundred goals and were unbeaten at home for over four seasons.

As titles were racked up and opponents swept aside, Torino became a byword for post-war pride and virtue. Mazzola's elegant facial features meant that his image was soon appearing on a whole host of commercial paraphernalia. A hero to football fans and a magnet for women, Mazzola's scandalous infidelities were his only failing, at a time when divorce was still illegal in Italy.

Tragedy curtailed "Il Grande" Torino's reign, but their records and achievements still resonate, symbolized by the brilliant and charismatic Valentino Mazzola.

ALBERTO MÉNDEZ

A ghostly Gunner

When people in London asked him what he was doing for a living, Alberto Méndez, who had just won the Premier League 1997–98 title with Arsenal, always answered: "I am a student". He thought nobody would believe him if he told them the truth.

In his five years with Arsenal, he remained virtually unknown to the public after playing just a dozen games for the club, but that does not take away anything from his merit: he was Arsène Wenger's weirdest signing ever. Wenger, who developed a splendid reputation for unearthing talent in his long career as Arsenal's manager, went down one spring day in 1997 to watch a German fifth division match between the railway workers' Club Nuremberg and SC Feucht. It was the equivalent of a UK game in the Dr Martens Southern Premier League. Wenger had received a tip-off from a scout about Feucht's 22-years-old, two-footed playmaker.

Méndez, a German of Spanish descent, who indeed *was* a university student at the time, had a bad game by his own admission. Feucht had already secured promotion and Méndez had drunk a bit too much the night before. But Wenger signed him anyway for £250,000.

Méndez told him: "Sorry, but I don't get it: I am an amateur player, I had a terrible game and you want me." Wenger muttered something about potential. So Méndez moved to London to join a world-class team alongside the likes of Patrick Vieira and Dennis Bergkamp.

There were, indeed, moments when he really looked in the same class, particularly in a League Cup game against Birmingham. But the rest of his career suggests that maybe, just maybe, Wenger saw something in him that was simply not there. After unsuccessful loan spells in the Greek and German First Division and three years involving two relegations in the Spanish Segunda División, he spent the remainder of his career travelling the German Third and Fourth Divisions, the clubs on his CV telling a unique story: Feucht, Arsenal, Sandhausen, Weiden. He did, however, manage to finish his economics degree at university.

BILLY MEREDITH

Boy from the black stuff

When **Billy Meredith** made his debut for Manchester City in 1894, the game was in Newcastle. The problem for Meredith was that he was employed full-time as a miner in his home town of Chirk, North Wales. After slaving in the pit throughout the Friday, he caught a train at 2.00am, arriving on Tyneside at 11.00am. He played the game, losing 5–4, then took a return train and went straight back down the pit.

> **"If Billy takes my advice he will stick to his work and play football for his own amusement when work is finished."**
> Billy Meredith's mother

It may sound like a "When I were a lad" sketch from *Monty Python*, but such were the realities of football shortly after the formation of the league. Billy Meredith went on to become its unlikely first superstar. Meredith didn't want to be a professional footballer – he was quite content in the mines (where he'd started straight from school, aged twelve). But his talents and fate conspired to push him into the game. He was already recognized as Wales' most talented player from his amateur heroics with Chirk, and a miners' strike meant he needed to supplement his income. Manchester City were ready to pounce.

Meredith refused to move to Manchester, instead commuting from North Wales. It didn't harm his career: the nippy right winger was nicknamed the Welsh Wizard and was bamboozling defenders over ninety years before **Ryan Giggs**. Meredith, who played with a toothpick in his mouth, was feted for his strength and skill. He was a key player as City lifted Manchester's first FA Cup in 1904, and by the age of thirty he was club captain.

But in 1905 disaster struck: Meredith was accused of bribing an Aston Villa player before an important match. He denied the charges strenuously, but was suspended by the FA for eight months. During his suspension, he engineered a transfer to City's lowly neighbours, Manchester United.

The severity of his punishment inspired Meredith to refloat the Players' Union and he became a union stalwart and campaigner for players' rights and the abolition of the maximum wage. He was a prominent member of the "Outcasts", the Manchester United players who went on strike in 1909 when the FA tried to ban the union.

Meredith was also remarkable for his endurance. With United he won two league titles and another FA Cup, before re-signing for City in 1915. A health-conscious teetotaller, who swore by hot baths and the copious application of "dog oil" (a mixture of rape oil and petroleum jelly, used for massaging racing greyhounds!) Meredith played on until the age of 49, picking up the last of his 48 Welsh caps aged 45. Still the oldest player ever to appear for City, he played a total of 1568 games, scoring 470 goals. He died penniless, his caps and medals in a suitcase under his bed, still contemptuous of the footballing authorities who treated footballers like chattels.

WILLIE MILLER

A towering ambition; a natural talent

When Sir Alex Ferguson ranks you, along with Bryan Robson, Eric Cantona and Roy Keane, as the only player in his managing career who "didn't need Alex Ferguson in order to succeed" it marks you down as something exceptional. Which is what William Ferguson Miller was as a footballer, captain and spiritual leader of Aberdeen football club for two decades.

Despite the historic dominance of Scotland's Old Firm, Rangers and Celtic, Miller is the only captain of a Scottish club to have lifted two European trophies – the European Cup Winners' Cup won in a dramatic defeat of Alfredo di Stéfano's Real Madrid in 1983 and the European Super Cup in a two-leg victory over European champions Hamburg. It is ironic that Miller and the greatest Scottish manager even shared Ferguson as a family name because they not only shared seven blistering years at Pittodrie but an identical burning, relentless hunger to win at almost any cost. Their ten trophies, including three Premier League titles, belie the fact that the two Glaswegians initially viewed each other with open hostility with a consequent frequent need to mark out territorial rights, after Ferguson arrived at Pittodrie in 1979.

Told that Miller was "slow and a poor trainer" the new Aberdeen manager spoke to reserve coach Teddy Scott about the player but was told to "wait until Saturday at three o'clock and you'll see how good Willie is". Miller recalls that Ferguson constantly goaded the sweeper that anything he did was "not as good as Jackie Copeland would have done" in reference to his former team leader at St Mirren. The love–hate relationship developed into mutual respect and, fuelled by the coruscating hatred of defeat they both shared, Miller and Ferguson dominated Scottish football for several seasons.

> **"the best penalty box defender in the world."**
> Alex Ferguson on Willie Miller

Miller originally learned his trade as a free-scoring striker, loaned out to Peterhead in the Highland League which he called "a field of conflict where no prisoners were taken" and even after captaining Aberdeen to victory over Kenny Dalglish's Celtic in the 1976 League Cup final spent the following summer on the roof of a friend's house building a loft conversion. He became what Ferguson called "the best penalty box defender in the world", made record league appearances for Aberdeen and was an inaugural inductee in the Scotland Football Hall of Fame. Categorized by opposition fans as Aberdeen's "referee", one immense ticking-off Miller gave to match official Kenny Hope at Ibrox actually led to Hope being disciplined and suspended from some Cup matches for accepting the tirade.

His towering moments were organizing brilliant 0–0 draws at Bayern Munich en route to winning the Cup Winners' Cup and the same result at European Champions Hamburg on the way to defeating Real Madrid in the rain-soaked

1983 final. He also headed the equalizer, against Celtic, which clinched the 1985 Premier League title – making him the last non-Old Firm player to score a league-winning goal. The 1982 World Cup finals might have offered similar glory as Scotland were on the verge of qualifying from the group stage for the first time until Alan Hansen barged into Miller, Russia broke away to score and Miller, ruefully, reflected later: "I'm probably the only human being who remembers that I played well in the game – except my mum."

GERD MÜLLER

"And it goes bang!"

He showed the world that there is no sharper weapon in football than a beefy backside. The ball at his feet, Gerd Müller turned and with his finest trick, stuck out his bum to keep the defender behind him at bay. His was always the smallest contribution to the game and at the same time the biggest. Because Gerd Müller, a three times European Cup winner with Bayern Munich, 1974 World Cup winner and 1972 European Champion with West Germany, did hardly anything but stand waiting in the opponents box and then, in a split second, turned the bum and scored.

His goals were never beautiful, often surreal, but they were, above all, plenty and decisive. Gerd Müller scored like nobody ever did and nobody ever will – 393 goals in 453 games for Bayern between 1964 and 1979. For Germany, 68 goals in 62 games – among them the winner in the 1974 World Cup final against the Netherlands. He was seven times the Bundesliga's top scorer, twice Europe's leading scorer. Twelve years in a row he managed more than twenty league goals each season, forty goals in the 1971–72 Bundesliga season being his best tally – unbeaten of course.

"Small, potty Müller", one of his managers at Bayern called him – and it sounded like a declaration of love. Gerd Müller – 5 feet 7 inches-small and looking, at least from afar, a tiny bit chubby – was the triumph of the ordinary. A polite and simple man who did not even look an extraordinary player, but who had that one special thing. Once he recorded a song with the title: "Dann macht es bumm!" – "And it goes bang!" Has his art ever been described with greater precision?

GÜNTER NETZER

Breaking the mould

When German football fans think of the 1970s, they think of Bayern Munich ruling Europe and of the best national team they've ever had. When they're asked to come up with images defining this era, one player invariably springs to mind – despite neither playing at Bayern Munich nor ever truly becoming a West German regular. That man is Günter Netzer.

One typical Netzer image has him leaping in the air on a June day in 1973. It was his last game for Borussia Mönchengladbach, the Cup final against Cologne. Netzer had been benched, mainly because he'd already signed with Real Madrid at that point, but during the interval before the beginning of extra time he brought himself into the match without asking for the coach's permission. Four minutes later he scored the winner.

Another image has Netzer surging through midfield, his blond mane illuminated by the Wembley floodlights. It was 29 April 1972, and West Germany were in the process of winning for the first time on English soil. Netzer was only playing because Cologne's Wolfgang Overath was injured, but it was largely his performance that has bestowed the match with near-mythic status in German football lore.

There are plenty more images though – some of which might explain why Wolfgang Overath, the reliable team player, won 81 caps to the 37 collected by this unfathomable and unpredictable genius. There are the pictures of Netzer in the bar he owned, Lover's Lane. Pictures that show him behind the wheel of a fast car (in June 1970, he almost died in a Ferrari). Pictures taken with his beautiful and mysterious girlfriend, a goldsmith. It could be an all-too-familiar story of a footballer going off the rails – but Netzer was not the average football player or typical 1970s maverick. He owned a bar but he didn't drink. He loved cars but he wasn't reckless. He was a sex idol but never a womanizer. He was an icon for all those who hated Bayern's clinical efficiency, yet he was a man with a keen business sense – he was Hamburg's commercial manager from 1978 to 1986, moulding the great side led by Kevin Keegan.

> **"Netzer broke through from deep midfield."**
> **Professor Karl Heinz Bohrer, German cultural critic**

Today, Netzer is mainly known as an acclaimed TV analyst, popular for his acumen and honesty. But at the same time, he led the group that bought the broadcasting rights to the 2006 World Cup from the bankrupt Kirch Media company. Some thirty years since his heyday, he still defies the stereotypes.

LUTZ PFANNENSTIEL

Globetrotting journeyman

Lutz Pfannenstiel almost became famous as "the man who stole the penguin". But he had second thoughts, and before anybody had noticed, he removed the penguin from his bath and delivered it back to the wildlife reserve in New Zealand, from where he had hijacked the poor animal the night before in one of his larger-than-life practical jokes. So, in the end, Lutz Pfannenstiel from a remote village in deepest Bavaria, became more justly famous as the only footballer to play professionally on all six continents. He is still trying to arrange a game in Antarctica, so that continent can be added to the list – for the pedants.

What's in a Name?

It doesn't say anything particularly positive about the footballing imagination that players' nicknames are generally formulaic. The simple substitution of a name's last three or four letters for an "o" – as in Thommo or Deano – or an "a" – viz. Gazza or Macca – is usually deemed enough. If inventors of such things are having an especially creative day they might come up with Psycho or Tank for the midfield hatchet man. Over the years there have been numerous Tanks, Rocks and Walls, plus at least one Rocket (Boudewijn Zenden), Cannon (Ronald Koeman), Axe (John Jensen), Hammer (Jörg Albertz), Nail (Wim Jonk), Lamppost (John van Loen), and even a Computer (the Kaizer Chiefs' Zacharia Lamola) too.

Then there are the vocations: the Professor (Arsène Wenger), the Philosopher (Lilian Thuram), the Doctor (Socrates), El Matador (Marcelo Salas), the President (Laurent Blanc), the General (Rinus Michels), the Butcher (René Trost), the Assassin (Ole Solskjær, albeit a baby-faced one), and there are hordes of Princes and Kings.

But professions and DIY boys' toys come a poor (joint) second in the world football sobriquet league. The indisputable champions are animals. Indeed football has so many – including of course *the* Animal, Edmundo (actually meant as a compliment rather than a reference to his violent streak) – it's surprising no manager to date has earned the nickname Noah. There's the Black Cat/Spider/Octopus (according to who you believe, Lev Yashin and any half-decent keeper

In 1993, aged twenty, the goalkeeper received an offer from Bundesliga side VfL Bochum. But they just wanted him for their reserve team and Pfannenstiel did not think of himself as a reserve-team keeper. So, rather than join Bochum, he accepted an offer from Penang FA in Malaysia. And so his globetrotting journey began. In the course of his career he played for Nottingham Forest in the UK, Orlando Pirates in South Africa, Sembawang Rangers in Singapore, Dunedin Technical in New Zealand. When he realized, fifteen years and some twenty-four moves later, that South America was the only inhabited continent where he hadn't been employed, he gave up a secure job at the Vancouver Whitecaps to join an obscure Brazilian side called Hermann Aichinger. Moving on had become a thrill for him – an obsession.

He was jailed (though his claims of innocence have some justification) for match-fixing in Singapore and is known as the man "who died three times for Bradford Park Road", after his heart stood still three times when he was knocked out by a furious tackle in a game against Harrogate Town. When announcing that his career was over aged 36, in 2009, he said: "my career has not been better or worse than I imagined at 18, just different." A few weeks later, he signed for a team in Namibia.

since), the Dutch Swan (Marco van Basten), the Vulture (Emilio Butragueño), the Black Panther of Mozambique (Eusébio), the Giraffe (Jack Charlton), the Goat (Shaun Goater), the Fox (various), the Horse (Oleg Luzhny), the Snake (Kanu), the Pit Bull (Edgar Davids), the Bat (Cle Kooiman), the Bald Eagle (various), the Gazelle (Faustino Asprilla), the Magpie (Winston Bogarde), the Buffalo (various), the Mosquito (Erik Mykland), the Flea (Jesper Olsen) and the Llama (Frank Rijkaard). All apparently are complimentary.

In Europe, the Italians and the Dutch show more imagination, boasting the Little Soldier (Angelo di Livio), the White Feather (Fabrizio Ravanelli), the Divine Ponytail (Roberto Baggio), the Snowflake (Ronald Koeman, again) and the Black Tulip (Ruud Gullit). Curiously, the not-particularly-squirtish Marco Tardelli is the Squirt. The Brazilians surpass these, however, with such pearls as the Encyclopaedia, the Possessed, the Phenomenon (Ronaldo), the Human Bullet (Roberto Carlos), the Helmet, the Hurricane, the Old Wolf, the Village Cannon, Tom Thumb, the Atomic Kick (Rivelino), Cry Baby and Mister Sadness. But even those don't compare in grandeur with the Bomber of Borovo (Yugoslav Siniša Mihajlović), the Emperor of Cameroon (Roger Milla) or the Prince of the Red Square (Russian Igor Korneev).

Cartoon characters are popular monikers too. There's Mighty Mouse (Marc Overmars), Dumbo (Edwin van der Sar), Goofy (Dejan Govedarica), Shaggy (Steve McManaman), Tin Tin (Ronald Koeman – again!), Spiderman (Walter Zenga), Batman (Marco Simone) and two Icemen (Dennis Bergkamp and Rudi Peter). Football, you'll be pleased to know, even has a Smurf (MLS' Antony De Ávila).

FERENC PUSKÁS

"Look at that fat chap over there … we'll murder this lot"

"I came away wondering to myself what we had been doing all these years." Tom Finney's stark assessment of England's 6–3 drubbing by Hungary at Wembley in 1953 heralded the end of England's era as a footballing superpower as the baton passed to foreign fields. Yet while we deify the Brazilians, Italians and Argentinians who have since risen to prominence, the protagonist of that epoch-defining defeat – a short, squat, former army officer from behind the Iron Curtain – is often overlooked.

It may be because so little footage of **Ferenc Puskás** exists that we forget what talents he possessed, but he was the first player to impose his individuality on the game to the extent that he overshadowed the rest of his team. While **Nandor Hidegkuti**'s role in "the hole" was credited with destroying England that day, it was the fact they couldn't get the ball off Puskás which had most to do with the outcome. Puskás won every domestic honour and scored 83 goals in 84 internationals, though his equalizing strike in the 1954 World Cup final was disallowed as

West German industry overcame eastern European flair. He also unwittingly became a symbol of resistance when he defected to first Austria and then Spain following the failed Hungarian uprising of 1956.

With Real Madrid, Puskás defied age and an ever-expanding waistline – one Wolves player described how Puskás amazed onlookers by demolishing countless helpings at a post-match dinner when Honved played at Molineux – to win three European Cups and score four goals in the thrilling 7–3 defeat of Eintracht Frankfurt in the 1960 final. When he finally returned home in 1993 to manage the national side, he was mobbed in Budapest by fans to whom he represented not just outstanding artistry but hope.

GIANNI RIVERA

The Young Monk

Nicknamed the Golden Boy of Italian football, and the first native Italian to win the European Player of the Year award, Gianni Rivera should really have been bigger than The Beatles. With his hairdo straight from *A Hard Day's Night* and the detached air of an intellectual, the graceful playmaker helped Milan to two European Cup victories in the 1960s. However, this was not enough for some observers, who clamoured for perspiration over perspicacity, and called attention to Rivera's spindly physique, which was more Twiggy than Tyson.

For while Rivera's laconic gestures set fans swooning, his particular gifts appeared starkly at odds with Italian football's central ethos during the 1960s, epitomized by the cautious, defensive *catenaccio* system favoured by Helenio Herrera's Internazionale side.

In contrast, Rivera would reside in the attacking third of the pitch, where he would conjure openings in the opposition's defence with delicate passes – bestriding the turf with elegance and poise. Rivera was a genius; a sorcerer of cunning and wit. Sadly, in the Italian age of defensive concern, Rivera's distaste for tracking back and working up a sweat would land him in hot water.

As rivals Inter excelled, claiming back-to-back European titles, renowned journalist Gianni Brera labelled Rivera "the young monk", an appellation that attempted to expose his hesitancy towards the bump and grind of Serie A.

The debate over Rivera would reach its height during the 1970 World Cup finals. Alongside Rivera in the Italian squad stood Sandro Mazzola, Inter's very own source of creative inspiration. Rather than find a way to accommodate both of his best players, Italian manager Ferruccio Valcareggi hit upon the idea of playing one player in each half. However, during the final, Rivera was only used for the dying minutes at the end of the game, with Italy already well adrift of a magical Brazilian team. A maverick operating in an age of conservatism, Rivera appeared a man born in the right place at the wrong time.

Nevertheless, the Golden Boy was always appreciated at Milan, where he won three league titles to go along with his marvellous performances in two European Cup finals. Following a customary sex scandal in the 1970s Rivera took the next logical step, into politics, where he served at the Defence Ministry. He is now an MEP. For a man well accustomed to stylishly dodging bullets both on and off the field, it appeared a most fitting reinvention.

ROMARIO AND EDMUNDO

Brazil nuts

Romario and Edmundo fit squarely within the category of flawless players who are flawed human beings. Yet even by football's standards, the pair are in a class of their own. Between them, **Edmundo Alaves de Souza** and **Romario de Souza Faria** have turned the soap opera of Brazilian football into full-scale tabloid opera involving nightclubs, carnivals and a monkey called Pedrinho.

Known as "the Animal", and labelled "a liability to mankind" by one journalist, Edmundo has been named as defendant in a paternity suit by a Brazilian TV presenter, been sent off seven times in one season, brawled on the beaches of Rio and once spent a week under arrest in an Ecuadorian hotel after destroying a TV camera. And in December 1995, a car that he was driving was involved in an accident that left three pedestrians dead. Edmundo was found guilty. His lawyers launched the first of a series of appeals, but Vasco da Gama sacked him, and he left for Italy two years later. He signed for Fiorentina and the club briefly had a chance of winning Serie A, but with striker **Gabriel Batistuta** injured, they needed Edmundo badly. His response was to go and party at the carnival in Rio.

A similar error of judgement cost Romario his job at Flamengo. The night before they lost against Gremio, he had been seen in a nightclub. Unimpressed by Romario's claims that he was suffering from insomnia, Flamengo sacked him. Romario's response was to launch a £1.5 million lawsuit for unfair dismissal. Not to be outdone, Edmundo got himself into trouble again, this time with animal rights organizations. He'd hired a circus to perform in his garden to celebrate his son's birthday, including Pedrinho the chimpanzee. His accusers say Edmundo wasted no time getting Pedrinho drunk on beer and whisky. Edmundo denied it.

Both players ended up with Vasco da Gama again (but not before Edmundo had been sacked by Cruzeira for deliberately missing a penalty against Vasco). The pair soon fell out when Edmundo saw a crude cartoon of himself on a toilet door in a nightclub owned by Romario. When it was suggested that Romario be captain of Vasco, Edmundo refused to play. It wasn't the first time that a toilet had got Romario into trouble. National team manager **Mario Zagallo** had already sued him after seeing similarly crude graffiti about himself in the same convenience.

If there's one thing Romario loves more than partying, it's sex. He told one journalist that "Good strikers can only score goals when they have had good sex on the night before a match" and one Brazilian priest was worried that Romario had had so much sex that he might pass on "bad spirits" to **Ronaldo** just by playing in the same team. As for Romario, though the Brazilian Supreme Court confirmed his earlier conviction, and he faced four and a half years in an open prison, he managed to evade jail and continue playing for Vasco.

But Romario and Edmundo did manage to hold it together long enough to annihilate Manchester United in the inaugural World Club Championship in 2000. It was a game that reminded the world why so many managers have indulged both players, and suggested that even "the Animal" might have a different side. Edmundo celebrated scoring by raising his shirt to reveal a picture of Rafael Barcelar, a five-year-old boy who had died from meningitis the week before. "The boy's wish before he died was for Vasco to beat Manchester United", he said. "The beauty of the goal was dedicated to him."

DEJAN SAVIĆEVIĆ

Frustrated footballing genius

The Montenegrin attacker Dejan Savićević has suffered a fair amount of flak in the course of his career. If it wasn't arch-disciplinarian Fabio Capello deploying him in strange positions, it was Yugoslavian politics – the latter keeping Savićević and a superb national side away from the 1992 European Championships. Savićević's career was plagued by interruptions, but his preternatural ability to dribble and exploit extra space around defenders redefined the boundaries for arch trickery and deception.

His career began in earnest at Red Star Belgrade, where, alongside Robert Prosinecki and Darko Pancev, he played a central role in the club's greatest era. Red Star managed four league titles in five years, and a crowning victory over Marseille in the 1991 European Cup final. Red Star were a primordial mixture of speed and devastating intuition, capable of startling interplay and quicksilver counter-attacks. Savićević's famous goal against Bayern Munich during the 1991 European Cup semi-final is a classic example. Taking advantage of a stray Stefan Effenberg pass, the ball was instantly propelled forward, before Savićević swept past the last defender with insulting ease and fired home.

Manchester United fans may recall Savićević's performance in the 1991 European Super Cup, when his mazy runs of labyrinthine complexity humiliated their defence. Red Star would go on to lose the game 1–0 against the run of play, but the gulf in quality play was as plain as paper.

In 1992, the team was cruelly broken up and Savićević shipped to Milan, largely as a result of the nascent Balkans conflict. Another sad corollary of the unrest – the national team were banned from Euro '92. Under the watchful Capello, Savićević

The field trails behind Savićević in the 1991 European Cup final, Olympique de Marseille v. Red Star Belgrade.

initially struggled to bed in to a magnificent Milan side already studded with gold. However, by the end of his second season, Savićević was being lauded as the star of the 1994 European Cup final. Barcelona's "dream team" were routed 4–0, as Savićević provided an assist for the opening goal and a stunning lob for the third.

Despite such mercurial bursts, Savićević was often criticized for lacking the tactical discipline associated with Italian football. With his truncated bob of hair billowing in the wind, he often cut an isolated figure.

After retiring at Rapid Vienna in 2001, Savićević endured a torrid spell as manager of the Serbian national team, before helping the successful political push for Montenegrin independence. Although the underachieving Savićević is rarely named among the greats, his intoxicating style inspired much admiration. Silvio Berlusconi described him as "the genius", and, for once, appeared to be telling the truth.

LEN SHACKLETON

The original maverick

What is it with the Northeast and footballing clowns? Forty years before Paul Gascoigne burped, joked and swore his way into the public consciousness, there was the original gifted joker, **Len Shackleton**.

On the pitch, Shackleton was one of the most entertaining players of the 1940s and 1950s, wowing the huge post-war crowds with his flamboyant skills and spectacular goals. Off it, he was a bolshie comedian whose approach sometimes got him into trouble with the authorities and meant his talents often went unrewarded. When one selector was asked why Shackleton had been left out of the England team again, he answered: "because we play at Wembley Stadium, not the London Palladium."

A Yorkshireman, Shackleton started his career at Bradford Park Avenue, often cheekily moonlighting as a player for Bradford City, whom he supported as a boy. He went on to play for Newcastle United, but really made his name at Sunderland, scoring 101 goals in 348 appearances – still a post-war club record. Via two FA Cup semis and a second place in the Championship, Shackleton soon earned his crown as football's "clown prince".

On one occasion, as Sunderland led Arsenal with five minutes to go, he dribbled into the opposition penalty area, stood on the ball and pretended to comb his hair while looking at his watch. Shackleton regularly bamboozled opposing full-backs by playing one-twos off the corner flag, and once deliberately lost a ball at Bramall Lane by booting it into a massive snowdrift. He could even kick the ball fifteen yards ahead of him with so much spin on it that it would screw back to him.

Shackleton further enraged the establishment when he published his autobiography, which contained a page headed "The Average Director's Knowledge of Football". It was blank. He was capped only five times for England, scoring a memorable goal in a 3–1 defeat of West Germany, but frustrated manager Walter Winterbottom. "If only Len would come halfway to meet the needs of the team, there wouldn't be many to touch him", sighed the boss.

Retiring from the game in 1957, Shackleton went on to work as an outspoken journalist. He became as much admired as an anti-establishment figure as he was as a player – even capturing the attentions of anarchist rockers Chumbawumba, who included "Song for Len Shackleton" on their 2002 album, *Readymades*. Shackleton died in 2000, aged 78.

ALLAN SIMONSEN

Valley of dreams

In 1977, Allan Simonsen was voted European Footballer of the Year. Five years later, he was playing for Charlton Athletic. But it wasn't drink, drugs or gambling which led to the Danish superstar's reduced circumstances: it was his own free will. To get an idea of how unlikely Simonsen's move from northeast Spain to southeast London was, imagine Rivaldo signing for Grimsby Town. The tricky attacking midfielder was a popular figure at Barcelona, with whom he spent three years and won the Cup Winners' Cup, but when Diego Maradona pushed the quota of foreign players above the permitted maximum, Simonsen was deemed surplus to requirements.

He was put on the market for £300,000 and was expected to move to Italy, but Addicks chairman Mark Hulyer was nothing if not ambitious and stumped up the cash to take the star to the old Second Division. Hulyer reasoned that the mid-table strugglers would recoup the outrageous outlay through sponsorship and additional gate receipts – more than two thousand saw Simonsen's reserve-team debut – but the big figures never rolled in, and his wages of £1500 a week (then an enormous sum) were another stumbling block.

On the pitch, Simonsen inspired Charlton with nine goals in sixteen matches and some performances which fans still talk about, but when it became clear his salary couldn't be paid he packed his bags, making his swansong in a dismal 7–1 defeat at Burnley. It was a decidedly unglamorous end to what might have been a fairy-tale season, and the outlay played a considerable part in Charlton's financial woes of years to come. Simonsen, though, had evidently acquired a taste for being the underdog: he rejected offers from Spurs and Serie A to rejoin Danish minnows Velje, his first club, and later resurfaced as manager of first the Faroe Islands and later Luxembourg. "I like a challenge", he later explained.

JOMO SONO

The burning spear from Soweto

Ask most South African footballers to name their idol and they will say Jomo "Black Prince" Sono. Born in the township of Orlando East in Soweto, he dreamed of playing for local club Orlando Pirates like his father. He would realisze that dream, although his father died in a car crash when he was a child and his mother abandoned him to be brought up by his impoverished grandparents.

He got the nickname Jomo (which means "burning spear") for his stellar performances for the Pirates in the years of apartheid, before moving to the nascent NASL where he played alongside Pelé for the New York Cosmos. With a sharp business as well as football brain, he was invigorated by US culture and returned to Johannesburg in 1982 brimming with ideas. He purchased the Highlands Park FC, one of the most successful in South Africa and renamed them Jomo Cosmos.

"He did that for the love of the game", says the former Leeds United defender Lucas Radebe, himself once voted the second most popular man in the country behind Nelson Mandela. "And to this day still gives young stars opportunities." Many of the best talents are spotted and later sold to European clubs by the shrewd Sono – players like Mark Fish, Phil Masinga and current South African captain Aaron Mokoena. Radebe admired him greatly as a player. "He had great skill and was the first person I saw do a banana kick", he says. "He could bend the ball in any direction. He was in charge of the South Africa team which I captained in the 2002 World Cup and brought a great team spirit. He was a true hero."

Jomo Cosmos are one of the most established teams in South African football, with Jomo the longest-serving coach in the country.

BERT TRAUTMANN

Keeping with the enemy

Many would say that Bert Trautmann had endured enough suffering by the time he turned up at Manchester City in 1949. During World War II he was captured by the French, Americans and Russians but escaped every time. He was buried in a cellar for three days while fighting as a paratrooper, and was later court-martialled for sabotage. After being taken prisoner by the British, he was shipped to a POW camp in Ashton-in-Makerfield, Lancashire, where his displays between the sticks began to catch the eye (though he had only performed as an outfield player in amateur games in Germany).

Somehow he ended up playing the 1948–49 season for St Helens Town in the Liverpool County Combination and was then poached by City to become the first German to play in the English Football League. And what a player he was – Trautmann's raw talent electrified Maine Road and he is regarded by many as the greatest-ever keeper to play within these shores. Fans who had threatened a boycott at the prospect of one of the "enemy" turning out at Maine Road, soon regarded him as a hero – and his legendary status was sealed when he played on with a broken neck to help win the 1956 FA Cup final for City.

When he retired, sixty thousand turned out for his testimonial. But there was also a more tragic side to Trautmann that few ever saw – the death of his son in a car crash led to the end of his marriage and he cast a lonely figure towards the end of his City career, playing football in the streets with kids after training rather than returning home alone to face an empty home. Truly, it's all a very long way from *Escape To Victory*. He got a warm welcome too in 2010 when he returned to promote a biography.

PONGO WARING

The sweet smell of success

There must have been something in the water in Birkenhead in 1906. Within four months of each other, two men were born in the town who would between them contest the country's record for goals scored in a single season. One was Everton's maestro **Dixie Dean**, the other was Aston Villa legend **Tom "Pongo" Waring**. Pongo still figures large in Midlands football mythology, and was recently voted the second-best player in Villa history. A giant forward with speed, power, strength and guts, he scored goals for fun in his first professional season at local side Tranmere Rovers (24 in 27 games), prompting a nationwide scramble for his signature. Villa won, paying a then-incredible sum of £4700 for the Merseysider. They were amply repaid: Waring banged in two goals every three games. It's a ratio unheard of in the modern English game, and only Dean could match him through history: Pongo's

49 goals in one season has only been beaten by Dean's staggering tally of 60.

> **"He kept chickens in the front room of his house in Nelson Road."**
> Villa fans remember Pongo Waring on the Internet

Even Waring's debut for the Villans was something special – an incredible twenty-three thousand spectators turned up to watch him score a hat-trick for the reserves against local rivals Birmingham City – always a good way to endear yourself to Villa fans. He ended up scoring 167 in a total of 226 appearances, although the management did have some trouble with Waring. Billy Walker remembered him as "a funny lad. There were no rules for Pongo, and nobody on the staff could do anything with him."

The King of the Holte End, also known in those more innocent times as "the Gay Cavalier", was such a maverick that he even managed to get his own dressing room. (We can only speculate as to whether this was due to petulance, status or team-mates' desire to avoid the smell from the chickens he kept in his front room.) Still, he earned five England call-ups, a remarkably small number considering his mercurial talents and eye for goal, scoring four times, and fired Villa to second place in the League in 1931. He found it hard giving up the game, playing for New Brighton during the War, and turning out for amateur sides well into his fifties. When he finally did retire, Waring gave away all his medals, awards and caps, although he remained interested in the game. He was often seen back on the Wirral supporting Tranmere. He apparently stood in the Paddock wearing wellies and – still known as Pongo – bantering with the fans.

GEORGE WEAH

Liberian superstar

On the opening weekend of the 1996–97 season, George Weah scored just about as perfect a virtuoso goal as can be imagined. He was playing for Milan, the best club team of that decade. From the moment Weah cushioned down a Verona corner in his own penalty box, to when his low shot drilled into the far corner of the goal at the other end of the San Siro pitch 14 seconds (and 85 metres) later, no other Milan player had touched the ball. Several Veronese had tried and failed.

At the time Weah held the World and European Footballer of the Year awards – the world duly replayed the goal on TV time and again. Alas, in his native Liberia, which had suffered the turmoil of political unrest and civil war on and off since the mid-1980s and where the national electricity grid had ceased functioning some years earlier, few of Weah's compatriots got to see it. Shortly before his wonder goal, Weah had moved several relatives out of the country, following an arson attack on his villa there, apparently in response to Weah's call for the United Nations to send a force to Liberia to control a civil war that had claimed two hundred thousand lives.

Before Weah, Liberia had been less than a backwater in African football. After Weah, it had a profile. If ever a national team revolved around an individual, it was Liberia under Weah. He was their star and for years their patron, too. In 2003 as war engulfed wider and wider areas of the country, Weah could be found desperately trying to charter airlines to fly Liberian players to Ghana for a qualifying match they were obliged, because of fighting in Monrovia, to play abroad. In the event the national XI, the "Lone Stars", had to make up numbers by fielding Liberians sourced from refugee camps in Accra, Ghana.

Two years later, retired from playing, Weah stood for election as state president of Liberia. After a first round of polling, 29 percent of Liberians chose Weah ahead of 21 other candidates. In the run-off, Weah polled just over forty percent of the vote, leaving him, narrowly, in second place to Ellen Johnson Sirleaf (who became, and remains, the only elected female head of state in Africa). But peace had returned to Liberia – and their standalone, superstar footballer took some of the credit for that.

FRANK WORTHINGTON

Northern star

Such is the romantic mist which now enshrouds such 1970s mavericks as **Frank Worthington** that he seems, in memory, to have exhibited Brazilian ball skills. In reality, Frankie was far more unusual than that. The hairstyle was pure Elvis, and the knee-manipulating comedy routine with which he started many matches was right out of Norman Wisdom. But just as you had begun reluctantly to conclude that he was just a music hall entertainer, he would show a touch of real Brazilian artistry, albeit not quite of the 1970 vintage. Bolton fans still talk in hushed tones of a legendary goal he scored against Ipswich. Back to goal, on the edge of the eighteen-yard box, Worthington controlled the ball with his knee, flicked it up and volleyed it over his head into the net.

In the 1970s, as George Best changed clubs faster than he changed pubs, Frankie was a blessed relief. A footballer who seemed to genuinely enjoy himself on the pitch, he even put on a brave face when his once-in-a-lifetime move to Bill Shankly's Liverpool fell through because – well, for all the rumours, only Frank really knows why. He played for a lot of northern clubs like Bolton and Huddersfield but seemed to find his niche as the star attraction in **Jimmy Bloomfield**'s enterprising Leicester City side of the early 1970s. He wouldn't have been quite as effective without Len "Solly" Glover thundering down the wing – with a lot more pace than any of Glover's horses ever showed. But Frank was a showman in a team which, on its day, could beat anybody – even if that day didn't come often enough to save Bloomfield's neck.

Worthington was too much of an individualist to fit **Don Revie**'s utilitarian vision of the perfect England side (although he got a look-in under **Joe Mercer**'s caretaker regime), but he consoled himself with the kind of off-the-pitch lifestyle which would fill today's *Sunday Sport* for a year. It's all chronicled in the nudge-nudge wink-wink autobiography *One Hump or Two*, the very title a sign that Frank could be as coarse off the pitch as he could be sublimely subtle on it.

The autobiography is, though, notable for its superb flickerama and a fine tale about a Caribbean pre-season tour which climaxed with Frank and Alan Birchenall meeting Omar Sharif at a party. The international playboy, upon meeting two of Leicester City's finest, pronounced himself "deeply moved".

Frankie's career eventually fell into the kind of nomadic pattern which marked Bestie's declining years, with spells at Bolton, Leeds, Birmingham, Tranmere, Brighton, Sunderland, Southampton, Preston, Stockport, Hinckley Town, even the Philadelphia Atoms and Mjilby AIF in Sweden. But he was of great service to Leicester, not just because of the goals he scored, or the skill he showed, but because his antics inspired a young Filbert called **Gary Lineker**.

The Gaffers

The geniuses, the alcoholics, the threads …

◀◀ Previous page: Crystal Palace manager Malcolm Allison wearing a fedora, watches the game at Scarborough, which Palace won 2–1, January 1976.

The Gaffers

"... after God, me."

José Mourinho

MALCOLM ALLISON

A touch of glamour

The enduring image of **Malcolm Allison** will be that of the fedora-wearing, cigar-smoking playboy, a model on each arm, posing for the cameras. That he was also one of the finest coaches England has ever produced is often completely overlooked. Allison's personality, high-profile managerial failings and even his headgear all overshadowed everything he achieved on the training ground. Had he stuck to what he knew, his life and career might have been very different, but then Allison was a man spurred on to ever-greater acts of showmanship by the twin demons of drink and a deep-seated need for the limelight.

The latter stemmed from his time as a player at West Ham; in 1958, Allison was the finest defender on the Upton Park books, but he contracted tuberculosis and was confined to a sanatorium. On his return, he lost his place to a young **Bobby Moore** and never really recovered from the blow. On the surface, at least, it spurred him on: after a managerial apprenticeship at Plymouth, he pitched up at Manchester City as Joe Mercer's assistant in 1965 and set about turning an average Second Division side into league champions playing with flair and style.

While Mercer's nous in the transfer market was responsible for much of City's success, it was Allison's work in making the Blues the fittest, most adept passing side in the country which really sealed the deal. His techniques were years ahead of their time and reflected his own, unlikely, hard-working habits as a player. When he stepped out of Mercer's shadow to take over the hot seat in 1972, however, the cracks began to show.

Within a year, he was off to Crystal Palace, where he changed the strip, widened the pitch, and posed in the team bath with porn star Fiona Richmond.

Razzmatazz was introduced to Selhurst Park, to the extent that players were even given nicknames in the club programme: **Don Rogers** was dubbed The Troublemaker, **Tony Taylor** The Road Runner and **Charlie Cooke** The Card Shuffler. The club shop began selling mini-fedoras and the fans were enthused, but Palace never achieved anything more than an FA Cup semi-final appearance and plenty of media coverage. Cue a return to City, via Plymouth once more.

This time Allison went mad with chairman Peter Swales' chequebook and blew millions on **Steve Daley** and **Kevin Reeves** to spark hyperinflation in the game. It became clear Allison was out of his depth, so off he shuffled for a world tour taking in Kuwait, Portugal and Bristol, a journey that ended in alcoholism, huge debts and life in a nursing home. But, his memory lives on. In 2007 Palace fans celebrated the anniversary of Allison's famous cup run as "Fedora Day" – complete with cigars and champagne.

"BIG" RON ATKINSON

Early doors

Used to be a decent defender at Oxford United, Ron Atkinson. Managed a few clubs too: Kettering Town, Cambridge, West Brom, Manchester United, Atlético Madrid, Aston Villa, Coventry City, Sheffield Wednesday and Nottingham Forest.

However respectable his achievements as a manager were, Big Ron will always be best remembered as an analyst, fashion icon ("Mr Bojangles", who kept a sunbed in his office at United), bon viveur and wit. His unique linguistic magic in the commentary box had inspired a huge cult following, and his addition of several gobbledegook phrases to the national vocabulary has led to the creation of "Ronglish".

Favourite Ronisms include: early doors; amusement arcade forwards with tricks in the locker; the little lollipop (a deceptive jink); sticking the big ugly whip on it (a fearsomely powerful cross); spotter's badges and the Wide Awake Club (membership awarded for defensive perceptiveness); giving it the full gun (a high-powered shot); the little eyebrows (a subtle, glancing header); and doing the ugly, old-fashioned things (tackling and giving). In Ron's world, a player would come out and "go bang" and some lads can throw a ball further than he goes on holiday. He's also seen the odd shot saved because a forward has hit it too well. And, I'll tell you what, that boy has got to be reading comics if he thinks he can score from there.

Ron's cheek sometimes got him into trouble. "You won't see that again now the Scouser's got it", he quipped as Liverpudlian **Steve McManaman** raised the European Champions Cup for Real Madrid. To be fair, Ron himself was born in Liverpool's Old Swan, and has had some trouble with Scousers. "Going to Anfield was like Vietnam", he said of his visits as Manchester United manager. He was once tear-gassed on a trip there, and had to put up with baffling Kop banners reading "Big Ron's Leather" and "Ron's Tart Is a Slag".

Still, not much bothered him. "I thought we might scrape a draw when it was only 7–1", he said after his Forest side had been hammered by Manchester United. "I'll be down to my last 37 suits", he quipped after United sacked him. It led to accusations that he cared more about wiseguy gags than his job, but this was wide of the mark. Beneath the mahogany tan lies a remarkable knowledge of football – ask him to name the Honved team of the mid-1950s and he can discuss their strengths and weaknesses – and a real love of the game, as he showed weekly in his excellent tactical columns in *The Guardian*.

But Big Ron fell from grace spectacularly in 2004 when he resigned from ITV and lost his *Guardian* work after a derogatory comment about Chelsea player Marcel Desailly was accidentally broadcast to various countries in the Middle East. He strenuously denied that he was a racist, citing his past record in promoting black players, but the damage had been done.

CARLOS BILARDO

Maradona's right hand

With every stride made by Argentinian football during the last fifty years, Carlos Bilardo has appeared somewhere close to the fore. Firstly, the man known as "big nose" was the tough and mature midfielder at the core of Estudiantes' legendary team of the late 1960s. Latterly, Bilardo was the manager and principal catalyst of Argentina's 1986 World Cup victory, alongside the mercurial Diego Armando Maradona.

Bilardo joined Estudiantes in the mid-1960s, and quickly became the fulcrum around which dictatorial manager Oscar Zubeldia built his feared team. Somewhat unfortunately known as the "killer juveniles", Estudiantes conquered South America on three consecutive occasions in the final years of the decade, before being crowned world champions following their defeat of Manchester United in the Intercontinental Cup final of 1968.

While Estudiantes' rise to glory marked a proud moment in Argentina's football history, the team was often criticized for its cynical philosophy and frequently unethical approach, and players like Bilardo rarely received the critical acclaim they deserved.

Yet as a manager, Bilardo's nous and tactical ability would be properly recognized. After skirting around South American football, Bilardo found success once again with Estudiantes, leading his former club to the 1982 title. Spotting his potential, the Argentine FA offered him the position of national coach.

Diego Maradona celebrates with Argentine manager Carlos Bilardo after winning the 1986 World Cup final against West Germany.

Bilardo would lead the country to two World Cup finals, while developing a clever plan to utilize the outright genius of Maradona in the process. While Maradona and Bilardo will forever endure criticism for the perceived cynicism of their characteristically Argentine styles, the 1986 World Cup marks the greatest collaboration between a manager and a single player. The perfect marriage of Bilardo's tactical intelligence and Maradona's unfettered expression charted new territory, and proved that "big nose" had a big brain to boot.

For the 2010 World Cup campaign the odd couple were back together: Maradona as Argentina national team coach, Bilardo (more behind the scenes) as general manager.

VIC BUCKINGHAM

International English eccentric

If any single incident best encapsulates the eccentricity of this much-travelled coach, it is the affair of the emergency team meeting. **Vic Buckingham**'s reign as Fulham manager (from 1965 to 1968) is not remembered by fans with much affection – he is usually blamed for dismantling the team and presiding over the sale of such talents as Rodney Marsh at bargain prices – but the players will never forget him. Or the emergency team meeting.

The Cottagers' form had dipped and Buckingham felt that an emergency meeting was needed to clear the air. The players turned up at the Fulham ground, anxiously wondering if they were to be subjected to one of Buck's two-hour team talks. Instead, Vic strolled into the dressing room, sat down, read the paper and, when he'd finished it, just got up without saying goodbye and left.

He may have done it just to wind the players up, but it could also have been to accentuate his carefully acquired reputation as the game's eccentric English aristocrat. Born in Greenwich, the wing-half-cum-left-back signed for Spurs in 1935. His playing career was interrupted by World War II but he was the kind of player who looked more stylish on a cigarette card than on the pitch.

He began his coaching career winning the FA Amateur Cup with Oxbridge side Pegasus in 1951, joining Bradford Park Avenue that same year, going on to manage West Brom (with whom he won the FA Cup in 1954), Ajax (where he helped discover **Johan Cruyff**), Sheffield Wednesday, Fulham, Ethnikos and Barcelona (where, as at Ajax, he was succeeded by Rinus Michels).

BRIAN CLOUGH

"Now listen to me, young man"

Brian Clough's reputation is proof that football will forgive a demagogue anything, provided he kept the common touch. Clough's legendary managerial status is based on the two consecutive European Cups won with Nottingham Forest and a gift for turning mundane players into great ones (see **John Robertson**), but it was his idiosyncrasies as much as his successes that made him a hero.

Clough delighted supporters – and bewildered **Terry Venables** – by holding hands with the Spurs manager as they led their teams on to the pitch for the 1991 FA Cup final. He insisted on referring to **Teddy Sheringham** as Sir Edward Sheringham and confidently told the people of Nottingham he could walk on water. The fans, used to well-worn homilies about boys who'd done well and games of two halves, loved it.

Just how much they would tolerate was demonstrated when two of them invaded the pitch after the team beat QPR in the Littlewoods Cup. Clough clouted them as they passed by his dugout but neither pressed charges; one reportedly turned down thousands of pounds offered by Robert Maxwell to tell his story, and both apologized on a memorable edition of the local news. "Sorry, Brian", they mumbled. "That's alright, lads", Clough replied ... and kissed them.

Clough was just as popular as a pundit. Commenting on the World Cup, he listened while another member of the panel praised the sweeper system, ending with the words "the Germans do it". Clough added "even educated fleas do it" and the studio descended into a nervous silence.

He was equally willing to get involved in politics. Described by former Labour leader Michael Foot as "one of the best socialists I've ever met", Clough signed the founding statement of the Anti-Nazi League, stood for parliament as a Labour candidate in Derby, and when the miners' strike divided the Nottingham miners, openly supported the strikers. But the abrasive egotism that elevated him to folk hero in Nottingham hadn't always worked so well. In fact, by the time Cloughie arrived at the City Ground in 1975, he needed Forest as much as they needed him.

He had been the youngest manager in the League in 1965 when, aged just thirty, he took charge at Hartlepool. He took over struggling Derby County two years later and managed them to the First Division Championship, becoming so popular that the Derby players threatened to strike when he left to join Brighton after an argument with the board over his work as a TV pundit. But he had a disastrous time at the Goldstone Ground – an 8–2 defeat by Bristol Rovers being one of the lowlights – lasting just nine months. Next stop was Leeds United, where he replaced **Don Revie**, who had stepped up to the England job. But his first, calamitous move was to tell Revie's players, respected and reviled in equal measure as the toughest and most successful team in the country, that they were cheats. He left, perhaps unsurprisingly given the circumstances, after 44 days.

After months in the wilderness, Clough joined Forest. He turned an average Second Division club with an average following into European champions, with an air of inspired lunacy that often disguised his genius for creating teams that were greater than the sum of their parts. He gave his son Nigel the job of handing out Kit-Kats on the team bus – and disciplined one player for asking for a Crunchie. He berated his players, punched them and sang to them (normally "Fly Me to the Moon"). He bewildered interviewers with kisses and bon mots prefixed with the famous words: "Now listen to me, young man …"

As long as he was successful it all held together, but it couldn't last. Clough had been fighting a private battle with drink and, as he lost, he surrendered his grip on the club. In his final season – and by now clearly unwell – Clough saw Forest relegated. He resigned and bade the supporters an emotional farewell.

In retirement, he showed a renewed appetite for causing controversy by declaiming on everything from **Posh Spice**'s shoes (too many) to foreigners in the Premiership (too much garlic). And he also provided a suitably humble epitaph to his managerial career: "I wouldn't say I was the best manager in the business. But I was in the top one." After his death in 2004, his fame has continued to grow, particularly after David Peace's "occult history" of his 44-day sojourn at Leeds, *The Damned United*, which was also made into a film. Michael Sheen portrayed a tormented and, critics said, highly misrepresented Clough.

JOSEPH GUARDIOLA

Cruyff's Catalan protégé

Catalan cult status was bestowed on Joseph "Pep" Guardiola long before he coached Barça to an unprecedented six trophies in 2009.

Born and raised in Santepdor, a town of seven thousand in rural Catalonia where his parents still live modestly, Guardiola is the most famous graduate of La Masia, literally "farmhouse" in Catalan, the building which houses Barça's academy.

Ask most *cules* to name two former players that symbolize Barça and they will say **Johann Cruyff** and **Guardiola**. Cruyff symbolized Barça's internationalism and flair, Guardiola their homegrown, stoic, Catalanism.

Awarded a debut by Cruyff in 1990, Guardiola played nearly 400 games, leading Barça to six league titles, one European Cup and two Spanish Cups. As elegant off the field as he was on it, Guardiola was adored in Catalonia, of which he was proud to be a nationalist. A sometime poet and model, it was difficult to overstate how highly regarded he is. And that was before he took over as Barça coach in 2008 after his career had petered out with spells at Brescia and Roma in Italy, Al-Ahli (Qatar) and Sinaloa (Mexico).

> **"Boys want to wake up in the morning and see Guardiola's reflection in the mirror."**
> Quique Costas

Guardiola's football philosophy is clear. "Players have to think quickly and to play with intelligence, always knowing the next pass", he says. "This is the Barcelona way. It is how we have all been taught to play and how the public expects us to play. It is attractive and effective."

He inherited his ideas from Cruyff and the two remain close.

"Johan Cruyff had a theory to how we should play," he said. "He taught us how to play by moving the ball quickly. He only used players with exceptional technique. When scouting for players for La Masia, the club still look for these qualities."

"Guardiola came to Barça at the age of twelve", recalls Quique Costas, the former Barça player now in charge of youth development. "He was very skinny, but you could tell straight away he was something special. He thought quicker than a normal player. And he's a lovely guy. That's maybe his secret now as a coach: boys want to wake up in the morning and see Guardiola's reflection in the mirror."

RUDI GUTENDORF

The ultimate coaching nomad

Largely unknown German coach Rudi Gutendorf holds the record for coaching the most national football teams. And he remains unknown because he's taken

Schalke 04 coach Rudi Gutendorf, in his 1970s pomp, stepping out of his hotel room.

charge of countries who are not regulars on the biggest stage like Tunisia, Tanzania, Peru and Mauritius. Or even more obscure places like Fiji, Tonga, Grenada or Antigua. Nor has Gutendorf been particularly successful – the only time he touched silverware was as player-manager of Lucerne in 1960 and in Japan, where he coached Yomiuri Tokyo to the 1985 championship.

Born in 1926, he left Germany aged thirty to work abroad. By forty, he had coached on three continents. The veteran first made his name by taking tiny Duisburg to runners-up spot in the Bundesliga in 1964. He then took over struggling Schalke 04 and led them to the 1970 Cup Winners' Cup quarter-finals.

His Chile side did qualify for the finals of the 1974 World Cup, but his friendship with the late Marxist president Salvador Allende made him *persona non grata* under General Pinochet's new regime. Gutendorf's few months in Chile were dramatic. He was shot at while driving through the countryside and an affair with a suspected CIA agent more than twenty years his junior led to another shooting. One night when the couple were in bed, a man entered their room and opened fire at the woman. She was killed instantly, while Gutendorf's jaw was shattered.

Gutendorf has written several autobiographies and managed **Kevin Keegan** when he was at Hamburg, where he fell out with his players whom he accused of blanking Keegan. By the age of 55 he was in charge of Nepal, becoming the only man to have coached a team on every continent. At 66, he coached China's team for the Olympics, his 50th job. In 2003, aged 77, he took on his 55th post at Samoa, claiming that he had an addiction to go on and on.

IAN HOLLOWAY

"Ollie, Ollie, Ollie"

"Who did they think they were playing – some nuggets from Blackpool?" asked the Tangerines manager Ian Holloway. He was criticizing the Cardiff fans whom he felt had disrespected his side and, just to put a sneaky dig in, asked: "Are they worried that Swansea are just behind them?"

Honest, passionate, loyal – three words which are used to describe "Ollie" on the back of his autobiography. Plymouth fans may question those words. Yes, they loved him when he was manager at Home Park. Especially when he spoke about their Green Army as if they were the best fans in the world and offered to buy all 700 travelling fans who'd made the 805-mile round trip to Sunderland a drink. Plenty took him up on the offer. They couldn't believe it when he stood up to Fabio Capello's Real Madrid, who tried to get Plymouth to switch hotels during their pre-season preparations in Austria.

"Who are they to move us?" he asked in his Bristolian accent. "I don't like it myself. We're Argyle, get out of our way." When a deal was reached whereby Argyle played Madrid in a prestigious friendly, he said: "We'll leave something on a few of them and I don't think they'll like that too much."

But Plymouth fans were less enamoured when, on 20 November 2007, he affirmed: "I'm not going to Leicester. It's total poppycock, if I'm allowed to use that word. It's absolutely pathetic. The media is a very powerful thing and, unfortunately, they can make a rumour into a bigger rumour. But ask anybody who knows me how I feel about Plymouth and they will tell you the truth. And if you need me to say it again, I will. I'm in love with the place. It's absolutely magnificent." Two days later he joined Leicester.

Holloway became a cult hero at his local club Bristol Rovers where he played for eleven years during three spells, including time as player-manager during his five years managing the team. A combative midfielder, he also played for Wimbledon, Brentford, Torquay and QPR. His after-match quotes were relished by journalists – he once compared a win to picking up a girl ten minutes before closing time in a nightclub – and always amused. But it is the many hurdles he has overcome in his personal life that make Holloway's career all the more remarkable: his wife Kim fought cancer and their three daughters are profoundly deaf.

ROBERTO MARTÍNEZ

The Wonder of Wigan

Not many football managers turn down the job at Glasgow Celtic to take charge at little old Wigan Athletic. But then there are not too many football players who desert the balmy climate of Catalonia to sign for a Fourth Division club in the North of England. That is where the love affair between Roberto Martínez and Wigan Athletic began.

Roberto – "Bob" to the locals – arrived in the UK in July 1995 from his local team FC Balaguer as one of the "Three Amigos". Lazy clichés aside, it was an unheard-of coup for Wigan at a time when overseas' players in the English game numbered the high-kicking Cantona and the low-diving Klinsmann.

The three lads lived in a tiny terraced house in the Poolstock area of Wigan, barely spoke a word of English between them and endured the kind of culture shock that saw the most highly rated of the trio, **Jesús Seba**, disappear within a few months. Isidro Díaz stayed for a couple of years and then moved back to the continent. Which left one, and somehow Roberto adapted, survived and learned to love the town of Wigan. His father also became a regular visitor and was often seen strolling the streets of Wigan in the early evening, as is the norm in Spain.

On the field Roberto played a pivotal part in the club's first League Championship – the 1996–97 Fourth Division title – as a classy midfielder with a range of passing ability and ball control which far surpassed the level he was playing at. Bobby made 227 appearances for the club and scored 23 goals. His departure was a less than welcome episode as Steve Bruce added his name to a lengthy release list at the end of the 2000–01 season, shortly before ditching Wigan Athletic himself to take the Crystal Palace job.

Roberto drifted up to Scotland to sign for Motherwell, leaving behind the club many thought he would stay at forever. Several seasons later, his footballing principles re-emerged at Swansea City, first as a player and then manager, as he took Swansea from the fourth tier to the fringes of the Championship play-offs.

At the end of the 2008–09 season, when Steve Bruce jumped ship (again) to join Sunderland, Roberto Martínez took the helm at the DW Stadium with Wigan Athletic now a Premier League club and the return trip was complete. Known recently as a small, gutsy club fighting to survive against much bigger teams with healthier budgets, Martínez has transformed Wigan into a smooth footballing outfit where more then five hundred passes per game is the norm. If his period as manager is half as successful as his spell as a player, he will achieve the impressive status of being both Wigan Athletic's favourite cult player and manager.

STEVE MCCLAREN

"Masshive"

McClaren became England manager in 2006 as "Second Choice Steve" on the strength of his excellence as a coach and his relative club management success at Middlesbrough when the FA bungled their attempt to appoint Phil Scolari as Eriksson's successor. As assistant to **Jim Smith** at Derby County and **Alex Ferguson** at Manchester United, McClaren was rated by his bosses and players for his modern and innovative methods and became known as a "thinking man's coach".

His England appointment divided opinion, his critics quick to point out that the former midfielder had neither played nor managed at the highest level, even though when he progressed into club management he brought Middlesbrough their first major trophy with the League Cup in 2004 and a UEFA Cup final appearance in 2006. Despite advice from PR expert Max Clifford, his dropping, then recalling of Beckham was badly handled.

Despite boasting the shortest term ever as England manager, when he was dubbed, "the wally with the brolly", for sheltering in an "unmanly" fashion while watching his players fail to qualify for Euro 2008, Steve McClaren has won enduring football fame and eternal ridicule for two minutes of widely viewed YouTube footage. In an interview with Dutch TV as manager of Eredivisie side FC Twente before a game with Arsenal, "Shteeve", as he is now known, swapped his softly spoken, educated Yorkshire brogue for a comic Dutch accent, lisping "fantashtic", "masshive" and mercilessly mangling sentence structure. McClaren responded to the furore which followed what was undoubtedly a misguided attempt to make himself more intelligible to Dutch viewers, with self-deprecating humour, claiming his new accent was a natural thing. "Going Dutch" did not stop him being given an extension to his contract with the "Tukkers" and completing an unlikely league win in 2010.

JOSÉ MOURINHO

The Very Special One

Appropriately for someone who coined his own nickname, the "Special One", José Mourinho is one of the few football managers to have his own website. Suave, handsome and supremely self-confident, Mourinho frequently promotes his own importance with an almost Cloughian turn of phrase and hubris: "If I wanted to have an easy job … I would have stayed at Porto – beautiful blue chair, the UEFA Champions League trophy, God, and after God, me." When appointed Chelsea coach in 2005, the impeccably dressed Mourinho provided a striking alternative to the brusque Celts, assorted craggy regional types and cerebral foreign professors then in charge of British clubs. He even won grudging admiration from Alex Ferguson, the man he is frequently tipped to replace at Old Trafford, as "the new young gunslinger".

The son of a Portuguese goalkeeper, Mourinho was unsuccessful as a player and became a physical education teacher before using his intelligence and linguistic talents (he claims to have learnt Italian well enough in three weeks to give a press conference in it) to return to football, working as **Bobby Robson**'s interpreter in Portugal and Spain. His managerial career began at Benfica, but it was at Porto that he made his name, notably by winning the Champions League trophy in 2004. Unafraid either to spend Roman Abramovich's money freely, or court controversy, he then took Chelsea to their first domestic title in fifty years and further success. His resignation in 2007, which followed a power struggle with the Russian plutocrat, was highly unpopular with Chelsea fans. Despite quick success in Italy with Internazionale, Mourinho's feuds with the press and other managers, as well as his public disdain for what he considers to be Italy's obsession with *cotorni*, intrigue his ambitions to reign in Spain and return to England mean another move many not be too far away.

> **"After all that has happened this season – and that is a lot – I've reached the conclusion that I am a good loser."**
> Mourinho after losing the 2007 Premiership title

BOB PAISLEY

Everyone's favourite uncle

At first glance, Bob Paisley didn't seem cut from the right cloth to become the most successful British manager of all time. For a start, he lacked ambition. Following the shock resignation of **Bill Shankly**, the Liverpool board had to gang up on Paisley to get him to take the job. Even when finally bullied into it, Paisley's speech to his players the next day consisted of: "I never wanted this bloody job. But it looks like you're stuck with me." A shy, avuncular figure, Paisley was the yin to Shankly's blustering yang. While the eminently quotable Scot talked about wanting to "conquer the bloody world", the quiet Geordie seemed barely able to express himself. "The team meetings with Bob would be hilarious because he'd struggle to string two sentences together", remembers **Alan Hansen**. "He was always getting names wrong. The laughter was unbelievable."

Paisley picked up the affectionate moniker of "Dougie Doins" as a result of his habit of referring to opposition players as "doins" rather than their real names. Dressing-room comic **Terry McDermott** even did an uncanny impression of Paisley's bumbling – sometimes getting caught out by the manager in mid-flow. It's hard to imagine **Alex Ferguson** putting up with that. But the cold, hard facts speak for themselves. Paisley masterminded six League Championship wins, three League Cups, one UEFA Cup, five Charity Shields and – truly amazingly – three European Cups. So how did he pull it off?

For one thing, Paisley knew the club inside out. He'd been there as a player, and then a coach, since 1939. Under Shankly he was renowned for his tactical acumen, and his judgement of players was better than the Scot's. Paisley also had a no-nonsense canniness learned during World War II, where he was a Desert Rat: rolling down a boulevard in Rome prior to their 1977 European Cup triumph, Paisley told his players: "The last time I drove down here, I was in a tank liberating Italy." (Appropriately, "Gunner" was his other nickname.)

> **"The whole of my life, what they wanted was honesty. They were not concerned with cultured football, but with triers who gave one hundred percent."**
> Paisley on the Kop

His straightforward style worked wonders. "Paisley's philosophy was simple – we played to our strengths and exploited their weaknesses", says Hansen. Paisley had an astounding knowledge of how the game worked, was a marvellous man-manager and was also a first-class physio, able to diagnose what was wrong with a player just from the way they walked.

Paisley remains loved not just for his achievements, but for the humble manner in which they were made. "Bob's the only man I know who had no ego", says **Kevin Keegan** of a guy whose great pleasure was a tinkle on the electric organ on Sunday afternoons. But the anecdote that sums up Paisley perfectly comes from **Graeme Souness**. "After the 1981 European Cup final in Paris, Alan Hansen and I decided to stay in the hotel", he says. "We went to Bob's room. He's sitting there in a jersey with soup stains on it. He's got his slippers on because he had problems with his ankles. It's like a night in watching *Coronation Street*." It was that kind of ordinary greatness that would bond Bob Paisley with the Liverpool fans forever.

GRAHAM TAYLOR

"Swedes 2, Turnips 1"

"I know I used the F-word 25 [38 according to others] times in a 50-minute programme. But I was being filmed for two years. Tell me anyone in football who wouldn't swear that many times over two years." So said Graham Taylor about his iconic performance as England football manager in the 1994 Channel 4 documentary *An Impossible Job*. Boasting a Facebook appreciation page, devotees swapping classic Taylor lines, such as "Whether he's ten stone or twelve stone, the Norwegians are in awe of Paul Gascoigne", the programme's enduring legacy is to present him unfairly as a provincial buffoon. Remonstrating frantically in his deliberate, quaint Scunthorpe turn of phrase, "Do I not like that!" or "Can we not knock it?" he presides impotently over England's disastrous 1994 World Cup qualification. Phil Neal, his lugubrious Little Sir Echo assistant, constantly repeats Taylor's judgements deadpan while Gascoigne gooses the marching band.

An ex-full back for Grimsby Town and Lincoln City, Taylor was appointed England boss in 1990 after being highly successful with Lincoln City, Watford and Aston Villa. With his brand of direct, attacking play, in five years he took Watford from the Fourth Division into the top flight for the first time. Watford also qualified for the UEFA Cup and lost the 1984 FA Cup final to Everton. Moving to recently relegated Aston Villa in 1987, he not only brought them straight back up, but helped them to second place in the First Division in 1990. He could not repeat this success with the national team. Although England narrowly qualified for Euro '92, they were eliminated before the semi-finals by the host nation, prompting the memorable *Sun* headline, "Swedes 2, Turnips 1", with Taylor's face memorably transmuted into the latter root vegetable. Resigning in 1993, he returned to club management until 2003.

Denigrators said his teams were no better than a collection of longball-playing journeymen with **Carlton Palmer** being Taylor's authentic archetype. Supporters – and there are a few – claim he pioneered the all-action "pressing game" now part of every top team's tactical repertoire.

NEIL WARNOCK

Scourge of the refs

Neil Warnock is always clear who is to blame and it's not himself. This outspoken, short-fused Yorkshireman is better-known for vituperative outbursts about referees and fellow managers, than a commendable managerial record (chiefly at lower league outfits with limited resources). Manager of eleven clubs since 1981, under him five of those achieved promotion to higher divisions – Notts County and Sheffield United into the top flight. The failings of referees (he qualified as one himself … and also trained as a chiropodist) are his "pet subject". He once described a David Elleray decision as, "given by some bald-headed bloke standing fifty yards away". After Sheffield United were beaten 1–0 in controversial circumstances by Arsenal in the FA Cup semi-final in 2003, Warnock called referee Graham Poll, "their best midfielder in the goal".

"Made in Sheffield", as his autobiography is titled, in 1999 he took over Sheffield United which he supported as a boy. When later asked how he would run rivals Wednesday he said, "I would buy some bad players, get the sack and then retire to Cornwall". Warnock left Bramall Lane following the club's relegation from the Premier League in 2007, claiming it was in response to a "foul-mouthed tirade" by club director, actor Sean Bean, witnessed by Warnock's wife and daughter, which Bean denies. Warnock has also never forgiven Liverpool manager **Rafa Benítez** for fielding a weakened team in a defeat to Fulham which saved the London club at the Blades' expense. A serial mover, Warnock is currently with QPR. For now.

In contrast, Warnock's weekly column in Saturday's *Independent* newspaper, "What I Learnt This Week", though awash with his standard bile about officials, contains nostalgic reminiscences about his twelve-year playing career with eight lower-league clubs – such as how he never washed his strip if Rotherham won, once wearing it dirty for seventeen games – and unexpectedly charming family stories.

GIANFRANCO ZOLA

Good guy and clever little so and so

When Gianfranco Zola came to the Boleyn Ground in 2008 on the departure of Alan Curbishley, it was to be his first management job after a glittering playing career in Italy and Britain. Surely if anyone could prove wrong the old adage that "Great players don't make great managers" it was the attacking midfielder once dubbed "the wizard" by Claudio Ranieri and a "clever little so-and-so" by Alex Ferguson? Zola had cut his teeth in Italian football, including a spell at Napoli where he learnt how to take free kicks from Maradona. Signing for Chelsea in 1996, he went on to be awarded an OBE and to be voted Chelsea's greatest-ever player.

The signs looked promising. West Ham were bankrolled by billionaire Björgólfur Guðmundsson, reputedly the second-richest man ever in Icelandic history, and the popular Italian was greeted with an outpouring of goodwill rarely seen in the British media. He made all the right noises, placing himself squarely within the "West Ham Way", although their first-ever foreign manager, by announcing, "the philosophy will be to play attacking football". However, by July

2009, after a moderate season where West Ham had finished mid-table, Guðmundsson had filed for bankruptcy and the club's default owner, Icelandic bank Straumur, was looking for a buyer.

Despite the help of ex-Chelsea colleague, Steve Clarke, Zola struggled in his second term – West Ham were plagued by injuries and straitened finances … but also an inability to win matches. Come 2010, new owners Davids Gold and Sullivan pledged their "support" and promised transfer funds for the manager who refused to sacrifice his principles. "I was appointed to play a certain way and I don't see why you cannot win games by playing good football." Bookmakers responded by making him favourite to be the first manager to be sacked in 2010 – and though he defeated the odds and West Ham survived the drop, the axe was wielded on 11 May by the club's new owners.

The Clubs

Kiss the Badge, win or lose

◀◀ Previous page: Zagłębie Sosnowiec captain Witold Majewski congratulates Dukla Prague's man of the match Svatopluk Pluskal on Dukla's victory, which won them the American Challenge Cup in New York, 1964.

The Clubs

"All I want for Christmas is a Dukla Prague Away Kit."

Half Man Half Biscuit

AFC WIMBLEDON

Football supporters often get a poor deal – yet even the most long-suffering fans would be hard-pushed to feel quite as aggrieved as the former followers of Wimbledon FC. On 28 May 2002, to almost universal disbelief, a three-man FA Commission gave official sanction to Wimbledon chairman Charles Koppel's plans to move the club almost seventy miles from their temporary base at Crystal Palace's Selhurst Park to the promised land of Milton Keynes, home of the concrete cow. Within two months, a new club born from the ashes of the FA's decision were playing their first game in front of a capacity crowd and signing a six-figure sponsorship deal. It was the start of one of British football's most remarkable and uplifting tales – and it isn't finished yet.

The roots of AFC Wimbledon (it stands for "A Fans' Club") can be traced back to 1991. That was when Wimbledon – the unfashionable, philistine underdogs who rose from humble non-league roots to unleash **Vinnie Jones** and land the FA Cup – abandoned their historic Plough Lane home on safety grounds and began sharing Selhurst Park, while ostensibly searching for a new HQ in the London borough of Merton. For a variety of reasons (mostly dubious, say former fans), such a ground never came and Koppel came up with a radical solution.

The weeks following the FA's ratification of this solution were a whirlwind. Within two days, the Dons Trust (a supporters' organization set up to spearhead a move back to Merton) had voted to walk out en masse, set up a new club and enter it in the Combined Counties League, seven rungs below the Premiership.

AFC Wimbledon played their first match on Wednesday 10 July 2002, in front of 4657 at Sutton United's Gander Green Lane. When their league campaign got underway, 4215 squeezed into the ground they now share with Kingstonian in southwest London, and many more were locked out. Meanwhile, Wimbledon opened to a crowd of 2476 and hit a record low in November when just 664 paying spectators turned up for Rotherham's visit in the Worthington Cup.

Animals

Africa is full of exotic, intriguing animals, African football even more so. Watch the Ivory Coast and you are admiring the Elephants, and if you are a real devotee, you'll be dressed up with a trunk and big ears to show your allegiance. Follow Cameroon, and you support the Indomitable Lions. Nigeria are the Super Eagles, Mozambique the Mambas, Tunisia the Eagles of Carthage, Algeria the Desert Foxes. Morocco refer to themselves as the Atlas Lions, the Democratic Republic of Congo, formerly Zaïre, the Leopards.

Others promise to devour opponents but seldom deliver. Little Lesotho go by the term the Crocodiles. Tiny Gambia are the Scorpions, as are the islanders of Madagascar. Benin are the Squirrels, a truer reflection of the weight they punch in world football. Rwanda are the Wasps, capable of the odd sting but no kings of the jungle. Others go for elegance, like Angola, the Palancas Negras, sable antelopes, Botswana are the Zebras, Burkina Faso the stallions. Animals roam club football, too, like the Black Leopards of South Africa or the brilliantly monikered Venomous Vipers of Ghana. Their local derby in the city of Cape Coast is against Mysterious Dwarves, former champions in a country where the power is usually shared between Hearts of Oak and Asante Kotoko.

Other national teams are simply stellar. Ghana's XI know themselves as the Black Stars, Liberia's as the Lone Stars, Kenya as the Harambee Stars. A vivid image is often more important than a sense of locale. One of Swaziland's more successful clubs is Eleven Men in Flight. One day, in a Cup competition, they could meet Mali's Eleven Creators, or Ghana's Eleven Wise of Sekondi. In several southern African countries, there is a Naughty Boys FC. In South Africa around the time the institutional system of racial discrimination, apartheid, was collapsing, a Dangerous Darkies entered the first division, cocking a snook at what had once been a league structure that kept white and black clubs and players apart.

All this is a commentator's dream, of course. "In African football, a squirrel can maul a lion and an eagle can frighten an elephant", the Ghanaian commentator Michael Oti Adjei told listeners at the 2008 African Nations Cup. Two years later, as Nigeria struggled to make the finals of the 2010 World Cup, fans thought up a new name. The Super Eagles were derided as "The Super Chickens" – flightless and occasionally headless.

At the end of their first season, AFC Wimbledon finished third (out of 24 teams), losing only 5 games and scoring 125 goals in their 46 matches, as well as mystifying opposing teams whose average gates were somewhere around the one-man-and-a-dog mark. Currently making their Blue Square Premier debut, AFC fans' eventual aim is to return their club to the Premiership with their own ground, preferably passing their ex-club on the way down. Given the fairy-tale nature of their short history to date, it isn't quite as far-fetched a dream as it might sound.

ATHLETIC BILBAO

Athletic Club Bilbao, commonly known as Athletic Bilbao or just Athletic, are historically Spain's third most successful team with eight championships and stand alongside Barça and Real Madrid as one of three teams never to have been relegated from the top flight. That proud record has been in danger in recent years, partly because of the self-imposed rule which makes Athletic unique in world football – they only employ Basque players.

Writing in the club's centenary book in 1998, Athletic president José María Arrate summed up the policy thus:

> Athletic Bilbao is more than a football club, it is a feeling – and as such its ways of operating often escape rational analysis. We see ourselves as unique in world football and that defines our identity. We do not say that we are better or worse, merely different. We only wish for the sons of our soil to represent our club, and in so wishing we stand out as a sporting entity, not a business concept. We wish to mould our players into men, not just footballers.

Their rivalry with Basque neighbours **Real Sociedad** is one of the most bitter in Spain (see pp. 148–50). The San Mames, Athletic's home ground, is known as "the cathedral". The ever-passionate Athletic fans fill it to the forty thousand capacity most weeks and there are plans to move to a new fifty-three thousand seater venue on the same site by 2015.

BRISTOL ROVERS

Any club which claims Jeffrey Archer among its celebrity fans and revels in the nickname "Gasheads" deserves a break. They've changed nicknames, grounds and managers with disturbing frequency, but Bristol Rovers are just that kind of club. The players run out to the depressive strains of "Goodnight Irene" – is it any wonder the team have underperformed in recent years, clinging to the lower reaches of Division Three for dear life?

Founded in 1883, Bristol Rovers win a trophy, on average, every sixty years: they were champions of Third Division South in 1952 and 1973 and of the Third Division in 1989–90. So the bad news for middle-aged Rovers fans is that they aren't due to win anything again until they're dead and buried in their number twelve shirts with "Gashead" on the back. Their nickname has changed several times – from the Purdown Poachers to the Black Arabs (after the colour of the founders' shirts and a local rugby club called Arabs), from the Pirates to the Gasheads (after the proximity of their old ground to a gasworks).

The club's golden age was in the 1950s when they dominated the Third Division South. They twice beat sides 7–0 (Brighton and Swansea) and reached the last eight of the FA Cup in 1951. In 1954, Rovers made the most astonishing signing in their history, buying **Youra Esha Pera**, aka the Assyrian Wizard, the first Iraqi to play League football in England. The forward almost didn't make it, getting lost at Victoria Station and then being refused a permit by the Home Office. Questions were asked in the House of Commons and Youra was allowed to stay and given a

United by Any Other Name

Liverpool won the League last season while unlucky Chelsea were denied promotion to the top flight after an FA committee gave Benfica extra points because some of their opponents hadn't turned up. In other words, last season was a pretty typical affair in the southwest African state of Namibia.

In Britain, naming football clubs is a simple, none-too-creative, business in which the three key factors are: location, location, location. But as the gospel of football spread across the globe in the early twentieth century (the unlikely missionaries often being British sailors, dockers and railwaymen), foreign clubs aped the Brits.

So forget all that nonsense about "there's only one..." There are at least two other Manchester Uniteds on the planet (curiously, neither has been sued yet) and three Liverpools, while the number of Arsenals reaches double figures, if you include the odd amateur side in an over-30s league in Tennessee.

ARSENAL LESOTHO

Roots This South African kingdom won independence in 1966 and the national side, gloriously nicknamed the Crocodiles, played their first international five years later. In 1983, a bunch of Arsenal fans in the capital Maseru thought it would be fun to found a club which, touchingly, and unimaginatively, they decided to call Arsenal. They are not alone in paying such homage: there are Arsenals in Argentina, Guadeloupe, Mexico and Guyana, where the Gunners played in the evocatively named Milk Stout League.

Uncanny coincidences The boys from Maseru are called Arsenal (okay, Arsenal Lesotho to be precise), their nickname is the Gunners, they play in red and white and they won the League and Cup double in 1989 and 1991. Yep – the very same years George Graham's Arsenal won the League. They have won the title once more since (in 1993) and clinched the Lesotho Cup (which, intriguingly, is run as a mini-league) in 1998, the year Arsenal beat Newcastle 2–0 to claim the FA Cup.

EVERTON (CHILE)

Roots Legend in Valparaiso has it that when a bunch of Anglo-Chileans decided in the summer of 1909 to start their own football club, they called it Everton because one of the founders had an Everton mint in his pocket. As the original Everton had toured South America that year, and ships from Liverpool often docked at the port of Valparaiso, the truth may be more obvious and much job at a local colliery. He played for the club's third team but, on the brink of earning professional terms, returned to Iraq.

Youra's departure meant that he missed out on the club's finest moment: a 4–0 victory over Matt Busby's Babes in the third round of the 1955–56 FA Cup. Of late, Rovers have been bedevilled by financial problems. They were forced to sell their old Eastville ground to a greyhound racing company to pay their debts, moving to Bath City's Twerton Park before sharing the Memorial Ground with a rugby club.

duller. The club was forced to move to the seaside resort Viña del Mar in 1942. Free-scoring René Meléndez, somewhat inevitably dubbed the club's "Dixie Dean", helped win the first two championships (1950 and 1952). The club won the Chilean League again in 1976, adding another in 2008 after 32 years.
Uncanny coincidences Corporacíon Deportiva Everton did win the Chilean Cup in 1984, the same year Everton beat Watford 2–0 to lift the FA Cup. And the Chilean club's ground Sausalito has staged three World Cup qualifiers involving Brazil and a semi-final (back in 1962) won by the tournament runners-up. Goodison Park did exactly the same in 1966. A deeply trivial footnote, but proof of what Sting famously referred to as "the devastating principle of synchronicity".

LIVERPOOL (URUGUAY)

Roots At the turn of the century, Montevideo played host to many English football teams trying to jazz up their pre-season training. Most of these teams sailed from Liverpool, which may explain why in 1915 a bunch of Franciscan students from the Colegio de los Capuchinos de Nuevo Paris in the Uruguayan capital, decided to call their new club Liverpool.
Uncanny coincidences Teams called Liverpool, Dublin and Bristol were all based in Montevideo and competed in the Uruguayan League between 1915 and 1923. And the Uruguayan Liverpool's first game of league football was a 1–0 victory against Newcastle. Montevideo's Liverpool have never finished higher than fourth in the Uruguayan Premiership and their best performance against a foreign club was a 1971 4–3 victory in a friendly with Werder Bremen.

MANCHESTER UNITED (GIBRALTAR)

Roots With a population of thirty-one thousand, this slice of limestone rock can only support amateur football. Manchester United were founded in 1962 by local football fans. "We wrote to Manchester United to ask permission to use their name and got a letter back from Sir Matt Busby telling us to go ahead", said United's former manager and player Brian Askuez.
Uncanny coincidences Manchester United FC have won Gibraltar's League seven times (1975, 1979, 1980, 1984, 1995, and 1999) and its Cup three times (1974, 1977 and 1980), a fitting display of domestic dominance. They also play other teams with such familiar names as Lincoln and Wolves (although they are officially known as the Rock Wolves). Gibraltar is not affiliated to FIFA and the team only play friendlies abroad, mainly in the UK, Spain and Morocco.

Plans for a super stadium on the site stalled frustratingly. A happy knack of discovering strikers (**Bobby Zamora, Marcus Stewart, Jason Roberts, Barry Hayles, Jamie Cureton**) has also been undermined by the practice of selling them at knockdown prices.

CORINTHIAN CASUALS

The next time a high-profile footballer is required to perform community service for misdemeanours of a criminal nature, he should be made to carry it out at the King George V Playing Fields just north of Kingston, southwest London. For it is on this underdeveloped patch of grass, where any noise from the few dozen spectators is drowned out by passing trains, that the true spirit of football lives on – in an odd sort of way.

Corinthian Casuals are indeed alive and well, and still linked in essence to the club which epitomized sporting virtue in the nineteenth and early twentieth centuries. It was in the 1880s and 1890s that the Corinthians – formed in 1882 as a side to challenge Scotland in a friendly – became one of the finest teams in the game, although this claim was never tested as their strict public-school ethos meant that they didn't enter a competition until 1900. The club was about playing well and, above all, fairly, rather than winning matches, though they did this pretty effectively too, seeing off Manchester United 11–3 in a 1904 friendly, the Reds' record defeat. Sportsmanship was paramount, and if Corinthians were awarded a penalty, their player would deliberately miss it as to score from the spot was the act of a cad; similarly, if Corinthians conceded a penalty, the goalkeeper would stand aside to leave an empty net (these rules survived until the 1980s).

The team quickly became ambassadors for football, visiting Asia, Africa, Europe and the US to play prestigious friendly matches; their global legacy can be seen most obviously in the famous Brazilian side who share their name and in Real Madrid's aping of their all-white kit. Corinthians merged with Casuals, a leading London amateur side, in the 1930s, and the club still exists in the lower echelons of the **Ryman League**, still fiercely amateur and still endearingly quaint. To this day, a red card is often punished by being sacked from the club, while swearing or answering a referee back brings a hefty fine. Handlebar moustaches are, however, no longer compulsory.

DINAMO ZAGREB

It's not exactly unusual for football teams to become the very embodiment of their community, or the pride of a particular region, but Croatian side Dinamo Zagreb have stridently transcended such meagre expectations. Their fans, so the myth goes, prepared the launch pad for the establishment of an independent Croatia.

Dinamo Zagreb's captain, Zvonimir Boban, attacks a police officer during soccer fan riots, prior to their match against Red Star Belgrade, Zagreb, Croatia, 13 May 1990.

In 1990, during a match against **Red Star Belgrade**, fans of both sides transported acute political tensions between Croatia and Serbia onto the hallowed dimensions of an ordinary green football field. After Croatian superstar Zvonimir Boban dropkicked a policeman caught dishing out some heady injustice to a Dinamo fan, nationalist fervour began to well.

As the civil war miserably sprang into view, it became clear that many of Dinamo's notorious ultras, the "Bad Blue Boys", were eagerly getting stuck in on the front lines of battle. With club crests diligently sewn into military uniform, and barracks draped in huge Dinamo flags, the infant Croatia and its leading football team were locked in a symbiotic relationship of totemic relevance.

Dinamo Zagreb had been the area's leading side since its formation in 1945, when Yugoslav invasion led to the amalgamation of two clubs, HAŠK and Građanski Zagreb. The club enjoyed massive support and racked up a host of championships and domestic cups, while their single European success came after defeating Don Revie's Leeds United in the 1967 Inter-Cities Fairs Cup.

After Croatia finally claimed independence in 1992, Dinamo then became the bizarre target of national politicking. Recognizing its beloved status and cultural import, Croatian president Franjo Tudjman renamed the club, first to HAŠK

Građanski, then as Croatia Zagreb. Fans reacted vehemently, and attendances immediately dipped. The club eventually reassumed its original moniker in 2000, and the nebulous blend of Croatian nationalism and fraternal militancy that characterizes Dinamo's vitality was reclaimed by its partisan support.

DUKLA PRAGUE

There's only one real reason anyone in the UK really remembers the name Dukla Prague. In 1986, Birkenhead punk satirists Half Man Half Biscuit released their debut single, "The Trumpton Riots". On the B-side was the now-legendary track, "All I Want for Christmas Is a Dukla Prague Away Kit", a celebration of the madness of Subbuteo (see pp. 213–14). Dukla remain a cult for men of a certain age to this day. You can purchase that very maroon and claret kit on the Internet, and the club itself still does a fair trade selling away strips to baffling English visitors. They'll set you back about 120kc (£4.00), including a badge which you have to sew on yourself. Unfortunately, this supplemental income hasn't helped Dukla's fortunes, and in 1997 the side reached the ultimate low, leaving their home ground to merge with Marila Pribram and assume their name. Dukla's decline has been a spectacular one.

In the 1960s they were one of the strongest sides in the whole of Europe, reaching three European Cup quarter-finals and one semi-final (losing to Celtic in 1967), beating the great Ajax side that had hammered Bill Shankly's Liverpool 5–1, and drawing 2–2 with the mighty Real Madrid.

But Dukla's strength was based on Communism rather than popular support. Formed in the 1950s from the Czech army (named after Dukla, the village where the Czechs had fought off the Nazis in World War II), the club could call up any player on their general's orders. The generals were good managers: they soon picked **Josef Masopust**, European Footballer of the Year in 1962, who led Dukla to five national titles. The fall of Communism meant iron curtains for Dukla. They clung on through the 1980s, even winning the national cup in 1990, but the army's support of the club collapsed in 1994, and there were "financial irregularities". Consequently, the club went through many different incarnations, until a new Dukla Prague was formed in 2007, preserving the iconic name.

EAST STIRLINGSHIRE

It's an unwanted honour, but "The Shire" were statistically the worst team in British senior football during the first decade of the millennium, so bad that they were attracting nationwide publicity.

Sky television's Jeff Stelling used to highlight their results on *Soccer Saturday*. "And East Stirlingshire have only lost by four today", he'd announce, grinning.

East Stirlingshire gave 32-year-old Alex Ferguson his first managerial job in 1974. There were only eight registered players when Ferguson arrived. "They were the worst senior club in the country", he wrote later.

"He was a frightening bastard from the start", said winger Bobby McCulley. Ferguson left for St Mirren after 117 days, having revolutionized the club and pushed them to the top of the table.

Things really started to go wrong at the turn of the millennium when the people in charge behind the scenes changed. **Alan Mackin**, a former player, took control and fans were suspicious of his motives. He introduced a £10 per week wage for all players which meant the best ones were lost. He was unpopular, rarely attended games and remained unperturbed by the huge amounts of negative publicity for failure on a grand scale.

The club began to decay. Firs Park, East Stirlingshire's home, was given a safety capacity of just 750. The standard official capacity of a roped-off football pitch with no stands is twice that.

By 2003–04, the Shire were legendarily bad. That season, they went on a 26-game losing run. Pools companies stopped including them on their coupons, bookies didn't take win/lose bets. They were well on their way to breaking the 27-game losing streak British record until they beat Elgin 2–1 in the last game of the season. "It was like winning the Champions League. We were jumping around like fools", beamed Ian Ramsay, chair of the Shire Supporters Club. "We'd achieved something at last – we'd stopped ourselves becoming the worst British team ever. We never thought about leaving, because without us there would be no club." And, you would assume, nothing to stop the ground being sold.

But the situation didn't improve and in 2005, the Scottish League came up with the notion that any club could be thrown out of the League if they finished bottom of the Third Division four seasons in a row. All the bad publicity attracted a saviour of sorts, a Sheffield businessman who put enough money into the club to prevent them finishing bottom and by 2008–09 they made the Second Division play-offs and looked to be doing the same in 2009–10.

ESTUDIANTES

There are bigger clubs in Argentina, but few are as iconic as Estudiantes from the coastal city of La Plata, which is twinned with Liverpool.

Known as "the rat stabbers", Estudiantes became the first club outside of Argentina's Buenos Aires-based big five (Boca Juniors, River Plate, Racing Club, Independiente and San Lorenzo) to win the title in 1967. Their notorious side accused of being *el antifutbol* and coached by Osvaldo Zubeldía, was South American champions three times in a row from 1968–70. They also beat Manchester United in two controversial and ill-disciplined matches to lift the 1968 Intercontinental Cup. During the game in Argentina, a bag of offal was thrown at Bobby Charlton.

Worse was to follow as Estudiantes lost to AC Milan the following year and Feyenoord in 1970. Such was their barbaric behaviour in Milan, the entire team was arrested on their return on orders from the Argentinian president. Goalkeeper Poletti was suspended from football for life (though later pardoned) and served time in jail together with team-mates Aguirre Suárez and Madero. They were not all thugs though – the team contained two physicians while Juan Ramón Verón (father of Juan Sebastián) was a gifted playmaker.

The "little witch", Juan Sebastián – his dad was known as "the witch" for his magic on the ball – broke into his home-town team in 1994 and returned in 2006 after a hugely successful career in Italy and a less than spectacular one in England with Manchester United and Chelsea.

In 2006, the veins were popping out of Verón's head as Estudiantes beat Boca Juniors 2–1 in a play-off to win the Argentinian League. Boca had won the previous two titles and led the Apertura from the start, but Estudiantes chased them down with all the tenacity of coach Diego Simeone. Ten straight wins – including a 2–1 injury-time win at Newell's Old Boys – clawed them back to equal points in the last week of the season, triggering a one-off decider, a delirious win, and the resignation of Boca manager Ricardo Lavolpe. Estudiantes won the 2009 Copa Liberatadores, which earned them a place in the FIFA World Club Championship of the same year. They reached the final, playing Barcelona, but were beaten, ironically by an extra-time goal from a fellow Argentinian, Lionel Messi.

Manchester United captain Bobby Charlton shakes hands with the Estudiantes captain before the infamous first leg of the 1968 Intercontinental Cup final in Buenos Aires.

HURACÁN

Clad in virginal white, with a reputation for vibrant, thrilling football, Club Atlético Huracán are the discerning purist's Argentinian team of choice. While every man and his canine will adopt globe-straddling giants like River Plate as their own, fans of *El Globo* could never be accused of taking the easy option. Since the professional era began in 1931, eight teams from the Buenos Aires Province alone have enjoyed greater league success than Huracán, who can recall one measly title back in 1973.

Yet, supporters of Huracán tap into something mythical, for the team's lonely 1973 triumph was achieved with a bolt of brilliance so radiant that Argentina is still marvelling over its beauty. Ironically, for a team often referred to as "the burners", due to a stretch of land near their stadium formerly used to torch garbage, their Championship-winning side is remembered as Argentine football's aesthetic ideal.

Huracán were dragged from the mire of mediocrity by legendary coach **César Luis Menotti**; a man so effortlessly cool he made Johann Cruyff look like Roy Cropper. Menotti's brand of cerebral, passing football roused crowds and split defences, making such an impression that he was asked to coach the national side the following year.

However, it was Huracán where Menotti made his name, with a side that combined the meaty grit and explosive flair of the great Argentine sides.

Playing in an Art-Deco stadium, defenders like Alfio "Coco" Basile anchored the coruscating pace of winger René Houseman, while Carlos Babington, a striker of English heritage, laid waste to the opposition.

Huracán would fade into relative obscurity upon Menotti's departure, until 2009, when Vélez Sársfield cruelly pipped them to a second Championship in the final match of the season. Yet a new incarnation echoing Menotti's magnificence had surfaced, and the team from the burning barrio was adored for its style all over again.

JUVENTUS

Italians have never made good losers. A football defeat can't simply be explained by the fact that the opposition were better than you – there's always an underlying, sinister reason behind defeat: the ref is bent, the opposition are cheats or on drugs. Perhaps in a land of the Mafia and widespread political corruption, this attitude is understandable, but one thing's for sure: as the team at the top of the Italian tree, Juventus are always going to be the side everyone else is accusing. Italy's favourite – and also most hated – team, Turin's Old Lady are controversial for numerous reasons. Bankrolled by Fiat's Agnelli family – and in part by Libyan leader **Colonel**

Gadaffi's family – the Zebras have long been regarded in Italy as fat cats using their huge spending power to buy the Serie A title. Their support in Turin is largely based around southern economic migrants (often treated with derision in the north), and they have an unhealthy contingent of glory-hunting fans to annoy those of other teams. And that's all before you get to the drugs and the allegations of bribery.

"We all know Juventus benefits from favouritism", said then-Inter star **Ronaldo** in 1998, after a controversial penalty incident had sent the title to Turin. "They can punish me but I won't stay silent. When it's eleven against twelve, soccer becomes sad. I feel like crying." The allegations were treated seriously, and were even raised in the Italian parliament, leading to a scuffle among politicians. The drug scandals are just as explosive. Roma manager Zdeněk Zeman caused a huge stir in 1998 by accusing Juve of using "the chemist" to transform the physiques of players like **Gianluca Vialli** and **Alessandro Del Piero**. "I was surprised by their sudden bulking up", he said. "I thought such changes only occurred after years of work." But the greatest blot on the club's name came in 2006 with their involvement in the Calciopoli referee-rigging scandal which rocked top-level Italian football. Juve were given the greatest punishment, relegated to Serie C (B on appeal), docked thirty points (nine on appeal), stripped of their 2005 and 2006 titles and barred from the Champions League for a year. The "Old Lady" bounced straight back into Serie A, but saw many of star players depart. Fans muttered darkly that Juve were singled out at the expense of Inter, perhaps rightly, as the investigation goes on.

> **"When it's eleven against twelve, soccer becomes sad. I feel like crying."**
> Inter star Ronaldo sticks the knife into Juventus

Such problems shouldn't detract from the club's greatness. In the 1930s the likes of Orsi, Monti and Ferarri thrilled Turin as Juve won five straight titles. In the late 1950s, Welsh giant **John Charles** became a folk hero alongside brilliant, temperamental Argentine **Omar Sivori**. And the period 1972–86 saw their awesome dominance. Vialli, **Zidane** and the **Baggios** would all come later, as Juventus amassed 27 titles. Their star has dimmed in recent years – losing to Fulham in 2010's Europa Cup was another low – but the club remains Italy's greatest footballing success story. Just don't expect other Italian teams' fans to admit it.

LENS

Lens, population thirty-six thousand. Racing Club de Lens, average attendance over the last decade: thirty-six thousand. To an outsider, it does not make sense, but try and tell that to the residents of the former mining town in the Pas de Calais in northeast France, surrounded by World War I battlefields.

Lens (and its satellite villages) is a football town in the same way of another former mining stronghold, Gelsenkirchen, home of Schalke 04 in Germany. Their *Les Sang et Or* (blood and gold) nickname purportedly comes from the blood of the miners and the black gold they mined. The coal slag heaps were a dominant feature of the town by the end of the Great War – the town's skyline flattened after four years of shelling. German prisoners, who later cleared the ruins of the town, were camped at the spot where the Stade Felix Bollaert now stands.

Lens' footballing fortunes began to rise when the local mayor André Delelis hatched a grand plan to redevelop the stadium with the intention of staging games during the 1984 European Championships – tiny Lens ahead of great cities like Toulouse and Bordeaux. The rest of France considered the Lensoise crazy for building a fifty-two thousand-capacity stadium (it had standing then) – but Championship games were successfully staged and unlike in Elche and Alicante (Spain '82) or several of the venues for Portugal 2004, the resident club subsequently filled their expanded home.

Lens also staged games during the France '98 World Cup, including France's golden goal victory over Paraguay. That year, Lens also won their first – and so far only – Ligue 1 title, with the Cameroonian midfielder **Marc-Vivien Foé** their star. (Foé tragically collapsed and died during a FIFA Confederations Cup match in 2003). The night they won the League, mayor Delelis ordered all the bars in the town to stay open until dawn.

The following season, Lens became the smallest town to host Champions League group stage football – an achievement repeated when nearby Lille played their European games in Lens against teams like Manchester United.

MACCLESFIELD TOWN

Macclesfield, twenty miles south of Manchester, has a love-hate relationship with the sprawling northern city on its doorstep.

The town gave the world such delights as Peter Crouch, Hovis bread, Joy Division's Ian Curtis, New Order's Stephen Morris and … The Macc Lads – but as the United and City flags hanging outside local hostelries illustrate, most people in this market town of fifty-one thousand do not support their local club. Macclesfield Town's average gates of two thousand place them among the worst supported teams in the Football League, yet just surviving in the 92 is an achievement for a club which has spent most of its history playing non-league football.

Macclesfield Town's hand-to-mouth existence contrasts starkly with the conspicuous displays of wealth to be found in this most leafy of boroughs that Wayne Rooney, Mark Hughes, Sir Alex Ferguson and many other big-name Premier League stars call home.

In the 1990s, Macclesfield Town made headlines of their own with a story of ambition, rejection, death, determination, gangsters and financial hardship. In six

Visiting supporters watch from the back of the terrace at The Moss Rose Stadium, Macclesfield – in stark contrast to the glamour of their Mancunian neighbours.

short years, Macclesfield went from being within a game of being relegated to a league where the average crowd was four hundred, to playing a League fixture in front of over thirty thousand against neighbours Manchester City.

Sammy McIlroy was appointed manager in 1993, with the club in a mess. With assistant Gil Prescott, he scouted hundreds of semi-professional players. In his first season the team finished seventh – going on to win the Conference the following year. And yet they were denied entry to the Football League on the grounds that their Moss Rose home hadn't made the grade at inspection eight months before. Macc were outraged. This was a stadium that had staged League football with Chester City as residents and was refurbished to standard by the time the League was won. Chairman Arthur Jones took the news so badly that he shot himself and died.

While Macclesfield's financial position worsened, their team spirit was indomitable. Refusing offers from bigger clubs, McIlroy kept his side together. They won the FA Trophy in 1996 and the Conference again a year later – by which time their ground was passed fit.

Best player by far was **Chris Byrne**, a pasty-faced midfielder born and raised in Old Trafford. He'd scored a hat-trick on his debut and another to get Macc promoted at Kettering Town – and yet his story is tinged with tragedy.

"It was by some distance the best performance I've ever seen in non-league", buzzed McIlroy. Macclesfield were promoted again the following season with a home record of P23–W19–D4–L0, but Byrne had moved on to Premiership Sunderland, where he was soon in the team alongside Kevin Phillips as they beat Man City 3–1. Soon after he was arrested in a Sunderland hotel room – but not charged – as part of a complex Manchester murder enquiry.

Seven months later, he moved to Stockport, then of the First Division for £200,000, but his career was derailed by two career-threatening cruciate ligament injuries. In 1999, Byrne was given 240 hours community service for his part in the burglary of a Manchester chemist and, in May 2001, rejoined Macclesfield after refusing to go on Stockport's pre-season tour of China. A month earlier, he had been arrested in connection with a stabbing but not charged.

In 2002, a bullet severed the main artery in his left leg after he was shot in an alleyway in Hulme, Manchester. It was believed that Byrne was trying to prevent balaclava-clad youths from taking his car. In 2006, police announced that they were hoping to speak to Byrne in relation to a number of boiler robberies from Lancashire plumbing merchants.

"I thought Chris could have gone on to become a fantastic player and make a lot of money, but he lives his life as he chooses", said McIlroy, sadly.

Despite the odds, Macclesfield Town have kept their Football League status ever since.

OLYMPIQUE DE MARSEILLE

Before Roman Abramovich and the boys with the big bucks invaded the Premier League, global gazillionaires rarely seemed interested in football. Then again, who needs a financial figurehead with a dextrous appreciation of hedge funds when your transfer targets include Marco Boogers? Back in the days when pitches looked like they might actually contain mud, it took a more eccentric type to get involved. Step forward Mr Bernard Tapie, a Gallic entrepreneur with an undoubtedly fragrant hand in every pie.

Tapie was a businessman, politician, and most famously, the president of Olympique de Marseilles. Although Marseilles were regularly successful, most notably during the presidency of media mogul Marcel Leclerc during the 1960s and 70s, they were prone to frequent slumps. Even Leclerc was accused of pilfering money, and Marseilles spiralled into France's second tier for almost a decade.

After a return to the top flight in 1984, Tapie soon took over. Marseilles rocketed to four consecutive League titles, and Tapie pumped the team full of superstars.

There was European football's first African of great note, Ghana's **Abedi Pele**, and future French legends Deschamps, Desailly and Barthez. Between 1989 and 1993, the team played gloriously, in a golden period culminating in victory over a superb AC Milan team in the 1993 European Cup final.

Yet the president's magic dust was laced with poison. In 1994, after revelations that Tapie had approached minnow club Valenciennes in an attempt to fix results and prevent injuries, the club was relegated and stripped of its 1993 League title, while the astonishing European success was tainted forever.

Tapie was indicted and imprisoned for corruption, while Marseilles have not been champions of France since. Braggadocio and bustle made him the king of this tough sea-port town, but vice and sleaze saw France's greatest club thrown mercilessly to the sharks.

NEW YORK COSMOS

For a few years in the 1970s, the New York Cosmos were the coolest team on the planet. **Pelé** and **Franz Beckenbauer** strutted their stuff in front of eighty thousand in the Giants Stadium, while the celebs hanging out in the dressing room read like a who's who of 1970s' cool: the Rolling Stones, the Monty Python team, Robert Redford, Alice Cooper. It all happened in a mad whirlwind that owed everything to American entrepreneurship and a go-getting attitude, but ultimately the foundations for this New York soccer dream were built on sand.

The Cosmos were set up in 1971 to join the recently established North American Soccer League. Initially playing in the decrepit Randall's Island Stadium and drawing crowds of around five thousand, it took a series of ambitious moves to propel them suddenly into the big time. Former Welsh international Phil Woosnam, NASL commissioner, asked Englishman Clive Toye to help build the club. English coach Gordon Bradley was installed, but Toye knew they needed a big signing to promote soccer in the Big Apple. The pair wooed major executives from Warner and Atlantic Records to help buy players, and Toye persuaded the now-retired Pelé to turn his back on offers from European clubs because "if you go there you can win a championship. Come here and you can win a country." The Brazilian legend went for it – and won. His arrival in 1975 put around fifty thousand on the gate straight away.

> **"The biggest challenge for us was not stopping and watching him play."**
> **Cosmos captain Werner Roth outlines training-ground issues after Pelé joined the team**

For a while, the glamour was irresistible. Teams including Pelé, Franz Beckenbauer, **Carlos Alberto**, **Giorgio Chinaglia** and **Johan Neeskens** (as well as former Aldershot and Hartlepool defender **Malcolm Dawes**, **Keith Eddy** of Barrow, Watford and Sheffield United and **Barry Mahy** who made 21 appearances for Scunthorpe) won 8 out of every 10 games they played. They scooped the title in 1972, '77, '78, '80 and '82, and during the evening they partied with the best of them at Studio 54. Alice Cooper charmed Pelé sufficiently to be given a shirt, which he later wore on stage in the city. It seemed things could hardly get better, but the bubble would eventually burst.

There was interference from executives, as Toye remembers: "We had one asshole telling us that we had to change the way the game starts, and have Pelé and Beckenbauer juggling the ball in the centre circle like a circus act." In addition, the quality of opposition was often appalling, leading to a lack of competition for the Cosmos, and when Pelé retired, the glamour disappeared. Sponsorship never came in, and the league gained a reputation as a retirement home for ageing talent. Like many other attempts to wean Americans off native sports, the style was never backed by substance.

PARTICK THISTLE

Alan Hansen recalls a pre-game Saturday morning training session at Partick Thistle, with the team in the middle of a bad losing streak. "The manager Bertie Auld said 'I'm going to announce today's team now, then we're going to have a practice game without any opposition. We'll knock the ball about a bit, score a few goals, and that will get our confidence back.' After fifteen minutes the score was 0–0 and Bertie was going mental. After thirty minutes it was still 0–0 and he had changed the team for the afternoon. It's actually quite difficult playing against nobody."

The story sums up the fortunes of Glasgow's third club, who are destined to be the bridesmaid to the giant Old Firm sides. But while they may never have won the League, Partick offer something entirely different to the Glaswegian football scene. Where between Rangers and Celtic there is loathing, at Partick there's just humour. They even see fit to mock their auspicious rivals' petty bigotry in their chants:

"Hello, hello, how do you do?
We hate the boys in royal blue
We hate the boys in emerald green
So f*** the pope and f*** the queen."

There have been glory years: between 1954 and 1959, the Jags contested three Scottish League Cup finals – unfortunately failing to win any. Their time finally came in 1971, when Thistle defeated a mighty Celtic side containing nine internationals using a young and largely untried team. **Rae**, **Lawrie**, **McQuade** and **Bone** were the goalscorers in a miraculous 4–1 triumph – it's kept the Thistle fans going ever since. The Jags have also enjoyed two outings in Europe – the 1962–63 Fairs Cup, where they beat Glentoran only to lose to Spartak Brno of Czechoslovakia, and 1971–72, when they were thrashed by Honved.

Firhill, which celebrated its centenary in 2010, has even become a favourite haunt for celebrity Glaswegian football fans. Billy Connolly is among the most notable, and was recently joined by actor Robert Carlyle and *Pop Idol* graduate Darius Danesh. A suspicion is often aired in Glasgow that any celeb proclaiming their love for the Jags is merely avoiding the abuse that will be heaped upon them from fifty percent of Glasgow if they nail their colours to the mast of either Old Firm side, but it all adds a touch of glamour to following the city's underachievers.

PENAROL

"Almost all South Americans are football mad", observed American writer John Gunther in his 1940 book *Inside Latin America*, "but none are madder than the stout citizens of Uruguay." It's fair to say that the passion for the game remains as strong as ever on the continent that gave us **Garrincha** and **Diego Maradona**. But while Brazil and Argentina may have best represented this obsession in recent years, Uruguay led the way in the first half of the twentieth century.

It all started in Montevideo in 1891, when British gentlemen working on the railways formed the Central Uruguayan Railway Cricket Club. Football rapidly became the preferred game, and twenty years later the team changed their name to Penarol and became the country's dominant force, forming an intensely passionate rivalry with city-mates Nacional.

Like a Latin version of Celtic and Rangers, the sides share virtually every League title, battling against familiar-sounding teams – Liverpool, Wanderers – whose names betray their English roots. Penarol (club motto "You'll be eternal like time and you'll flower each spring") have the upper hand, and in the 1960s were a truly great side – defeating European champions Real Madrid on several occasions with fabulous players like **Pedro Rocha** and **Pepe Sasia**.

> **"The sight of a Penarol shirt makes me sick. I want them to lose every time, even against foreigners."**
> A Nacional supporter expresses his feelings for his Montevidian neighbours

"We Uruguayans belong to Nacional or to Penarol from the day we are born", says writer Eduardo Galeano. "That's the way it's been since the beginning of the century." Prostitutes in the Montevideo bordellos used to compete for fans' trade by sitting in doorways wearing club strips, and Galeano recalls a fellow Nacional fan's sentiments that "the sight of a Penarol shirt makes me sick. I want them to lose every time, even against foreigners." Even other South American nations recognize the fervour of Uruguayan support: "Other countries have their history, Uruguay has its football", runs the popular phrase.

But passion has its ugly side. Uruguayans have developed a reputation for professional fouls and mindless thuggery (profiled effectively at numerous World Cups) and this win-at-all-costs mentality is at its height during the Montevideo derby. Recent highlights include a huge, ugly brawl in the centre circle during a 2000 fixture and the multiple arrests for fighting of bad-boy Nacional striker **Richard Morales**.

On the world stage it remains incredible that a nation of just 3.3 million has made such an impact (including two World Cup wins, in 1930 and 1950).

RAPID VIENNA

Rapid Vienna have clapped their way into football history. Fifteen minutes from the end of every game at the Gerhard Hanappi Stadion, the home fans start clapping frantically – known as the *Rapidviertelstunde* – even (with a fine sense for English puns) rapidly, to encourage the boys in green and white. The tradition dates back to the pre-war years and a game, lost to memory but enshrined in myth, when Rapid were on the wrong end of a humiliating scoreline (4–1 or 5–1, opinions differ) and the fans started clapping after 75 minutes, their applause inspiring the team to snatch a draw.

Why the fans behave like this is probably, ultimately, less important than the fact that they do still do it – at every game. And although, through repetition, the inspirational effect has worn off, you can still detect a glimmer of extra urgency in the team. Rapid were big in the 1930s, bigger still in the 1950s (when, inspired by midfielders **Ernst Happel** and **Gerhard Hanappi**, they beat Real Madrid and Milan in the European Cup), and still quite good in the 1980s, when **Hans Krankl** was the genius in residence. Rapid still pride themselves on a passionate never-say-die kind of play which comes straight out of the English football school – but then the club was founded by hat factory employees who changed the name from Wiener Arbeiter-Fussballklub to Rapid to give their club a more English-sounding name.

Rapid still proudly call themselves a people's club and the people have been known to take matters into their own hands, staging a peaceful sit-in on the pitch after one barren spell of form in 2001–02. Their great rivals Austria Wien are the posh club, said to "have been founded in coffee house smog" by the working-class fans of Rapid.

Unlike a lot of clubs, for whom the past is a burden to be borne or something to be redefined according to the needs of this season's marketing campaign, Rapid are proud of their past and give seats for life to legends. On matchdays, the club erect a massive marquee where beer and sausages are dispensed at decent prices, and even the players have been known to drop in for a chat. It's all a long way from the world of the high-pressure English club – and all the better for it.

SKONTO RIGA

If you think the Old Firm's dominance of Scottish football is boring, just be grateful you didn't live in Latvia before 2005. Since independence, the club's primary professional club, Skonto Riga, won the league fourteen times on the bounce, until 2005, when it finished second, to an audible sigh of relief. With only eight teams in the top flight, and only four of them properly professional, it was once a walkover for Skonto, who had attracted the best players and coaches over recent years. The dominance was getting embarrassing. In two consecutive seasons, they didn't lose a single game.

"I'm bored", admitted Georgian international midfielder **Alexander Rekhviashvili**. He went on to say that he wanted to play in Italy or England, as well as adding (and something may be lost in the translation here) that "Ireland is not a bar of chocolates".

Even when they were not playing well, things went right for Skonto. They were almost pipped to the title by rival club Ventspils, as the two sides finished equal on points, with Skonto holding a better goal difference. Excited at the prospect of somebody else winning the League, the Latvian FA decided to waive the rules and ignore the goal factor; instead there would be a league play-off. Skonto won 4–0.

SSV MARKRANSTÄDT

It says something about the success of a club when its only famous footballer was a referee. Rudi Glöckner, ex-SSV Markranstädt, was in charge of the 1970 World Cup final between Brazil and Italy. It was about the only time people noticed that the club existed. Until 2009, when the marketing directors of Red Bull, the soft drink company with a 2.6 billion euros turnover, decided that SSV Markranstädt was the ideal club for their aim to create a Red Bull-run German Bundesliga side. Markranstädt play in a division equivalent to the Isthmian League. But Markranstädt, a small town of fifteen thousand, is only five miles away from Leipzig. That was the unique selling point for Red Bull.

Leipzig is the second biggest town in East Germany, has a World Cup stadium, but no team above the fourth division, so Red Bull saw it as the strategically perfect place for their assault. The only problem with Leipzig is that the supporters of its two traditionally big clubs Lokomotive and Sachsen are among the most radical in the country. Red Bull feared violent resistance from their supporters if they took over either of the two clubs. So they went for the suburban side nearby, instead. They acquired Markranstädt's licences and when German football laws forbade them to rename the club Red Bull Leipzig, they christened the team Rasen-Ballsport Klub (Lawn-Ballgames Club) to make it RB Leipzig anyway. Their squad includes professionals like Ingo Hertzsch, the 33-year-old two-times Germany international, in the equivalent of the Isthmian League and they want to be in the Bundesliga by 2017.

Their games already regularly attract around two thousand fans, though maybe not all of them the ones they were hoping for. Hooligans and protesters from Lok and Sachsen Leipzig are regulars, trying to drive out the intruders with their marketing plans. Suffering the most in this feud is Markranstädt's groundsman. Three times in RB Leipzig's first month, Lok and Sachsen fans seeded the pitch with weeds under cover of darkness.

TORINO

Whether it's the resurrection of Christ or Kylie's chart-topping comeback, behind every epic tale there resides a punctuating dollop of tragedy and redemption. However, for Italian outfit Torino, there appears no escape from football's longest and most glittering shadow. Once Italy's greatest team, and a sty in the eye of Fiat-sponsored neighbours Juventus, Torino seem almost paralysed by history.

In the 1940s, Torino were possibly the world's greatest side. Led by the iconic "Captain Valentino" Mazzola, *I Granata* ("The Clarets") romped to five consecutive Serie A titles and notched up an array of astonishing records that still hold sway over Italian annals.

The team was devastatingly torn apart in an air crash in May 1949. Returning from a friendly in Lisbon, their plane lurched into the mountains above Turin amid murk and misty rain. With the pilot's view obscured, Italy's most feted footballers perished near a basilica atop the Superga hillside, to the south of the River Po.

The ensuing years had a bitter taste. Juventus regained Turinese bragging rights, while Torino's supporters endured cruel taunts that mocked the Superga tragedy. The club's solitary title since the disaster arrived in 1976, thanks to an indefatigable goal-scoring partnership between Paolo Pulici and Francesco Graziani, yet this isolated spring served only to expose the surrounding drought.

The crumbling Filadelfia stadium, home to so many of Torino's stirring triumphs, only amplified the misery. As its inner-city site, the very soul of the club, crumbled into ruin, hopes of reconstruction were repeatedly dashed. By 2010, Torino fans were resorting to turning up at local restaurants to dish out a few slaps to first-team players, so inept were the club's performances.

Kylie has triumphed again, but will Torino?

TSG 1899 HOFFENHEIM

When the South African football agent **Rob Moore** travelled for transfer negotiations to Germany's most admired Bundesliga club in 2008, he could not get off the train. Hoffenheim is so small that the train just stopped half a minute and was gone again before Moore even realised they had been there. A village of 3264 inhabitants near Heidelberg, Hoffenheim on first sight does not look to most people what it is: the latest hot spot of German football, the laboratory to create the football of the future.

In 1990, Dietmar Hopp, who had played for the village team in his youth, saw TSG 1899 Hoffenheim go down 2–3 in a relegation play-off against mighty FC Stebbach. Hoffenheim were relegated to the Kreisliga A, the third league from the bottom of the German football pyramid. Hoffenheim had never played much higher. The club asked if Hopp could help them out with a few thousand

> **"Just sometimes, we have to remind ourselves that we have not invented football."**
> Peter Zeidler, assistant manager

Deutschmarks to get back to the fourth lowest league. Hopp, a founder of the software-giant SAP with a private fortune worth some €6.3 billion, paid the money. And some more since then. Eighteen years later, Hoffenheim reached the Bundesliga and a club from a village of 3,263 now fills a stadium of 30,000 – which Hopp had built, investing roughly €100 million. But, unlike most patrons, he would earmark only a small amount for big-name players. Hoffenheim keep on amazing people not with their money, but with their stylish football, the development of young talents and their scientific approach to the game. They signed, for example, the national hockey coach to invent new training methods, and a so-called *kinetik* coach. This is a coach who trains the eyes of the players to widen their vision during games. "Just sometimes", says assistant manager Peter Zeidler, "we have to remind ourselves that we have not invented football."

UNION BERLIN

A free-kick for Union Berlin in any game in Communist East Germany was not only a rare chance to score a goal for the team frequently fighting relegation from the GDR-Oberliga, but also the unique opportunity for thousands to show their disaffection with the regime. As soon as the rival's defence lined up for the wall, the Union support started singing: "The wall has to go, the wall has to go!" Nobody could miss the double-meaning at times when the Berlin wall had become the symbol of a nation's imprisonment.

Although Union was run by loyal Communists who had no intention of creating an opposition movement, the club became the team of opposition and dissidents in the GDR. As in most Communist bloc countries, the regime tried to control football strictly, running most teams through government organizations like the army or the secret service. But thanks to the intervention of an important unionist, Union was organized like a traditional club. As the one team with a degree of "differentness", it attracted all sorts of malcontents. Not all of them were political dissidents, but simply youth who just wanted to be different like punks or rockers. Even hooligans, a well-hidden secret of the GDR, frequented the club. Any opposition to the party line had to be subtle, but in the heat of the East Berlin derbies against BFC Dynamo, the pet team of the secret service, the singing often became overt: "I'd rather be a loser than a *Stasi*-pig!" There was no other place in the country to get away with such statements.

Today, Union plays in the second Bundesliga, higher then ever since the wall came down, and still cultivates its underdog mentality. Although supporting Union today is for most fans the expression of a far more anodyne opposition: against the ever boring football of Berlin's Bundesliga-side Hertha.

WEST HAM UNITED

In the official history of West Ham United, **Trevor Brooking** notes that "Football at Upton Park has always been about more than just results, it's about playing the game the right way, playing with style and flair". This is the so-called "West Ham Way", which hasn't stopped the Hammers fielding "hard men" such as **Julian Dicks** and **Neil Ruddock**. Obviously the exceptions which prove the rule.

West Ham is, famously, the club that founded its own unofficial football academy decades before the shiny official academies sprang up like mushrooms across Britain. In Cassattari's Café in the 1950s, Malcolm Allison, Dave Sexton, Frank O'Farrell, John Bond and Noel Cantwell would discuss football tactics, trying out ruses with salt and pepper pots. Although the name of **Ron Greenwood** is usually associated with the Academy, he didn't become the club manager until 1961, although, like Allison, he thought English football should learn from the havoc the Hungarians had wreaked on England in 1953. Allison's views would have a massive influence on **Bobby Moore** and John Lyall. But, from the style of play adopted by Coventry City under Cantwell in the 1970s, one can only assume the Irish defender wasn't listening. The terms "progressive football" and "Ernie Hunt" don't often appear in the same sentence.

But that's West Ham for you, a club whose reputation for playing good football was cemented by the holy trinity of England's 1966 World Cup triumph: Moore, **Martin Peters** and **Geoff Hurst**. The club conveyor belt continues to deliver such talents on an astonishingly regular basis (Alan Devonshire, Ray Houghton, Rio Ferdinand, Joe Cole, Michael Carrick, Frank Lampard, Jermain Defoe). The tradition that such talent is cherished by the club's discerning fans lasts as long as it takes you to go to the Boleyn Ground on a frustrating Saturday afternoon and hear the Hammers faithful baying "F***ing kick it!" at the wonderboys.

The club is perceived, with some truth, to have stuck to its guns, and indeed, its latest manager is football wizard and devotee of all things skilful **Gianfranco Zola**. Sometimes you wonder if the fans themselves might not have preferred a different tradition: that of winning trophies. Still, being renowned for playing fluent attractive football is a happier fate than being famous for being infamous (Millwall) or for being the team of the 1980s (Crystal Palace).

LEOPARDS
ZAÏRE
3

The Games

Thrillers, spankings, giant-killings and the match that never was …

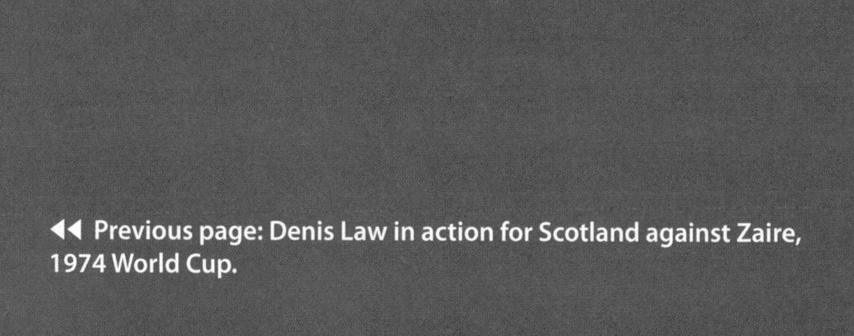

◀◀ Previous page: Denis Law in action for Scotland against Zaire, 1974 World Cup.

The Games

"This game had all the beauty a fantasy can offer."

Günter Netzer, 1971

AJAX 5–1 LIVERPOOL, THE FOG GAME (1966)

Johan Cruyff was one tricky customer. When Liverpool met Ajax in the second round of the 1966–67 European Cup there were a couple of factors that weren't in their favour. First, they had never heard of the nineteen-year-old Cruyff and knew nothing of his capabilities; and second, the pitch was inundated by a thick inpenetrable fog. Cruyff, Ajax and the match would never be forgotten.

Bill Shankly's Liverpool were among the favourites to win the competition, while Ajax were unknown, unfancied opponents. Having made a scouting trip to witness Ajax in defeat to lowly opposition, Shankly returned to Merseyside unassailably confident.

On the day of the match, consuming mists surrounded the Olympic Stadium in Amsterdam. Schiphol airport was shut, and Shankly pleaded with officials to postpone the game. But, with sixty thousand spectators packed in and the goals barely visible, the referee refused due to popular demand.

Liverpool were soon caught in a whiteout of a different kind, as Ajax stormed to a two-goal advantage. In a blind fury, Shankly ventured unseen onto the fog-bound pitch to instruct his players, but Ajax possessed new purpose, new discipline and ideas that would revolutionize football in the coming decade. Led by progressive tactician Rinus Michels, Ajax drove Liverpool into the ground. The crowd cheered each goal instinctively, but were unable to accurately discern the flow of the game.

The game finished 5–1 to Ajax, leaving Shankly humiliated. He strove to convince the whole of Liverpool that a miraculous comeback was likely. The crowds poured into Anfield for the second leg, but were met by an implacable Ajax. With Cruyff, their chief sorcerer, Ajax progressed 7–3 on aggregate, and the genesis of a new force in European football was underway.

Cruyff would become the most famous player of the 1970s, but it was here, clad in divine white, that he made his name in a mystical, otherworldly battle with the elements. Ajax had leapt headlong into the ether and emerged transformed.

MÖNCHENGLADBACH V. INTERNAZIONALE MILAN, EUROPEAN CUP (1971)

Interviewed amid the sublime calm typical of a football ground in the hours after a great victory, Mönchengladbach's playmaker **Günter Netzer** mused that: "This game had all the beauty a fantasy can offer." A young and attacking team from a German provincial town had beaten the adored Italian champions Inter 7–1 in the second round of the European Cup; yet only a few days later, this stunning victory had been returned to the realm of mere fantasy once more. Sensationally, the game was nullified by UEFA, as a result of post-match allegations that Inter's Roberto Boninsegna had been hit on the head by a can thrown from the stands 29 minutes into the game.

"Let's put it this way", said one Jef Dorpmans decades later. "Inter were going down and when the can came flying, Boninsegna saw his chance. We can assume that he was play-acting." And that was the fixture's Dutch referee speaking. "But I had no proof that Boninsegna was putting on a show. Anyway, personally it never occurred to me to abandon or nullify the game. But the Italians were well connected on UEFA's committees at the time."

It was an era when a manager, with clear ideas and a good crop of local players, could still turn a small-town side into potential world-beaters – it happened with **Brian Clough** at Derby and it happened with manager **Hennes Weisweiler** at Mönchengladbach. The flying long hair of their wingers Jupp Heynckes and Rainer Bonhof became a renowned trademark.

There were still highlights ahead of them – they were runners-up against Liverpool in the European Cup final of 1977 – but they never again played such overwhelming football as they did that night in 1971 when the can came flying. The nullified game had to be replayed on neutral ground. After having lost the still-standing first leg 2–4 in Milan, the teams drew 0–0 in Berlin and Mönchengladbach were out.

Referee Jef Dorpmans took a small souvenir from the game and handed it over to the museum of his club, **Vitesse Arnhem**. There in a glass cabinet, the infamous Coca-Cola can remains today … seemingly undamaged.

MILAN V. LEEDS (1973)

Unlike the cheerleader-assisted carnivals of the modern era, the 1973 Cup Winners' Cup final between Milan and Leeds was no festival of football. With a rich cast, including a bribed referee and Norman "Bites Yer Legs" Hunter, the match was basically the Battle of the Alamo, transported to a piece of grass in Greece.

Following ninety barbed minutes under wet, stormy skies in Salonika, Milan emerged victorious, thanks to a third-minute free kick from centre-forward Luciano Chiarugi. Awarded with some generosity by Greek referee Christos Michas, the decision sent the contest careening towards carnage.

In classic Italian fashion, Milan spent most of the match in their own half, peppered by long balls and rugged aerial affronts from a Leeds side not known for its timidity.

Famously derided for their ruthless style, Don Revie's Leeds had left a trail of bloody conquest throughout England. However, bereft of the inventive Johnny Giles through injury, an impotent Leeds failed to cope with an equally dogged Milan side.

As Leeds desperately sought an equalizer, Michas turned down penalty after penalty. With both sides increasingly irascible, fouls became more frequent. Iron defender Norman Hunter eventually lost it, chasing down Milan's svelte artiste Gianni Rivera and administering an inelegant thump. Officials flooded onto the field in an attempt to quell the subsequent melee. Hunter saw red, and the game ended under a cascade of boos.

The usually sanguine commentator **Barry Davies** declared that the match had "done European football no service whatsoever", but when Michas was retrospectively convicted of match fixing, Milan were shamefully allowed to keep the trophy.

In 2009, twelve thousand persistent Leeds fans signed a petition, headed by MEP Richard Corbett (who was incidentally defeated by the BNP in the 2009 European elections), demanding that the trophy be awarded to their club. But for the team now remembered as Revie's "Damned United", there was scant sympathy.

YUGOSLAVIA 9–0 ZAIRE, WORLD CUP (1974)

Zaire were the first team from sub-Saharan Africa to make it to the World Cup finals and they trailed a continent of supporters expecting a boost to collective pride ... and, perhaps, a little glory. Unfortunately, Zaire lost their first match, 2–0 to Scotland.

But in defeat, they nonetheless displayed glimpses of the form that had seen them become the reigning champions of Africa. *The Times*, reporting on the Scotland game, stated that: "Zaire were an eye-opener ... Their movements are snaky, with the accent always on attack, as fresh as a summer breeze on a lovely summer night."

> **"Their movements are snaky, with the accent always on attack, as fresh as a summer breeze on a lovely summer night."**
> *The Times* on the elegant Zairian team

Back at the team hotel after the match, the summer night got hotter, as arguments erupted between players and officials over disappearing match fees. There was talk of a players' strike – a foolhardy idea given the autocrat tendencies of state president Mobutu, who took a close personal interest in how Zaire performed on the world stage. Thus it was an unhappy team who took to the field against Yugoslavia in their second group game.

From the first kick of the ball, things progressed from bad to worse for the Zairian team, and by the 23-minute mark Yugoslavia had already hit the back of the net four times. Then Zaire's leading goalscorer, **Mulamba Ndaye**, was shown the red card in a case of mistaken identity – punished for defender Mwepu Ilunga's aggressive berating of referee Omar Delgado.

Zaire's coach Blagoje Vidinić substituted goalkeeper **Mwamba Kazadi** and his replacement, **Dimbi Tubilandu**, had barely run onto the field before Zaire conceded their fourth. Conspiracy theories abounded: that Vidinić had purposefully weakened the team because he wanted his native Yugoslavia to win and boost their goal-difference; that Vidinić had bowed to pressure from a senior, pushy Mobutu crony who had a preference for Tubilandu, the 5ft 4in goalkeeper from AS Vita Club of Kinshasa, over Kazadi, from Lubumbashi's Tout-Puissant club. A darker rumour spread, suggesting that the players had stopped trying because they felt ripped-off by their bosses.

Ahead of the match, a Zairois mystic, one Mama Tuseya, had forecast a "small accident, which will be the sacrifice the gods of victory need for Zaire to win." Evidently, whatever misfortune occurred and to whom, the sacrifice was considered unsatisfactory by the deities concerned. The only consolation, at the full-time whistle, was that Zaire had narrowly avoided defeat by double figures.

EGYPT 1–0 LIBYA, ALL AFRICA GAMES (1978)

Egypt knew, when they sent their national squad to Algeria for the African Games in 1978, that they would encounter hostility from the grandstands. Football relations between Cairo and the other North African countries had long been strained by the perception that Egypt preferred to look east rather than west for its influences and alliances, that the descendants of the Pharaohs were a bit snooty about the rest of Africa and confused about which continent they belonged to.

By the late 1970s, political tensions had added to this atmosphere of distrust. Anwar Sadat, the Egyptian head of state was pushing forward peace initiatives with Israel, engendering fierce criticism from across Arabic Africa. Algeria and Egypt's next-door neighbours, Colonel **Muammar Gaddafi**'s Libya, were particularly vocal among the "rejectionist" lobby.

The football strand of the Games kicked-off in mid-July, in a hot and sticky Algiers. Algeria and Egypt drew in the first group game and by the third round Egypt and Libya were effectively playing one another for a remaining place in the semi-finals. Neither would fill it, because what happened on the pitch led to a major international incident and to both sides leaving the competition. As the whistle blew on a 1–0 Egyptian win, several Egypt players were assaulted by their Libyan opponents. Spectators armed with metals bars and clubs joined in on the Libyan side. Two Egyptian players suffered broken arms, others were treated for blood wounds, severe bruising and head injuries.

Egypt withdrew from the Games; Libya were kicked out. But that was not the end of it. In Cairo, the offices of Libya and Algeria's national airlines were attacked. Egypt threatened to boycott all events in "rejectionist" countries. Fully eleven years later, persistent bad blood would mar a crucial World Cup qualifier between Egypt and Algeria, with an arrest warrant (finally dropped in 2009) being issued against Lakhdar Belloumi, the Algerian star, for his alleged assault on a member of Egypt's coaching staff.

MÖNCHENGLADBACH 12–0 DORTMUND (1978)

The scoreboard at the Rhine Stadium in Düsseldorf, where Borussia Mönchengladbach still staged their home games in 1978, could not add another goal. It was simply full. The names of twelve goalscorers blinked on the scoreboard under the big golden numbers "12" and "0". It was the highest victory ever in the Bundesliga on a day when every goal counted.

Mönchengladbach went into that last match day of the 1977–78 season equal on points with leaders FC Cologne, but ten goals behind on goal-difference. Cologne were playing that day at the already relegated St. Pauli – there seemed no chance that Mönchengladbach would catch them. Or, at least, that's what everybody thought.

Then Mönchengladbach's Jupp Heynckes scored in the first minute. Sometimes it just needs a spark and the heat of the moment sweeps away everything – the players, the teams, any sense of tactics. After just 38 minutes, Mönchengladbach were 6–0 up. Meanwhile in St. Pauli, Cologne were winning 1–0. Separated by 300 miles, a fierce goalscoring-contest started. After 66 minutes, Cologne were 2–0 up. But Mönchengladbach led 9–0. Cologne's lead was down to three goals. There was one moment, which said it all. A shot by Mönchengladbach's striker **Kalle del'Haye** went wide, and the referee had to fetch the ball and put it down for Dortmund's goal-kick. The Dortmund goalkeeper **Peter Endrulat** just did not want to get on with it anymore. Match-fixing, obviously, has been mentioned, but the suggestion can be disregarded from the evidence. It was just Mönchengladbach getting high on goals.

"Torhagel (Goal hail)"
Nickname given to Dortmund coach, Otto Rehhagel, after the defeat. He was also fired ... with immediate effect.

In the end, Cologne held on to their lead, victors by 5–0, winning the league by three goals on goal difference. The Mönchengladbach players went out to party anyway, elated with the sense of an extraordinary achievement. Endrulat never played another Bundesliga game. Today he sells welding equipment. He never told his workmates about his most famous game.

WEST GERMANY 1–0 AUSTRIA, WORLD CUP (1982)

"It felt", wrote the *Süddeutsche Zeitung*, "like the sinking of the *Titanic*." The opening round of matches at the 1982 World Cup in Gijón, Spain, had produced a sensation: Algeria 2, West Germany 1. The European champions had just been beaten by the utterly deserving novices from North Africa, thanks to goals from Lakhdar Belloumi and Rabah Madjer – and inspired performances from the likes of Djamel Zidane (no relation), Salah Assad, Chaabane Merzekane and Noureddine Kourichi. The World Cups of 1982 and 1986, as well as European club football over the following years, would continue to hear a good deal more of these names.

Alas, Algeria lost their next match, to Austria, 2–0, leaving the group delicately poised: Austria on four points, West Germany and Algeria on two each, with Chile bottom of the table, having lost twice. The West Germans held a superior goal difference. Then there was the ominous scheduling: Algeria were to meet Chile in Oviedo on Thursday 24 June. Austria v. Germany had been timetabled for the following afternoon in Gijón. That meant the two European teams would know what result would guarantee their progress, while Algeria – and indeed Chile, who had a remote chance of going through if they won by a large score in their final game – could only throw caution to the winds.

"the most shameful day in the history of our Football Federation"

German television's verdict on the game.

Algeria went hell-for-leather. Within 34 minutes of the off, the Africans were 3–0 up against their opponents. But an alarming loss of stamina and authority in the second half would reduce their advantage. Their eventual 3–2 victory left them with an overall goal difference of zero, worse than that of Austria.

What happened in Gijón on the Friday stank, as Africa's World Cup hopes were hijacked. West Germany needed to beat Austria to go through; Austria could afford to lose by up to two goals and still join the Germans there at Algeria's expense.

West Germany's Horst Hrubesch scored after ten minutes. From that point, all pace and urgency was wilfully sucked from the contest by almost every player on the pitch. The crowd became agitated. Algerians there waved banknotes at the conspiring German and Austrian players: but that's how the score remained at the final whistle. German television called it "the most shameful day in the history of our Football Federation." Others struck on another way of describing how Austria and Germany had come to this mutually agreeable result. They called it "The Anschluss".

The Algerian Federation lodged a complaint with FIFA – in vain. However, FIFA did change the rules for future tournaments as a result of the flaccid

German–Austrian ceasefire, so that matches deciding final table positions would from then on take place simultaneously. But it was too late for poor Algeria's class of 1982.

BAYER UERDINGEN 7–3 DYNAMO DRESDEN (1986)

Years later, they would all say, "I was there ... I saw it". But the truth is that by half-time that night, many of the 18,000 spectators at Uerdingen's Grotenburgkampfbahn had already gone home. Uerdingen were trailing 1–3 against Dynamo Dresden after 45 minutes, having already lost 0–2 in the first leg of this European Cup Winners' quarter-final, which was more than a game, more a political show-contest between the capitalist West Germany, represented by Uerdingen, and Communist East Germany. "Please do not expect", said Uerdingen's manager **Kalli Feldkamp**, "that I can explain what happened next."

Uerdingen needed five goals in 45 minutes to go through and scored six in the last half-hour. It was obvious that this defeat carried a political dimension for an East German regime that regarded sports as a tool to showcase the supposed supremacy of Communism. The Stasi, the infamous secret service of the regime, itself forced the sacking of Dresden manager **Klaus Sammer**, the father of Matthias Sammer, who would captain the reunited Germany in the 1990s. Klaus Sammer, the Stasi claimed, "could not be trusted anymore", particularly as one Dresden player, Frank Lippmann, fled from the team hotel at four in the morning, the night after the defeat, to ask for political asylum in the west.

The Stasi though, had played its own part in Dresden's downfall. The secret service had excluded substitute goalkeeper Jörg Klimpel from the trip to Uerdingen, identifying him as a potential defector due to his "western contacts". When Dresden's number one **Bernd Jakubowski** got injured and had to come off at half-time, the utterly inexperienced Jens Ramme took his place. With a couple of terrible blunders he helped Uerdingen to their comeback.

By comparison, the winners only had one minor problem. As nobody had expected this victory, there was not enough beer at the ground to celebrate.

ORLANDO PIRATES V. JOMO COSMOS, SOUTH AFRICA (1986)

Orlando Pirates, the Buccaneers, are the oldest of the so-called Soweto Giants. They are South Africa's "People's Club", born in the district of the famous township where Nelson Mandela and Desmond Tutu once lived. The trouble, at the beginning of the 1986 South African League season, was that too many people were claiming ownership of the mantle "People's Club".

Various disputes at boardroom level had ushered in a new season of a league that was busily resisting apartheid and trying to unite teams of all colours against the background of a fraught and violent society. No fewer than three different factions claimed to control Orlando Pirates. Shortly before kick-off at their opening day fixture against Jomo Cosmos at Ellis Park, Johannesburg, thirty thousand spectators were startled to see no fewer than 22 players on the pitch in Pirates' strip. One set of eleven had emerged from the dressing room. Another had arrived in a minibus, brought there by rotund businessman China Hlongwane, who claimed to be the "true" chief of the "real" Pirates. Before too long, he was surrounded by representatives of the "other" Orlando Pirates, who set upon him in front of a horrified crowd. Hlongwane was stabbed seventeen times.

The journalist Peter Auf der Heyde was taking photographs pitch-side that day: "When the administrators of the first Pirates team saw Hlongwane encouraging his players to get ready for the game, they advanced towards him, like a pack of lions about to pounce on their prey", he recalls. "It all happened so fast that nobody intervened."

Hlongwane's "Pirates XI" fled back to the minibus, while Hlongwane himself was rushed to hospital once his attackers had returned to the bench. Remarkably, he survived the assault, apparently protected by his bulk and the vast rolls of fat he carried. His "rebel" Orlando Pirates, needless to say, did not survive much longer.

CAMEROON 1–0 ARGENTINA, WORLD CUP (1990)

Everybody assumed Cameroon would fail in first fixture of the 1990 World Cup, that their initial task would be merely to act as the welcome mat on opening night for the title-holders, Argentina, and their celebrated captain **Diego Maradona**. Cameroon's odds for the tournament had been set at 500–1, and that was by bookmakers unaware of events unfolding up near Lake Como, where the so-called "Indomitable Lions" were billeted. The Cameroon goalkeeper, **Joseph Antoine Bell**, had been effectively sacked on the eve of the tournament for slamming the squad's preparations and laughing at the decision, imposed by presidential edict, to select the 38-year-old striker Roger Milla, who had been retired from serious football for over a year.

Once on the field, Cameroon offered some threat from wide positions, but lived dangerously. The mammoth centre-half Benjamin Massing was booked after ten minutes for fouling Maradona, Victor Ndip cautioned for targeting the same man midway through the first-half. Cameroon looked set mostly on roughing up the reigning world champions. At the interval it was still goalless, and then, after the hour – sensation. From a lofted free kick, François Omam Biyick hung high and long in the air to power a header that Nery Pumpido, the unfortunate Argentinian goalkeeper, let wriggle from his grasp and over the line.

Cameroon had been reduced to ten men barely a minute earlier when Omam Biyick's brother, André Kana Biyick, was dismissed for pushing and tripping the substitute Claudio Caniggia. Poor Caniggia was brutalized. A lunge at him by

Dejected Argentine players Nestor Gabriel Lorenzo (left) and Jorge Luis Burruchaga walk off the pitch, past unidentified celebrating Cameroon players, after the opening match of the 1990 World Cup, in Milan.

Massing after Caniggia had slipped past two other attempted muggings had such force behind it that the collision separated the massive Massing from his own boot. Massing then walked, one shoe off, one shoe on – red-carded. Cameroon were down to nine men; or, eight plus a man close to his fortieth birthday. Milla had come on as a late substitute, made a robust tackle on Maradona and prepared himself for the run of amazing goalscoring that would, over the following matches, sweep Cameroon to within minutes of a place in the semi-finals.

KAISERSLAUTERN 3–1 BARCELONA (1991)

It was the night Kaiserslautern became something bigger than a city: a symbol of resilience and a hallowed word for Catalans – even if they found it impossible to pronounce. There is a Catalan belief that Barcelona must always suffer the spectre of almost certain humiliation, but that at the end of all the pain, they are destined to triumph. At Kaiserslauten, this mythology was deeply enriched. A goal from José Mari Bakero three minutes from the end, a goal against all logic, saw Barça

Denmark in Mexico (1986)

When Denmark hitched a ride to the 1986 World Cup in Mexico, few in the football world predicted fireworks. Saddled in a group with West Germany, Uruguay and Alex Ferguson's Scotland, Denmark's first journey to the finals looked daunting and potentially brief. Yet, only weeks later, they emerged top of Group D, leaving the back pages rhapsodizing over their refreshing, breezy, attacking football.

Having reached the semi-finals at Euro '84, a modest optimism oozed through the squad bound for the Americas, and with the emergence of promising Juventus playmaker Michael Laudrup, some detected the nascent blossoming of a golden generation. The 1986 World Cup would confirm the "Danish Dynamite" sobriquet granted to the team at home, as their rugged opponents were swept aside.

First up were the Scots, including hard-nut Graeme Souness and witty midfielder Gordon Strachan. Despite some agricultural tackling, Denmark easily made holes in the rigid Scottish formation. A thrusting run from midfielder Frank Arnesen fed livewire striker Preben Eljkaer for the only goal, as Denmark starved Scotland of the ball.

Next came the rabid Uruguayans, who, predictably, tore into the feted Laudrup with relish. After Denmark took the lead through the relentless Elkjaer, Bossio was sent off for a wild challenge, and the Uruguayan team, despite featuring the magical Enzo Francescoli, was brought to swift justice. Smooth, sinuous runs from Laudrup created endless openings, and Uruguay were tortured to the tune of a 6–1 tanking. The world's eyes were now fixed upon these Danish upstarts.

A flawless start was completed against West Germany. Acclaimed scrooge Lothar Matthäus was nullified, and a penalty from shaggy-haired Jesper Olsen was crowned with a beautifully paced team goal finished by John Eriksen.

Denmark's campaign came to a premature end in the next round against Spain, but 1986's brief bedazzlement christened the emergence of a thrilling team from the North.

through on the away-goal rule in this second qualifying round of the brand new Champions League. Six months later they won the European Cup for the first time in their history.

That night in the German province, Barça were overrun and out-powered by an opponent playing on a pure adrenalin rush. After 76 minutes, Kaiserslautern were 3–0 up, having annihilated Barça's 2–0 lead from the first leg. Almost twenty years afterwards, Pep Guardiola, the Barça legend who starred in that game, would say: "I still start to shiver, I can still feel the fear, every time I hear the word Kaiserslautern. I never, ever want to experience something similar." And then Bakero scored.

It was a single, banal goal, headed in after a free-kick – but with the power to change destiny. Barça went on to finally win the European Cup after many years of waiting, and because of this success, became totally dedicated to the attacking–passing game their manager Johan Cruyff had installed that season. Hence Barça became a refuge of the beautiful game. They gave the world wonderful teams such as the 2006 Champions League winners led by Ronaldinho or their 2009 successors built around Leo Messi. But it all started in Kaiserslautern. In 2009, when Andrés Iniesta scored that mad, wonderful goal in the last minute against Chelsea to get Barça to the Champions League final, one Catalan radio reporter just shouted: "Kaiserslautern! It's Kaiserslautern again!"

INTERNAZIONALE V. SAMPDORIA (1991)

In the early 1990s, Italian football was enjoying a golden age. Serie A showcased the globe's finest players, and millions tuned in to appreciate its operatic magnificence.

However, the triumphant Sampdoria side of 1991 is but a speck against the league's grand history. In a league overflowing with totemic clubs, Sampdoria's success was surprising. Plucky outsiders, their strengths were spirit and healthy reserves of old-fashioned luck.

After landmark victories over Milan and Juventus, the Genoese side topped Serie A with only four games remaining. Lying in wait were Internazionale, and their German superstars, Jürgen Klinsmann and Lothar Matthäus.

Savouring the opportunity to supplant Sampdoria and propel themselves towards top spot, Inter filled the San Siro to the brim for a contest that seethed with tense drama. Inter attacked relentlessly, but chances were fluffed and a Klinsmann goal ruled offside. The game reached an excruciating impasse.

Tempers frayed, and a brawl broke out between Sampdoria striker **Roberto Mancini** and Inter defender **Giuseppe Bergomi**. Both sides were reduced to ten, though the departed left the pitch arm-in-arm, like star-crossed lovers reconciled after a petty tiff.

The second half provided no respite for embattled Sampdoria, but after a defensive lapse in Inter's ranks, the veteran Dossena snaffled a ridiculously undeserved opener. Inter regrouped, and were quickly granted a penalty. Incredibly, the redoubtable Lothar Matthäus fired straight at Gianluca Pagliuca, and Sampdoria grasped another breathless reprieve.

The siege continued, but when the irrepressible Gianluca Vialli rounded Zenga and whipped home a second, the title was Sampdoria's in all but name. Amid the exhausting excitement, Inter could have done nothing more.

On the league's final weekend, Sampdoria's players dyed their hair peroxide blond – a humorous symbol of the unity that had oiled their path to glory, and repelled the superstars of Serie A.

CHELSEA 4–4 LIVERPOOL (2009)

Champions League encounters between Chelsea and Liverpool became something of an annual event at the beginning of the twenty-first century, as much a result of English football's prominence in Europe as of pure coincidence. Though the conspiracy theorists divined a continuing (and, in the previous year at least, unsuccessful) UEFA plot to prevent an all-English final. Chelsea carried a 3–1 win at Anfield into the quarter-final second leg, leading most commentators to believe that they would progress easily into the semis. What followed was an extraordinary match which defied all such expectations and where the outcome was in doubt to the last.

Liverpool, jettisoning coach **Rafa Benítez**'s previous tactical caution and staging a barnstorming charge to the end of their season, were also buoyed by the heightened emotions which surrounded the twentieth anniversary of the Hillsborough tragedy. They scored two first half goals, one courtesy of a goalkeeping blunder by Petr Cech which saw him stranded out of position unable to stop a thirty-yard free kick by Aurelio. Xabi Alonso also coolly converted a spot kick awarded when he was fouled.

Then Chelsea, supposedly treated to a half-time tirade from coach **Guus Hiddink**, came out after the break and scored three times without reply to lead 6–3 on aggregate, and seemed to once again have put the tie beyond Liverpool's reach. Cech's earlier jitters seemed to infect José Reina at the other end, fumbling Didier Drogba's shot into his own net. Chelsea's Brazilian defender Alex scored with a stunning free kick from 25 yards, and Frank Lampard made it three with fifteen minutes to go. Until the 81st minute the tie seemed decided, until a long-range shot from Lucas deflected off Michael Essien giving the hapless Cech no chance and a Dirk Kuyt header that brought the score back to 6–5 over the two legs. Liverpool were now just one strike from the semis on the away-goal rule.

Yet the drama was not quite over: Lampard scored again in the 89th minute with a shot which hit both posts on the way in, then Chelsea's Michael Essien had to clear off the line courtesy of another Cech mistake. Rafa Benítez's verdict was that it was disappointing to be eliminated: "But to lose in this way … you have to be really proud with your head up."

The Rivalries

The fixtures not to miss …

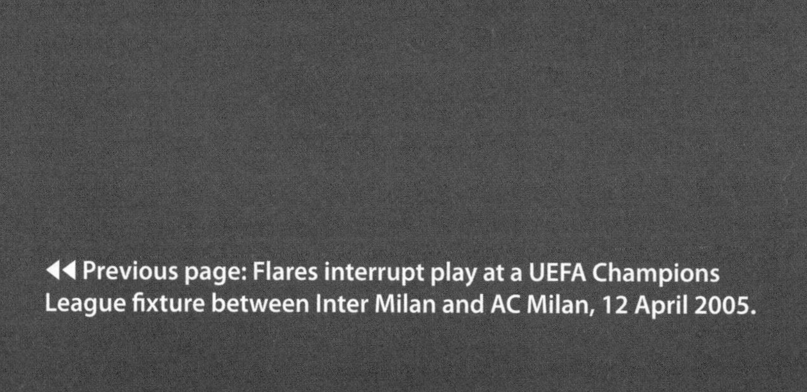

◀◀ Previous page: Flares interrupt play at a UEFA Champions League fixture between Inter Milan and AC Milan, 12 April 2005.

The Rivalries

"Nothing else matters."

Paolo di Canio on the Rome derby

AJAX AMSTERDAM V. FEYENOORD

Some wish their enemies dead. In Holland, the situation became so bad between fans of Ajax Amsterdam and Feyenoord of Rotterdam that such wishes came true.

In 1997, in a field by a motorway intersection between Amsterdam and Rotterdam, mobs from the two clubs clashed in a pre-arranged meet. Hundreds moved towards each other, armed with makeshift weapons: bats, knives and poles. The few police could do nothing to prevent what became infamous as the "Battle of Beverwijk".

Feyenoord outnumbered their rivals and as Ajax retreated, **Carlo Picornie**, a solidly built asthma sufferer, was stranded. Aged 35, he had been a prominent hooligan in the past, but came out of his hooligan "retirement" that day, fobbing his partner off with a story that he was going to get something to eat.

Picornie was beaten to death in a muddy field. The sole Ajax fan who went back to help him was stabbed twice in the lungs. The death stunned the Dutch public.

Consequently, the security operation when Holland's biggest two teams from its two biggest cities meet is the most sophisticated in European football. Feyenoord fans travel the 43 miles to the Amsterdam ArenA (capacity 51,000) on two double decker trains carrying 800 fans each. The journey should take an hour, but these trains deliberately travel slower with the heat turned on full and the windows closed to create a soporific atmosphere.

When they arrive, they are escorted from the platform to the stadium through a covered tunnel straight into the away end. Thousands of angry Ajax fans are held back by two lines of police in "robocop" gear, waving batons and shields. Behind them wait the serried ranks of police horses, two phalanxes of police vans, assorted security officials and officers with surveillance cameras to provide extra security. A clutch of plain clothes officers loiter nearby. Every few minutes

> **"While Amsterdam dreams, Rotterdam works."**
> Traditional Dutch saying

they identify a problem fan and cunningly close in, before dragging him into a van where they administer their own form of justice, which never makes it as far as a jury. Most of the fans cover their faces with scarves in an attempt to preserve their anonymity.

Ajax call Feyenoord "cockroaches", Feyenoord accuse Ajax of being arrogant and bloated by the success which has seen their team achieve far more than Feyenoord.

As with all great rivalries, it transcends football. Amsterdam is a tourist magnet while Rotterdam is a hard, predominantly working-class city, the second largest in Holland (metropolitan population 1.1 million) after Amsterdam (1.5 million). It boasts the largest port in Europe and only Shanghai is bigger. Politically, the cities vary, with Amsterdam liberal to socialist, whereas Rotterdam has become more right-wing.

Civic pride counts for more in Rotterdam and locals are fiercely proud of their home. Several Dutch sayings reflect this: "While Amsterdam dreams, Rotterdam works" or "Amsterdam to party, Den Haag [The Hague] to live, Rotterdam to work". These divisions are given full expression each time the two teams meet.

ATHLETIC BILBAO V. REAL SOCIEDAD

Until 1989, Real Sociedad – The Royal Society Football Club of San Sebastián, to give them their full title – had a similar policy to their Basque neighbours Athletic Bilbao of using locally born players nurtured through the youth system. Indeed, La Real's policy was even more exclusive since they only took players from the immediate province of Guipúzcoa while Athletic were prepared to twist their own rules by recruiting from French Basque country, the partly Basque neighbouring regions of Navarra, or La Rioja, famous for its wine output rather than being Basque. Sociedad's strategy had endured for decades and frequently prospered, bringing them the League twice in succession and a European Cup semi-final in the early 1980s.

It was this competition for Basque-born players with Athletic that forced Sociedad to loosen their recruitment policy. Athletic are the bigger club and were using their higher status and financial muscle to snare the best Basque quarry, poaching players from Sociedad, Alavés and Osasuna. Sociedad broke with tradition to sign an outsider, Basque nationalism dictating that he could not be a Spaniard but a moustachioed Scouser, **John Aldridge**, who'd never heard of the beautiful beach-flanked city of San Sebastián, let alone understood the intense local politics. Aldridge arrived to "Foreigner Go Home" graffiti. Some 40 goals in 75 games later, there wasn't a problem. Goals, it seems, are a global currency. Dalian Atkinson and Kevin Richardson followed him.

Brits brought football to Spain and Athletic were best known for their Anglophilia, demonstrated by the appointment of a series of English managers. The best was Frederick Pentland, a stereotypical English gent known as "the bowler

Barcelona v Real Madrid – El Clásico (1970)

Nowadays, there exists a lengthy inventory of items prohibited inside a football ground. Flares, penknives and glass bottles are all banned because of their capacity to inflict injury, but absent from that list is the potentially deadliest weapon of all, the Catalan cushion.

During the second leg of a 1970 Cup match between Barcelona and Real Madrid, a hail of soft pillows, more usually to be found easing buttocks aching from the hard seats, caused not only the abandonment of a match, but a full-blown riot.

After decades of repression under the tyrannical General Franco, Catalonia was hungry for change. As the regional flag and the Catalan language were banned, Barcelona's matches became an opportunity to celebrate local culture. No team roused the Camp Nou quite like Franco's favourites, Real Madrid. Both clubs were engaged in a running battle for prestige, but Madrid had dominated the 1950s and 60s, thanks to a raft of international superstars and help from suspect referees.

Barça lost 2–0 in the first leg of the 1970 tie, but sensing an uplifting comeback for weary Catalonia, a huge crowd gathered for the return. With Barcelona leading by a goal on the night, young referee Emilio Guruceta caused uproar. Stranded upfield as Madrid countered, Guruceta awarded a dubious penalty. The Camp Nou was not bashful in expressing its disgust; Madrid forward Velazquez had been fouled metres outside the area.

A great malevolent hiss seethed from the crowd, and cushions began floating towards the turf. Despite protests, the game restarted, but after cushions continued to rain down, Guruceta sprinted towards the changing rooms to escape the enveloping venom. The crowd loped onto the pitch in a great swelling of Catalan frustration. Fires were ignited and rebel songs erupted. The long pent-up resentment of injustice was pouring forth.

The game was awarded to Madrid, but a greater victory had been achieved. Catalonia was fighting back, using little more than a football club and its cushions.

hat". He had trained Racing Santander until Athletic snared him, a clever move as Pentland won two successive League titles for the club in the early 1930s. Another English manager, William Garbutt, also won the League with Athletic in 1936.

Howard Kendall managed for a time in the 1980s. He was unsuccessful but popular after eschewing a penthouse apartment offered by the club for a spartan one overlooking the training ground.

Until the 1990s, Real Sociedad and Athletic had co-existed without real problems. The fans shared the same Basque ideology, a healthy respect and suspicion of all things Madrid. The first time the two clubs met after the death of Franco in

1976, the two captains held the Basque flag together on the centre circle before the game to reassert their Basque identity. This was the first public display of the flag since the end of the dictatorship and was accompanied by the playing of an ETA anthem, "Basque Soldiers". In 1977, Athletic reached the UEFA Cup final, only losing on away goals to Juventus. Athletic fans were pleased when Sociedad won those two League titles in the early 1980s, pipping Real Madrid to the title in 1981 on the last day of the season with a goal twelve seconds from the end of time. The feeling was reciprocated when Athletic followed up with consecutive titles bagged by their famously aggressive team in 1983 and 1984 under young coach Javier Clemente. To the Basques who agreed with the policies of both their main clubs, this was justification of their historic sporting prowess.

Relationships soured in 1988 after Sociedad scored just 38 League goals in one season. Manager **John Toshack** left for Real Madrid and Athletic poached the source of those few Sociedad goals, striker Loren. The usual solution, that of recruitment from the *cantera*, offered no strikers of the required class. But this was nothing compared to what happened seven years later when Athletic bought Joseba Etxeberria, the young Spain international and Basque winger, from Sociedad for £3 million. Sociedad were outraged that their great young striking hope was joining their main rivals and felt that a gentlemen's agreement not to poach each other's junior players had been broken. The two clubs broke off formal relations for two years and they've never quite recovered since.

BELFAST: CLIFTONVILLE V. LINFIELD

It's not even the biggest game in Belfast, but given that Linfield have a reputation for being a predominantly Protestant club and Cliftonville a predominantly Catholic one (the only one in the top division since Belfast Celtic folded and Derry City started playing games south of the border) encounters between the pair have a history of being problematic. East Belfast's Glentoran (whose fans have taunted Linfield with chants of "Gerry Adams is your MP" because Linfield's Windsor Park is close to the Sinn Fein territory of West Belfast) may be a truer rival to Linfield when judged by success and support, but the Cliftonville–Linfield clashes have always had religious connotations and been viewed as a microcosm of sectarian strife in the province. And that was too big a chance for the security services to take.

"We were standing behind the goal and the UDA threw a hand grenade over the wall towards the Cliftonville supporters."
Stephen McKillop, Cliftonville FC

"During the Troubles, the police argument would have been that they were too tied up to police a Cliftonville v. Linfield match in what is a largely nationalist North Belfast", suggests the BBC's Ireland correspondent Mark Simpson.

Between 1970 and 1998, it was indeed not deemed safe for Linfield to make the journey to the wonderfully named Solitude, the home of Cliftonville.

Known by various epithets including "murder mile" and "the killing fields", more lives were lost in the area around Solitude during the Troubles than in any other part of Northern Ireland. This part of North Belfast is a patchwork of working-class communities living cheek by jowl, but divided by religion. It may not have the iconic status of West Belfast's Shankill or Falls Roads, but there are political murals, flags and painted kerbstones aplenty.

Every time Cliftonville played Linfield the game was staged at Windsor Park, Linfield's home. "The police are not as acceptable in Nationalist areas of Northern Ireland as they are in Unionist areas and Windsor Park is in a Unionist area", explains Simpson.

For 28 years, this arrangement held sway, despite the unhappiness of both sets of fans. Windsor Park, the venue for Northern Ireland internationals, was not only considered safer territory by the police, it was also adjacent to a motorway which aided pre- and post-match segregation. But this didn't guarantee that there were no incidents.

"We played at Windsor Park three days after an IRA bomb which killed two soldiers in November 1991", said Cliftonville's **Stephen McKillop**. "We were standing behind the goal and the UDA threw a hand grenade over the wall towards the Cliftonville supporters."

Cliftonville were known as "Sporting Sinn Fein" by some Linfield fans who barely differentiated between them and Gerry Adams. Football fans are about exaggerations, and the more Cliftonville fans were portrayed as Nationalists, the more Nationalist they became – bringing Irish flags and singing IRA songs. Linfield did likewise, choosing players according to their Unionist politics or Protestantism and emphasizing their Loyalism.

Thankfully, as politics in Northern Ireland have changed, so have relations between the two clubs. Games are now played at a redeveloped Solitude between the pair and players are chosen for their ability alone.

BLACKBURN ROVERS V. BURNLEY

England's oldest derby was first played in 1888 between the teams from the East Lancashire towns of Burnley (population 89,000) and Blackburn (115,000), eight miles away. Both clubs have a rich pedigree stretching back 130 years. Blackburn were formed in 1875, seven years before Burnley. When the clubs first met in a friendly, Blackburn won 10–0 and by the time the Football League was formed in 1888, they had won the FA Cup three times. When Burnley finally beat Blackburn for the first time, in the Lancashire Cup final of 1890, their victorious players were carried back through the town on a wagonette. They were proclaimed best team in Lancashire – which to the locals was a synonym for the best team in the world.

The enmity flourished. A game between the two clubs at the end of the nineteenth century had to be stopped because of crowd violence. The rivalry between the clubs defies a rational, geographical explanation, and has waxed and waned over the decades. Blackburn could just have easily crossed swords with Preston North End to the west or Bolton Wanderers to the south. For Burnley the choice was simple. With Yorkshire to the east and the Pennine hills to the north and south, they had to direct their invective squarely west towards Blackburn.

Both were founder members of the Football League and both have been champions of England, Burnley as recently as 1960 and Blackburn in 1995.

Before their recent resurgence, The Clarets slid down the divisions and, in 1987, almost out of the Football League. In 1991, someone hired an aeroplane trailing the message "U R Stayin down 4 ever, luv Rovers – ha, ha, ha", which flew over Turf Moor as Burnley struggled to overturn a 2–0 deficit against Torquay United in the second leg of the Fourth Division play-offs semi-final.

Blackburn fans call their Burnley counterparts "The Dingles" after the social misfits in the ITV soap *Emmerdale Farm*. They claim that they are from Yorkshire – while Burnley joke that Blackburn fans are gloryhunters who only started supporting their team when steel magnate **Jack Walker** pumped millions into the club and rebuilt their Ewood Park home.

They might be loathe to admit it, but the towns have got quite a lot in common. The textile mills which turned the wheels of the industrial revolution and made them prosperous have long departed, leading to a post-industrial decline that has had a corrosive effect on the social and economic fortunes of both towns. European money has been invested in the region as it tries to shed the cloth-cap, Hovis-bread-commercial image so often reinforced by visiting journalists ... but the 966-page *Rough Guide to England* doesn't find space for even the merest mention of either town. At least The Beatles were more forthcoming, namechecking Blackburn in "A Day in the Life", even it was only for having a reported 4,000 holes – whether these were in the roads, as John Lennon later explained, or in its inhabitants' arms, as Fab Four aficionados claim.

CARDIFF CITY V. SWANSEA CITY

Given their cities' battle for supremacy in South Wales, it's natural that the country's two biggest football clubs should also be great rivals. Perhaps more surprising is that in a 2008 study commissioned by the New Football Pools, the battle between the Bluebirds and the Swans was seen as bigger than Spurs v. Arsenal, the Sheffield derby, Aston Villa v. Birmingham and Newcastle v. Sunderland.

The survey result becomes all the more surprising if you consider that the teams' respective yo-yo histories up and down the leagues have ensured that they have avoided each other in league competition for decades at a time. When the clubs did clash, the rivalry was intensified and the South Wales derby has a history steeped in football hooliganism.

Whereas some derbies are defined by events on the pitch, in South Wales it's often what happens off it which makes headlines. A dart was thrown at a policeman's head during a Welsh Cup final in the early 1980s and in 1993, what became known as "The Battle of Ninian Park" saw pitch invasions, seats thrown and multiple arrests. The scenes were not unique and the game became the first in Britain to see away fans banned as police sought to prevent both cities becoming virtual war zones as they tried to keep rival firms of marauding young men apart.

Intending an element of surprise, Swansea's hooligans even travelled in several stretch limousines to one game in Cardiff, before eventually being rumbled by police. And such was the likelihood of trouble, both teams were frequently instructed to run immediately back to the sanctuary of the dressing rooms at the final whistle.

Despite not clashing since 1999, the hoolie book *Swansea Jacks* is full of cloak and dagger stories of the two sets of hooligans fighting their way through the decades – even when they're both abroad following Wales. Italian police were baffled in 2004 as they escorted hooligans from both clubs into the cells, after clashing with each other before a Wales game.

Even the derby-starved players have been fully aware of the simmering rivalry. Following their 2006 success in the Football League Trophy at Cardiff's Millennium Stadium, Swansea players **Lee Trundle** and **Alan Tate** carried a Wales flag daubed with "Fuck Off Cardiff". Fans' hero Trundle also wore a t-shirt depicting a Swansea supporter urinating on a Cardiff shirt.

The fortunes of both clubs have changed considerably in recent times, with new stadiums, much improved crowds and ambitions to reach the Premiership. Yet when they play, away fans have to travel on escorted coaches and the police operation to keep fans apart involves closed motorway junctions as the phalanx of away coaches, with 25 police vehicles and a helicopter in close formation, makes the 40-mile journey.

CHESTER CITY V. WREXHAM

No Chester or Wrexham fan pretends that the game is the biggest derby in football, but they believe their match is genuinely a unique encounter that's as much about class and national identity as football. Given that Wrexham have historically tended to play in a higher division than Chester, border skirmishes between the teams from middle-class Chester of England and working-class Wrexham of Wales are not played out with much regularity.

They play just ten miles apart; but Wrexham is the antithesis of well-heeled Chester. Many Wrexham lads are happy that it stays that way and are proud of their town's hard-bitten reputation.

> **"By scoring for Chester against our arch rivals, the goats, they have genius shining from every orifice."**
> Chester FC website

Chester never relied on traditional industries like Wrexham, rather a large white-collar workforce involved in financial services. Chester with its riverside setting, cathedral, Roman walls, the oldest racecourse in England and gothic town hall has long been a tourist mecca. The clock on the town hall only has three faces, with the Wales-facing side remaining blank because, according to local cards, "Chester won't give Wales the time of day". An archaic law states that any Cestrian (resident of Chester) may shoot a Welshman with a longbow if he loiters within the walls after sunset – although this law no longer offers legal protection against prosecution for murder.

Chester's population of ninety thousand is over the twice the size of Wrexham's, yet their support was around half, partly because Wrexham attract support from all over North Wales. Both teams have had major ups and downs over recent decades: Wrexham are currently playing non-league football and, following repeated financial problems during the 2009–10 season, which also affected many of their fixtures, Chester were served with a winding-up order by HM Revenue & Customs, put up for sale and later expelled from the League. Sadly the club was formally wound up in March 2010.

The 1970s are fondly remembered by Wrexham fans, with their side playing in the European Cup Winners' Cup (as Welsh Cup winners) four times and reaching the sixth round of the FA Cup twice. Anderlecht, Manchester United, AS Roma, Porto and Hadjuk Split have all played Cup Winners' Cup ties at the Racecourse Ground. Chester never reached such heights, but they were the club where **Ian Rush** made his name. A succession of turbulent owners left them playing at Macclesfield for a time, before they moved into a new ground which straddled the English–Welsh border.

When Wrexham and Chester met, you could expect to hear chants of "England" and "Wales" – plus flags from both countries. One Chester website had a section named: "They've scored against the Wrexham". "In a perfectly ordered society, streets would be named after them", it boasted. "When it comes down to heroes they're right up there with Spartacus, Hercules, Theseus and, yes, even Biggles. By scoring for Chester against our arch rivals, the goats, they have genius shining from every orifice." When they were not calling Wrexham "Wrectum" or "Sheepshaggers", Chester called them the "Goats". Wrexham used many profanities to describe Chester, one of the least offensive being "Jester Pity".

THE FAROES: HB V. B36

When the Faroe Islands' two biggest clubs HB and B36 meet in the Torshavn derby, the diminutive stands don't seethe with paranoia, hatred or religious strife. Love, as the song goes, is all around. What few chants are started have been carefully chosen so as not to offend too deeply. Small occasional displays of fervour by one or two of the more passionate, such as drum-banging, are tolerated – as long as they don't go too far. Fans have no choice but to get on because they can't escape to another city. There aren't any. HB and B36 are the two biggest teams in Torshavn – the world's smallest capital city, home to sixteen thousand weather-beaten souls.

HB – short for Havnar (Havnar is the local word for "Torshavn") Bóltfelag – are the older of the two teams, having been formed in 1904. It took until 1935 for B36 – Bóltfelag (Faroese for "football') to be formed by disenfranchized supporters in 1935. The working-class founders of B36 found that HB were snobbish and formed their own club – yet they are not called B35 because "6" is locally regarded as a more powerful number. And they think it sounds better in Faroese.

The teams share the five thousand-capacity council-owned Gundadalur stadium, but each club has its own stand which contains their own dressing rooms and fan facilities. With scrupulous Nordic fairness, both stands are identical and are situated on the same side of the pitch, seating around six hundred. Both ends are open, one of which features a grassy knoll with wooden boxes for fans to perch on. A stream gushes behind one goal and sheep idly graze nearby. Crowds can reach four thousand for a big derby game between the two.

When the national team started playing in 1990, games were played in Sweden as there were no suitable grass pitches in the Faroes. With little flat land to build on, in 1994 explosives (some fifty tonnes) were used to blow up some rocks behind the village of Toftir (population one thousand) so that a pitch could be laid that met FIFA regulations. The duly erected Toftir stadium held six times the village's population – and visiting teams hated it. After arriving at the Faroes' tiny airport, the likes of Spain and Scotland would take an hour-long drive around the islands' rugged contours, through scattered settlements of simple housing, before boarding a ferry for a 45-minute crossing. Although lashed by wind and waves, visitors couldn't have failed but be impressed by the stunning scenery of jagged green peaks tumbling into the ocean – and the passion for football. Even the smallest villages have their own artificial football pitches.

"If we get things to work, then I think we have a team that can compete at the very top."

B36 coach, Sigfrídur Clementsen

By 1997, pressure increased for Torshavn to have a grass pitch capable of holding international games and a stadium was built without any shelter. If any national stadium should have a roof then it's in the Faroes, which averages fifteen wet days per month.

With five thousand registered players – over ten percent of the population – the Faroese are big into football, although their team names need deciphering: GI, NSI, KI, IF, VB/S, EB/S. It's not a good idea to read the League table after a beer unless you support bottom club VB/S – and confuse them with top club EB/S.

MANCHESTER UNITED V. LIVERPOOL

In the 1980s, **Ron Atkinson**, then United's manager, described a visit to Anfield as like "going to Vietnam". He had just been tear-gassed, on the way to the dressing room. Though it is hard to top the away team being gassed, current rivalry between Manchester United and their close neighbours in Liverpool seems only to be growing stronger, in stark contrast to the cordial relations which existed between the two clubs as late as the 1960s.

Manchester United and Liverpool both hail from largely working-class, immigrant cities with huge Irish populations. Just 35 miles apart in England's northwest, both were economic powerhouses which enjoyed a friend–foe relationship by the nineteenth century. Liverpool revered itself as the greatest port in the world, gateway to North America for millions and a key trading post for the Empire. Manchester was "Cottonopolis", the first city of the industrial revolution and so the phrase "Manchester made and Liverpool trade" ensued. But once the worldwide trade depression of the 1870s took hold, relations between the two cities began to sour. Liverpool was blamed for charging excessively high rates for importing the raw cotton spun in Lancastrian mills. Manchester subsequently built the Ship Canal, connecting the city to the sea – cutting out Liverpool and becoming in the process Britain's third busiest port, despite being forty miles inland.

Northwest derby – Anfield, 20 August 1971. Manchester United's George Best (second right) and Alan Gowling (right) look nonplussed as a pre-match pitch invasion by teenage fans is swiftly quelled with a couple of well-placed police headlocks.

That was then. With the end of British colonial rule and the introduction of container shipping, Liverpool's port became less viable. The withering disintegration of the UK textile industries hit Manchester hard and both cities suffered generations of economic decline and depopulation. Growing working-class poverty and social exclusion led to violent riots in Manchester's Moss Side and Liverpool's Toxteth districts in 1981. Yet, throughout these times of socio-economic misfortune, when it came to football and music, both cities excelled – making them special to millions around the globe, but also reinforcing and extending their intercity rivalry.

On the pitch, enmities were not clear cut. Manchester City were the bigger Mancunian club until World War II, while Everton were often the pre-eminent Merseyside force. If anything, the rivalry between United and Liverpool was one of respect until the 1960s. Indeed, leading players like **Pat Crerand**, used to watch Liverpool when United didn't have a game.

United were top dogs in the 1960s – League champions twice and the first English team to win the European Cup in a decade that saw the clubs have transfer dealings for the last time. Liverpool were far superior to United in the 1970s and 1980s, winning four European Cups and numerous League titles as United went 26 title-free years, but United were usually the better-supported club and matched Liverpool in head-to-head encounters. By the 1990s, with United and Liverpool established as the two biggest clubs in England, the enmity grew. Unlike Liverpool, the Sky-led football boom allowed United to capitalize on their success and the Mancunians accelerated into a different financial league by regularly expanding Old Trafford while Liverpool were hampered by Anfield's limited capacity. Each team boasts eighteen league titles a piece.

MILANO: AC MILAN V. INTERNAZIONALE

The world's capital of fashion and opera, Milan was never going to stage just any old footballing rivalry. The Milan clubs are of similar stature, with similar average crowds of fifty thousand and spells in their history when they have dominated both domestic and European football, so it is seen as a rivalry between equals, unlike other derbies where one team predominates.

Milan Cricket and Football club were formed on 16 December 1899 with profound English roots. Herbert Kilpin, the 29-year-old son of a Nottingham butcher, was largely responsible (along with one Alfred Edward), becoming their first captain. Their name was even anglicized by the dropping of the final letter "o" from Milano. Their original pitch was close to what is now Milano Centrale station.

Eight years later, a splinter group led by the artist **Giorgio Muggiani** formed a new club – Internazionale Milano – because they were unhappy about the dominant presence of Italian players. They were dismissed as splitters and upper-class intellectuals, but Inter won their first League title in 1910.

> **"We would have won this game even with seven men. Maybe with six we would have struggled, but we would have won with seven."**
> Inter manager José Mourinho after 2–0 victory over Milan, January 2010

The two teams met for the first time in Switzerland (for reasons unclear) with AC Milan seen as the team of the working class and Milanese dialect gave nicknames of *Casciavit* for Milan and *Bauscia* for Inter – which translated as "spanners" and "braggers". These original socio-economic differentiations are now well outdated, and any notion of Milan's political persuasions being to the left ended when the centre-right **Silvio Berlusconi** became club president in 1986 and changed the fortunes of the club. Both clubs also have an even spread of support geographically with the city, though Inter have more support across Italy.

Inaugurated in 1925, the San Siro was originally the home and property of AC Milan. But in 1935 the stadium was sold on to the city authorities who expanded the capacity and Internazionale moved into the stadium as tenants during the war years to accommodate their huge support. The deal was made permanent in 1947 – and the two teams have been sharing ever since.

The seven thousand away fans in the eighty thousand crowd make for an atmosphere amongst the best in the world and there is fervour aplenty on display, but fighting is rare as a result of an understanding between the rival ultra groups which was agreed after a notorious clash in 1983.

The lack of animosity between the supporters also extends to the clubs, with players switching between them regularly. And when Milan were relegated to Serie B in 1982 with their finances in a parlous state, Inter loaned them three players which helped them bounce straight back to the top flight. **Giuseppe Meazza** – donor of the official name of the San Siro since 1980 – was a footballing legend who played for both clubs during a 20-year career (1927–47) in which he scored 283 goals in 408 matches.

Yet there are supposed differences between the teams' traditional styles of football. Milan's classic game is founded on a patient passing approach, dubbed "square-ball" football by detractors. Inter's game is traditionally built around one outstanding world beater – **Sandro Mazzola** in the 1960s, **Ronaldo** in the late 1990s, **Christian Vieri** and **Zlatan Ibrahimović** in more recent times.

PRESTON NORTH END V. BLACKPOOL

"The rivalry started with arguments over whether Stanley Matthews was better than Tom Finney in the fifties", says **Jimmy Armfield**, the Radio 5 pundit who played a record 568 times for Blackpool between 1952–71 and was capped 43 times by England. Given that Preston North End and Blackpool don't always play in the same division only seems to add to the intensity.

Former Preston manager **Gary Peters** took it so seriously that he publicly refused to utter the name Blackpool, always referring to the Seasiders as "that lot with the tower". It almost earned him a kicking when he was cornered on the car park outside Bloomfield Road after one game, but he faced his assailants and managed to get away unharmed.

Both these warring Northern clubs have proud histories. Preston North End were one of the founder members of the Football League in 1888 and were England's first League champions. Playing through the entire 1888–89 season without losing a game, their "Invincibles" became the first team to win the Double. Only Arsenal, in 2003–04, have managed to spend a season unbeaten in the top flight since.

Blackpool, relative newcomers, joined the Football League in 1896. FA Cup finalists in 1948 and 1951, they went one better and won the competition in the legendary "Matthews Final" of 1953, when the Seasiders came from 3–1 down to beat Bolton 4–3. During the post-war period, Blackpool finished runners-up to Manchester United's Busby Babes in the race for the 1956 title.

In the late 1940s and 50s, Preston–Blackpool derbies were in their heyday, with the pair meeting eighteen times in the First Division. These were flamboyant, free-scoring encounters; in one season they shared fourteen goals between the two matches. It hurts even more that Preston's heaviest defeat, 7–0 in 1948, was inflicted by Blackpool, five goals coming from **Jimmy McIntosh**. **Tom Finney** was rated as one of the world's top players, while Blackpool supplied England with several internationals – four of them, including the great **Stan Mortensen**, for the infamous 1953 Wembley defeat to Hungary.

In the subsequent slide of both clubs down the divisions, solace has been sought through derby glory. Preston owed their 1970 relegation to the Third Division to a 3–0 humiliation by Blackpool. The Tangerines had the added satisfaction of gaining promotion to the top flight by their victory.

Preston and Blackpool also have claims to fame that extend beyond the distinguished histories of their resident football clubs. Britain's first motorway, opened in 1958, was Preston's M6 bypass. The first Kentucky Fried Chicken outlet was also in Preston, as was the last major battle on English soil – the Battle of Preston in 1715.

Blackpool attracts more visitors each year than Greece and has more hotel beds than Portugal. It consumes more chips per capita than anywhere on Earth and boasts Europe's second most popular tourist attraction, the Pleasure Beach … only topped by the Vatican. But while Blackpool is struggling to shake off its tag of decayed Northern seaside town, Preston is on the up, much to Blackpool's envy and seems to receive the much better press, in all aspects of life. "If someone farts at Deepdale", remarked one Blackpool fan, "Radio Lancashire have a special programme about it." Author Bill Bryson lambasted Blackpool in his satiric *Notes from a Small Island*, as "ugly, dirty and a long way from anywhere, its sea is an open toilet, and its attractions nearly all cheap, provincial and dire."

Preston, meanwhile, boasts England's sixth biggest university with thirty-three thousand students, better transport links and a confidence brought about by its new city status. Plans for Preston to build an "iconic" city-centre tower were objected to by neighbouring Blackpool council for fear the development could damage the resort's own regeneration hopes. There is some good news for Blackpool – Preston is about to lose the National Football Museum, situated since its foundation at Deepdale, to Manchester.

RANGERS V. CELTIC

On the face of it, the Old Firm game barely seems to deserve its reputation as the ultimate derby. It fails to attract the biggest derby crowds, nor is it between two of the world's biggest clubs. The atmosphere, too, is surpassed by the biggest derbies in Spain and Italy, hosted in far more splendid stadiums than Ibrox or Celtic Park.

The answer to this conundrum lies in a combination of factors, not least religion. Old Firm matches have taken place since 1888. Celtic became champions of the Irish Catholic immigrants who flocked to the city while Rangers stood as the standard-bearers for the native Scottish Protestants who feared the impact of this influx. The complex clash of cultures was acted out in the riots and other trouble which marked many of these games, reflecting contemporary social and political frustrations during high periods of unemployment and deprivation.

"Anything that you ever thought about yourself will be tested in this fixture. Your bottle, your courage, your self-control."
Mark McGhee, whose Celtic career included eighteen Old Firm matches.

The religious affiliations attached to Glasgow Rangers and Glasgow Celtic became supercharged with tension as the politics of Ulster descended into troubled times from the late 1960s on. Rangers fans wave Ulster flags, in support of Protestantism and British Unionism. The tricolour of the Irish Republic flies wherever Celtic are supported, because of Celtic's historic association with the people of Ireland and Scots of Irish extraction, who are both predominantly Catholic.

"Unlike many other derbies, Old Firm matches normally have something at stake, usually a league title", says **Mark McGhee**, who played in eighteen Old Firm matches.

> In other British cities rival teams have their origins in different social and in some cases cultural backgrounds. None enjoy the added spice of religious difference as the main reason for supporting a particular team. Around the world, similar such conflicts of religious ideology have resulted in far worse things than two sets of football supporters who hate each others' guts.

The days have gone when Rangers would not sign a Catholic player and vice versa. Celtic legend Kenny Dalglish grew up in a tower block opposite Ibrox, a

Protestant Rangers fan who waited and waited for his childhood heroes to sign him. They never did. But Jock Stein, who was happy to sign players of either religion at a time when Rangers restricted themselves to Protestants, took him to Celtic.

Striker Maurice Johnston wasn't the first Catholic to sign for Rangers, although his signing in July 1989 caused huge controversy on both sides. Not only was he a Roman Catholic who had been a fan then a hero at Celtic before playing for Nantes in France, he had agreed to rejoin Celtic when Rangers boss **Graeme Souness** stepped in. Many of Rangers' heroes are Catholic, though mostly born outside Scotland. Even today, when religion no longer exerts a powerful grip, perceived religious slights generate enormous amounts of bile. **Paul Gascoigne**'s supposed mimicry of a Loyalist flute player in front of Celtic supporters made international headlines in 1998. In 2006, Scottish football authorities considered punishing Celtic's Polish goalkeeper Artur Borac for crossing himself before kick-off on similar grounds of incitement.

"Playing in an Old Firm match is one thing, playing well in one is something else altogether", says Mark McGhee. "For the players, particularly the indigenous ones, pressure builds as the match approaches. Anything that you ever thought about yourself will be tested in this fixture. Your bottle, your courage, your self-control."

ROMA V. LAZIO

"Apart from the Old Firm, nothing compares with the derby of the Big Dome [St Peter's in the Vatican]", says former Lazio ultra and player **Paulo Di Canio**. Having encountered five different derby configurations in the course of his career, from Milan to London, he should know. "The build up is huge, nothing else matters," adds Di Canio. "Roma and Lazio fans care more about winning the derby than where they finish in the league." It forms the focus for the most intense rivalry in Italian football.

Only five *scudetti* have ever been won by teams from the Italian capital. Roma and Lazio rarely find themselves chasing a title. Unlike the Milanese teams, points rarely matter, while honour is everything.

And the Milanese derby is diluted by the existence of Juventus in nearby Turin – indeed the Internazionale–Juventus clash is known as "the derby of Italy" because both clubs boast nationwide fan bases. The Rome derby is intensely, unashamedly parochial.

"Roma and Lazio focus on each other", observes local journalist **Aurelio Capaldi**.

> Football is a serious issue in the eternal city and it affects Roman life. With good weather, Romans live outdoors far more than people in Milan or Turin. They talk football in the squares, parks and bars. Roma and Lazio fans always tease each other about the derby. The Romans' personality is suited to football – ironic and

A flare explodes between Roma's Michael Konsel (right) and Aldair during a derby match at the Olympic stadium, 11 April 1999 – Roma won 3–1.

> humorous. The Milanese character is far more reserved and the population of the north is diluted by many southerners who moved for work. In Rome, you are Roman. And you're either Lazio or Roma.

Taking their name from the region around Rome, Società Sportiva Lazio was founded in 1900 by an Italian army officer, Luigi Bigarelli. They adopted Greek colours and played in wealthy northern suburbs like Parioli, close to their Rondinella home between 1914 and 1931. Fascist leader **Benito Mussolini** was a fan and took his kids to games. Lazio moved to the Fascist Party Stadium (the PNF) in 1931. The stadium staged the 1934 World Cup final but by this time, Lazio had a rival.

Associazione Sportiva (AS) Roma were formed in 1927 from a merger of four small clubs driven by local patriot and Fascist politician Italo Foschi. Lazio resisted the pressure to join the merger to form a super-Roma fit to challenge the northern giants from Milan and Turin. Mussolini wanted to promote Rome as the capital of a new rationalized Italy partly through football.

Roma played their games in the timber-built Campo Testaccio to the south of the city, a working-class district which is still an area of high Roma support. It was a glorious venue full of character and the *giallorossi* (red-yellows) lost just 26 games there in 11 years up to 1940 as Roma overshadowed their rivals and provided two of Italy's 1934 World Cup winners.

Il Duce took Italy into World War II and Roma reluctantly left their much loved but too cramped ground to share the bigger Fascist stadium with the *biancocelesti* (light-blues). The ground-share has never been popular. Older Roma fans declare they have been homeless from that day. In 1953, both clubs finally left the PNF stadium for the new Olimpico across the Tiber, built for the 1960 Olympics.

Derby games are still played there to this day, with the eighty thousand crowd arguably the loudest of any derby game in Europe.

SOUTHAMPTON V. PORTSMOUTH

Southampton and Portsmouth, two coastal ports just seventeen miles apart along the M27, have a centuries-old rivalry based on geography, and social and economic grounds. Oh, and football. The "skates" are Pompey, the "scummers" Southampton and the names are redolent of a rich maritime history. "Skates" comes from disreputable old slang for a sailor, while "scummers" has its roots in a dock strike across the two cities by employees of the same firm. Legend has it that the "Southampton Company Union men" were the first to buckle and go back to work.

Portsmouth is unique in being an island club and many would say having an island mentality. The home of the Royal Navy, they have a solid working-class support. Across the Solent, Southampton is no upper-class yachting enclave, but it always welcomed great liners like the *Titanic* and was more cosmopolitan.

The football rivalry became more pronounced when Southampton were relegated from the top flight in 1974 – but while Portsmouth achieved two League titles between 1949 and 1950, the Saints had the upper hand for the best part of forty years until the 2000s. Southampton won the FA Cup as a Second Division club, beating Manchester United in the 1976 final and big names such as **Kevin Keegan**, **Lawrie McMenemy** and **Matt Le Tissier** became associated with the club.

> **"There is no fiercer, more passionate, more hostile derby in British football."**
> Lawrie McMenemy, Southampton manager, 1973–85

Portsmouth, on the other hand, floundered and ended up in the Fourth Division at one point, though the pair did meet in an 1984 FA Cup tie at Fratton Park – eight years after a goal from Southampton legend Mick Channon had condemned Pompey to Division Three and sparked running battles around the ground. Southampton's players were spat at and bananas were thrown at their black players like Danny Wallace in a hate-filled atmosphere. One Southampton player, Steve Williams, was threatened in the players' lounge. That was after Southampton had won the game in stoppage time. The needle had been aggravated by a head wound sustained by Saints defender Mark Dennis after a coin was thrown from the terraces. The *Portsmouth News* described the game as the "Battle of Fratton", with 59 arrests and damage done to local properties.

When Portsmouth were promoted to Division One for a season in 1987–88, 116 fans were arrested during a derby game at the Dell – with all but three of them Portsmouth fans, including many from the club's infamous "6.57" hooligan firm.

And when Portsmouth reached the big time in 2003, all police leave in Hampshire would be cancelled for clashes between the clubs. True to form, for Britain's least-played derby, Southampton were relegated in 2005 so the clubs were destined not to meet again. Worse followed with several up-and-down years in the Championship capped with a ten-point deduction for insolvency followed by relegation to League One. But the future may hold the promise of further league clashes between these rivals with yo-yoing fortunes: in an ironic repetition of history, in March 2010 Portsmouth went into administration, were docked nine points and were subsequently relegated.

SUNDERLAND V. NEWCASTLE UNITED

Lifelong Newcastle fan Lee Clark was photographed wearing a "SMB" (Sad Mackem Bastard) t-shirt at Wembley before Newcastle's 1999 FA Cup final against Manchester United. Clark, who just happened to be captain of Sunderland at the time, was immediately transfer listed. The Tyne–Wear (or Wear–Tyne if you are from Sunderland) derby is largely greeted by indifference outside the Northeast. Yet to the populace of both cities, just twelve miles apart, the derby matters – and is cherished. Mutual insults abound, with Sunderland fans called "dirty Mackems" or "The Great Unwashed", Newcastle fans simply as "scum" or "skunks" – a reference to Newcastle's black-and-white stripes.

The enmity began way back with shipyards and coal, two of the key industries which gave Sunderland and Newcastle their prosperity. In the1600s **King Charles I** bestowed the East of England Coal Trade Rights on Newcastle, rendering the Wearside coal merchants redundant. They even went to war about it, Newcastle lining up behind King Charles I in the English Civil War and Sunderland lining up with the anti-monarchist Scots at the battle of Boldon Hill. Newcastle lost that one, and has never forgotten its occupation by the Scots army.

In the nineteenth century both became famous for their shipyards. Swan Hunter on the Tyne became a symbol of Newcastle. By 1840, Sunderland contained some 65 shipyards and by the boom years of the early 1900s, those yards employed over 12,000 men, a third of the town's (Sunderland only became a city in 1992) adult population. Stories were rife of Wearsiders not being employed in Tyneside yards and vice versa. Sunderland's last shipyard closed in 1988 and the Swan Hunter cranes have been sold and re-assembled in India.

When Sunderland were founded in 1879, they were giants from the start, their "Team of all talents" English champions four times between 1892 and 1902. The first Tyne–Wear derby took place in 1883, the first competitive fixture an FA Cup tie in 1888, with Newcastle winning the inaugural league meeting at Roker Park on

Christmas Eve 1898. A 1901 Good Friday meeting at St. James' Park was abandoned as up to seventy thousand fans made their way into a ground which held less than half that number. The subsequent cancellation prompted rioting.

Sunderland's two other titles followed in 1913 and 1936. Newcastle have won two fewer titles, and three of those four were between 1905 and 1909 – when the pair dominated. The other was in 1927.

"It's the most intense rivalry in English football", says one Sunderland fan. "Anything you can think of for a rivalry, it's there. And such is the feeling; it's not unusual for someone from Sunderland to have never visited Newcastle in their life. Translate this rivalry away from football into contention on the pitch and it's pretty tasty."

TEL AVIV: MACCABI V. HAPOEL

Tel Aviv may not strike you as the obvious destination for one of football's most vicious rivalries, but what Israeli teams lack in quality, their fans make up for in passion. No club has brought a greater away following to Old Trafford in the Champions League than the 4,800 febrile fanatics who followed **Maccabi Haifa** there in 2002. Hapoel Tel Aviv, meanwhile, took ten thousand to the San Siro for a UEFA Cup game in 2002.

Mention Israel and the world thinks of the Jewish–Palestinian divide. People are conditioned by BBC and CNN images of bloodshed and bombs. Yet the everyday talk in café bars or on the beach isn't of politics, but of football and basketball.

Domestic Israeli life contains great fissures which are represented graphically in every area of sport. Football in particular becomes a microcosm of Israeli life at large, where rivalries burn every bit as deeply as they do in Milan, Manchester or Madrid. And nowhere is the rivalry deeper than in the biggest city, blessed as it is with a sunkissed Mediterranean beach front closer in appearance to Miami's South Beach – all conspicuous high-rise chain hotels and beautiful people.

Hapoel were founded in 1923 and have always associated themselves with socialist ideology and the Histadrut, Israel's largest trade union association. They've won the League thirteen times and reached the quarter-finals of the UEFA Cup in 2001–02, knocking Chelsea out en route. Their main slogan: "The whole wide world hates Hapoel and only I love her!" isn't really true in Israel, let alone the rest of the planet. Neighbours Maccabi are loathed and loved in greater measure still.

Maccabi Tel Aviv are the older club, dating back to 1906. They've won a record number of League Championships and played in the Champions League in 2004–05. Israel's best-supported team, Maccabi's fans are proud of their right-wing reputation and the fact that they attract strong support from Tel Aviv's wealthy northern suburbs.

Average crowds of twelve thousand make Maccabi the best-supported team in Israel, with Hapoel fourth with crowds of eight thousand. Despite engrained enmity, the pair share the 17,500 capacity Bloomfield Stadium, which is filled to capacity when they meet, including up to 3,000 away fans.

The vitriol at these games is staggering, with loathsome songs about concentration camps, suicide bombers and Hamas. A hardened MAGAV unit, usually responsible for the border patrols with Palestinian territories is brought in to keep the peace.

Hapoel fans may sing: “We wish you another Holocaust” or “We hope you burn in Treblinka” (the World War II death camp). The Maccabi fans retort with chants such as “Communists” or “Get out of this country, you are not Jewish”. Or “Gate 5 [the main Hapoel section] is like a Gaza refugee camp”. “You don’t have any fans”, “Hapoel are Hezbollah” (an extremist terrorist group whose main political objective is the destruction of the state of Israel).

This is not a fixture for the faint of heart.

The Culture

Movies, music and media: football at large

◀◀ Previous page: Footballer Kevin Keegan with his "hit" record "Head over Heels in Love", "on the head", May 1979.

The Culture

"If you like a drink go to the players' bar/Oh no, let me think, we haven't built it so far"

Wealdstone FC from "We are the Stones"

FOOTBALL GOES TO HOLLYWOOD

You're 4–1 down at half-time. You're also down to ten men as your star player has been carried off with a broken rib; the referee is bent in the opposition's favour; and your goalkeeper is a big-mouthed tosspot with two left feet and an understanding of the beautiful game that could be written on the back of a postage stamp with a thick black felt tip pen.

In a situation like this most people would pray for the ground to open up and swallow them. Incredibly, this is exactly what happens. A huge hole appears in the changing room bath, giving the players a heaven-sent opportunity to escape from the inevitable humiliation of the second half. Do they take it? Do they hell.

For reasons unfathomable to those watching, the players remain convinced they can win the game, and duly ignore the gaping hole. The only one who takes persuading (understandably in view of his first-half performance) is the keeper. But instead of hanging him upside down from a clothes hook and administering Deep Heat to his genitals, his team-mates beg him to continue. He justifies their touching faith with a blinding second-half display, saving a penalty in the last minute to secure a remarkable 4–4 draw.

John Huston made some great films, but *Escape to Victory* (the climax of which is outlined above) is not one of them. Its biggest flaw can be summed up in two words: Sylvester Stallone. Playing a character inspired by Steve McQueen's part in *The Great Escape* – minus the charm – Stallone is the solitary American internee in a German POW camp otherwise occupied by stereotyped British officers, instantly recognizable by the stiffness of their upper lips.

Unlike the Brits, Stallone – or Hatch as he is called in the film – is granted certain privileges by the Nazis. These include a personal supply of biological washing powder to keep his singlets and grandpa T-shirts sparkling white, and access to huge quantities of high-protein rations and a body-building gymnasium, to make sure he's fit enough to knock out Dolph Lundgren in his next feature film.

Unlike Hatch, John Colby (Michael Caine) has a scruffy uniform and a middle-aged paunch. Despite his appearance, he is in fact a former West Ham United and

"What kind of game is this anyway? For old ladies and fairies?"
Sylvester Stallone struggles with the concept of *Escape to Victory*

England footballer, whose working-class origins are revealed in his London accent and his contempt for his fellow British officers. Colby accepts a challenge posed by Max von Sydow (playing the honourable German: the sort of role James Mason used to specialize in) to organise a football team from the prisoners to play a local German outfit.

Colby knows that British officers play rugger not soccer, so he insists on being able to choose his team from the enlisted men. This gives him access to several star players, all of whom seem to be called Terry, but are really **Bobby Moore**, **John Wark**, **Kevin Beattie** and **Mike Summerbee** in disguise. When the Germans move the goalposts by deciding to field a full international side, Colby strengthens his squad by demanding players from other Allied nations. A Trinidadian prisoner bearing an uncanny resemblance to **Pelé**, and a skinny fellow who looks just like **Ossie Ardiles**, join the team. And from the labour camps of eastern Europe come **Kazimierz Deyna** and some skeletal actors with non-speaking parts.

Displaying a modicum of judgement, Colby decides there is no place in his all-star eleven for Hatch. But by listening to a radio made from paper clips and bits of string, the senior British officers realize the game – now due to be played in the centre of Paris – is really a fiendish Nazi propaganda exercise, the damage of which can only be averted by arranging a daring escape for the whole team. So Hatch has to slip out of the prison camp, make his way to Paris, contact the Resistance, have a brief fling with a gorgeous, pouting French minx, and then allow himself to be recaptured so that he can relay the escape plan to the rest of the team – a mission he accomplishes with such ease it's a wonder the other prisoners haven't bothered to try it.

But Hatch gets locked up in solitary confinement on return to the camp, and Colby can only get him released in time to learn of the escape plans by insisting the brooding, muscle-bound hero is his team's goalkeeper, now that his first-choice player has broken his arm. The Nazis find this sufficiently unlikely to insist on seeing the shattered limb, so Kevin O'Calloghan displays true British pluck by volunteering to have his arm subjected to heavy assault.

Before the game gets underway it's revealed that the referee has orders to ensure the Nazis win. Once the whistle has blown it also becomes clear that the ref is unaware of any FIFA directives outlawing the cynical tackle from behind, even when Dutch veteran **Co Prins** is scythed down like a tree uprooted by a Panzer tank. Typically, this is ignored by the German match commentator (**Anton Diffring** performing a second-rate impression of David Coleman in jackboots) who raves as the ruthless Nazis rack up the goals.

"He might be a great action man, but when it comes to football he hasn't got a bloody clue."
Kevin Beattie on Sylvester Stallone

Cult German Football Movies

***Fußball wie noch nie* (Football As Never Before)**
In the 1960s, there emerged in Germany a group of experimental filmmakers who were obsessed with testing the limits of the medium rather than telling a story. One of them was Hellmuth Costard, who made a 1969 film called *The Oppression of Women Is Mainly Discernible through the Behaviour of Women Themselves*, in which a woman – played by a man – does housework (and nothing else). A year later, Costard went one step further and filmed the 12 September match between Manchester United and Coventry City. All six cameras were on only one player – George Best. The resulting film runs for 105 minutes and has virtually no dialogue. Sometimes you can catch a glimpse of other players or even the ball, but for the most part you stare at Best standing on the pitch, and you listen to the crowd reacting to something you don't see.

***Das grosse Spiel* (The Big Game)**
Das grosse Spiel was made in July and August 1941 and released a year later, yet it is not a Nazi propaganda film. In fact it's a rather old-fashioned love story. The new player for the fictitious club Gloria 03 falls for an official's daughter but has to prove his worth before winning her heart. He does that by leading his team to the championship final and scoring the sudden-death winner. What sounds mundane is made remarkable by Sepp Herberger's contribution. The national manager (who would win the 1954 World Cup) brought many internationals to the set to make the match sequences more credible – and to get them away from the battlefront. He also came up with the idea of mounting movable cameras behind the goals, something which became commonplace only in the 1990s.

With the help of a distinctly dubious penalty, clinically dispatched by the unsmiling German captain, the Allies approach half-time four goals behind and without Pelé, who has been forced to retire to the dugout after his efforts to play the beautiful game have been thwarted by defensive techniques learned from unarmed combat training manuals. But then the impossible happens: an unmarked Bobby Moore makes a late run into the German six-yard box to tap in a long cross from **Russell Osman** at the far post. Terry has scored and the Allies have discovered total football.

After refusing the chance to escape, Colby and the boys come out for the second half to give the complacent Master Race a good stuffing. Bewildered by the Allies' free-ranging movements and revolutionary tactics, the Third Reich's marking goes to pot. Ardiles is given the freedom of the park and, before you know it, the Allies have pulled two back and are looking for an equaliser. This is Pelé's cue, and he returns to the pitch, ignoring the pain of his broken rib. After his dazzling footwork leaves the whole German team falling dizzily into crumpled heaps, he crops up again to power an overhead kick into the gaping mouth of the Nazi net. In fact he does it several times, from different angles, twice in slow motion, and each time it goes in.

Ze Parisian crowd zey go wild, and just to prove again that he really is the decent, honourable sort of German who will go on to become a leading light in the post-war world, Max von Sydow leaps to his feet in spontaneous applause.

They thought it was all over. But it wasn't. An innocuous challenge by Ardiles in his own penalty area gives a German striker the chance to perform a manoeuvre later perfected by **Jürgen Klinsmann**. The referee has no hesitation in pointing to the spot. Can Hatch make the catch to save the match?

Natch. The penalty is feebly struck, and at just the height goalkeepers like, even this one. Before the ref can order it to be retaken and caution Hatch for wearing a jersey unbuttoned to the navel, the crowd follows the time-honoured Millwall practice of invading the pitch, encouraged by the Wehrmacht's unaccountable failure to provide any of their guards with ammunition for their guns. The barricades are swept aside and the players, disguised in suspiciously 1970s-looking clothing, are carried shoulder-high through the exits.

The film ends with Max von Sydow smiling enigmatically, doubtless dreaming of a European Super League, leaving unanswered the question of whether Michael Caine was recaptured on the outskirts of Paris wearing a hooded Adidas tracksuit top and platform shoes. Football, as they say, is a funny old game, but it's rarely funnier than when the filmmakers get hold of it.

In fact, *Escape to Victory* is one of the better football films. The plot is no more ludicrous than, say, *Where Eagles Dare*, and there's even a shred (only a shred, mind you) of historical evidence for a propaganda-inspired football match between the Axis and Allies during World War II. The use of professional players also lends some semblance of authenticity to the training and match scenes. But the football itself rarely rises above the Stallone standard – clearly following the Method school of acting, Stallone trained so hard he broke a finger and damaged both knees; afterwards, he said that keeping goal made him "a walking blood clot" – and the film fails to escape the conventions of football coverage. It even provides a commentator talking in clichés to describe what we can already see.

The plot of *Escape to Victory* is not a million miles removed from two earlier east European films. *Két Félidö a Pokolban* (also known as *Two Half Times in Hell*, *Eleven Men*, and *Last Goal*) is a Hungarian film made in 1961. This time it's Hungarian prisoners who play against the Nazis and they make their mass escape before the match, only to be recaptured. The Nazis sentence them all to death but insist on the match going ahead first. Like Michael Caine's team, they start badly, but get on top in the second half. Unlike *Escape to Victory*, however, the guards in this film do have live ammunition, and when the other Hungarian prisoners threaten a pitch invasion, they start shooting. The entire Hungarian team is mown down and the spectators disperse, leaving a solitary football on the pitch.

A similarly downbeat ending is preferred in the 1964 Russian film, *Tretiy Taym* (aka *The Last Game*). This time the action is set in Kiev and the Russian prisoners of war don't even get the chance to escape. They are given a simple ultimatum: lose or die. As you might expect, the Russians make a tardy start, but end up overwhelming the dark forces of the jackbooted oppression, only to be hauled in front of a firing squad when the final whistle blows. According to one source, the Russian actor **Gennardi Yukhtin**, who played the heroic Soviet keeper, was so impressive he was later invited to play professional football. It's hard to imagine Stallone having been granted a similar opportunity.

Neither *Two Halves in Hell* nor *The Last Game* are readily available on DVD, but if you're very unlucky, you just might come across *Hotshot*, a 1987 American film that is unmitigated crap. Rich kid wants to play professional football but God-fearing Republican-voting parents disapprove. Rich kid incurs wrath of local coach, so heads for Brazil to receive homespun wisdom and intensive coaching from retired, reclusive South American star (guess who?) and returns to Big Apple to score winning goal in crucial match, etc etc. *Variety* described it as "amateurishly made and acted", and damned the football scenes as "dull and uninvolving". Pelé is spared the hatchet – "Though he is not a professional actor and doesn't seem to speak much English, Pelé is a delight to watch for his smile and handling [sic] of a soccer ball" – but another review said simply that "there's not a single honest moment in the film".

It's doubtful, though, whether *Hotshot* is the worst football film of all time. A much stronger contender is *Yesterday's Hero*, scripted by Jackie Collins. **Ian McShane** (whose father once played for Manchester United) stars as the heavy-drinking wreck of a great player (can't imagine who inspired that), given one last chance by an ambitious Third Division club, managed by **Adam Faith** and owned by an international rock star (**Paul Nicholas** plays Elton John with hair). The football bits aren't up to much, McShane's genius seemingly limited to extraordinarily little movement off the ball and side-footed square passes on it. But even these are works of cinematic genius compared to the rock star scenes, which consist of Paul Nicholas yelling, "Hello Amsterdam, New York, Paris, Tokyo" etc in front of the same twenty extras who have been told to move about a bit and impersonate a crowd.

What do you mean, what happens? The Third Division club gets to the FA Cup final, McShane leaves the bottle in the locker, and comes off the bench to score the winning penalty in extra time. There's a surprise then. John Motson supplies commentary and a cameo performance.

Ladybugs is another film about football that is rarely seen and deservedly so. It's a 1992 American feature about a girls' "soccer" team who are so utterly hopeless they can only be saved by the new coach per-

"Pelé is a delight to watch for his smile and his handling [sic] of a soccer ball."

US review of the risible *Hotshot*

suading his nephew to dress up as a girl and wear a wig. *Empire* described this entirely believable scenario as "a five star no-no" and "a hopeless effort". *Variety* said it was "sexist, homophobic and woefully unfunny", singling out director **Sidney J. Furie** for being "so bored with the material that he doesn't even bother to stage his soccer scenes correctly."

It isn't difficult to find dreadful films about football, but where do you find some good ones? Phil Crossley, a researcher at the British Film Institute (and a Blackburn Rovers fan), has tracked down more than five hundred films, including documentaries, that have some connection with the game. These vary from the sublime – thirty seconds of a game between Blackburn Rovers and West Bromwich Albion in 1898, believed to be the oldest existing footage of a first-class match – to the ridiculous (*Carry On Emmerdale* contained a saucy serial rogering scene in the dressing rooms during an FA Cup final).

Crossley's research suggests the oldest surviving feature film about football is a 1911 silent melodrama called *Harry the Footballer*. The plot (dashing centre forward kidnapped by opposition, but escapes just in time to lead his team to victory) probably wasn't new even in 1911. A rather more sophisticated storyline was employed for *The Great Game*, a 1930 British feature. One of the first films to intersperse genuine action scenes (Arsenal against Huddersfield in the FA Cup final) with the drama, it concerned a split between the manager and chairman of a club on the eve of a big match. The manager wants to pick a young player who just happens to be in love with his daughter. The chairman thinks there may be a degree of favouritism. The manager resigns in a huff and his players go to pieces in the first half, but he manages to get word to them to inspire them to victory.

A contemporary review of *The Great Game* described it as "an authentic and thoroughly interesting picture of Association Football", a sound recommendation if ever we heard one. The only known surviving print is now being restored by the British Film Institute, so there is a chance it will reappear one day. When it does, you will be able to see what is possibly **Rex Harrison**'s first appearance in a feature film.

One film that is accessible (it crops up on Channel 4 at times when nobody is watching) is *The Arsenal Stadium Mystery*, made in 1939. Taking a leaf from *The Great Game*'s book, it used action from a match between Arsenal and Brentford as the backdrop for a murder mystery melodrama played as a light comedy. In the film, Arsenal are playing an amateur team called Trojans, whose centre forward suddenly drops dead on the pitch. The detective (**Leslie Banks**) suspects foul play, perhaps excessive use of the offside trap, but finally deduces that the striker was poisoned.

The plot twists and turns, but the real stars are the Arsenal team and manager **George Allison**, all of whom are heavily featured. During the newsreel sequence at

"Those patrons who think they will see a fine display of football will be disappointed."

Nul points for *The Great Game*.

the start (a device to introduce the Arsenal team), Allison is described as "born with a silver football in his mouth" – an image worth lingering over.

In 1952, *The Great Game* was remade with rather less success. This time it was played as a comedy starring **Diana Dors**, Thora Hird and John Laurie, with the football scenes cut to a minimum. "Those patrons who think they will see a fine display of football will be disappointed", snapped one critic. "There are only about three minutes' play in the whole film. While others expecting a sincere attempt to investigate the evils of the transfer procedure will be bored by the film's stupidity."

Stupidity and lack of decent action are the culprits in most football movies. Take, for example, *La vida sigue igual* (*Life Goes on the Same*), a Spanish feature from 1969 starring **Julio Iglesias**. Strange as it may seem, Iglesias really was on Real Madrid's books as a goalkeeper, but that's a poor excuse for this melodrama. With his career with Real out of the window due to a crippling car crash, he becomes a reclusive minstrel, composing execrable songs about love and pain and the futility of it all. Equally worth blowing up the telly to avoid is *L'arbitro* (aka *Football Crazy*), a 1974 Italian comedy about a pompous referee and his love life. The presence of **Joan Collins** provides further incentive to steer well clear.

Collins might actually have enlivened the Yugoslavian epic, *Comrade President the Centre Forward*. This 1962 masterpiece sounds like it ought to star Josip Tito as the striker-cum-revolutionary hero who scores a hat-trick in the World Cup final against the running dogs of imperialism, but it doesn't. Other obscure footy flicks include three Czech offerings: *Ivana in the Forward Line*, *Women Who Have Run Offside* and *The Goalkeeper Lives In Our Street*. Israel has also produced a film called *Fish, Football and Girls*, which features roughly equal amounts of each.

British football films found a new credibility in the noughties, with two excellent, intimate offerings. Ken Loach, Bath City fan and nostalgic lamenter of the disappearance of traditional working-class institutions, directed *Looking for Eric*. As one critic put it, "This may be your only chance to see Cantona play 'La Marseillaise' on a trumpet on the balcony of a Manchester tower block." Loach was also responsible for the brilliant playing field scene in *Kes*, in which **Brian Glover**'s bullying schoolteacher assumes the role of **Bobby Charlton**, in a hysterically funny scene which tells you more about the British attitude to the game than a dozen lesser films.

The Damned United is a funnier and softer version of David Peace's coruscating novel of the same name about Brian Clough's famous 44 days in charge of Leeds United. Michael Sheen's terrific performance as Clough, battling his own demons and the all-pervasive, cynical legacy of Don "Readies" elevates it to potential classic status.

The noughties also saw a mini renaissance in football documentaries, World Cinema football movies and even World Cinema documentaries as Hollywood, not surprisingly, continued to misfire with straight to video fare like *Air Bud: World Pup*. Though credit where credit's due, this was a better title than the nauseous *The Game of Their Lives*: a celebration of *that* 1–0 USA victory over England. One for the Scottish market maybe? Global highlights included *The Miracle of Bern* from Germany – though best avoid this if you are Hungarian or English any time near a World Cup – and *The Other Final* about a match between the planet's worst-ranked national teams. Cult director Emir Kusturica knelt at the shrine of Maradona whereas Zidane got the French auteur treatment in *Zidane: A 21st Century Portrait* with his every move in a game recorded for posterity.

Perhaps the only filmmaker who looked at the pitch from the goal line was **Wim Wenders** in his 1971 existentialist feature *The Goalkeeper's Fear of the Penalty*. In this, the central character fails to save an easy one for no apparent reason. He then goes on to commit a murder, ditto. Football as a metaphor for life, or life as a metaphor for football?

The history of football in films proves two things. First, not even a star cast, big budget and expert advice on the action scenes can make the drama created on the wide screen match that of a real game. And secondly, actors usually kick a ball with the same conviction as footballers time a punchline though the jury still remains out regarding Eric Cantona and Vinnie Jones who can seemingly make a living from either.

BEAUTIFUL GAME, SHAME ABOUT MOST OF THE FILMS

The good, the bad and the inexplicable – those football movies in detail.

The Arsenal Stadium Mystery* (1939)** Good football movies are almost as rare as good Elvis Presley movies. This British thriller has the unusual virtue of actually having a plot, which centres on the murder of a centre forward of an amateur team playing Arsenal. Detective Leslie Banks sifts through the usual suspects (**Tony Adams**, the victim's agent) and ensures justice is done. The plot twists and turns admirably, but the real stars are the Arsenal team and manager George Allison, all heavily featured. *

***Life Goes on the Same* (1969)** Little-known Spanish drama with Julio Iglesias as a football-playing troubadour. Deserves to be even less known. *

***The Goalkeeper's Fear of the Penalty* (1971)** Popular in arthouses, this exercise in cinematic existentialism takes the goalkeeper's predicament as a metaphor for contemporary angst (i.e. "We are all just waiting to pay the ultimate penalty"). This is actually a very respectable, if occasionally pretentious, movie which loses two stars only because there's not much footie in it. **

***Football Crazy* (1974)** Not a movie based on the famous song but the English name for an Italian comedy of manners about a self-important referee who finds it hard to focus on what's happening on the pitch as opposed to what's happening in his bedroom. This is understandable, as one of the things in his bedroom is Joan Collins. Under the new FIFA directive, this film deserves an automatic red card. *

***Yesterday's Hero* (1979)** Ian McShane does his best impersonation of George Best. Jackie Collins takes responsibility for the script. Adam Faith is in charge of the team, Leicester Forest, who appear to have been named after a service station on the M1 and languish in the old Third Division. Suffice to say that if, as FA coaching director Charles Hughes maintained, running off the ball is ninety per cent of the game, McShane wouldn't even play for non-league Leicester United. **

***Gregory's Girl* (1980)** Bill Forsyth's charming tale of adolescence, football and sex has proved enduringly popular. Former *Crossroads* star Dee Hepburn pulls off a triumph of method acting as the fleet-of-foot female forward. John Gordon Sinclair looks so gawky he could be a natural for the movie of Darren Anderton's life story. The Czech film *Ivana in the Forward Line* covers a similar theme but the would-be striker has to dress up in men's clothes and speak Czech. The other Czech film in the same genre is *Women Who Have Run Offside*. ***

***Hotshot* (1987)** Proof that Pelé can be dull. Tired old tale of poor little rich boy who flees to South America to learn about the beautiful game. Critics liked Pelé's smile. Unfortunately the script also gave him some dialogue. *

***When Saturday Comes* (1996)** They opened wide the big book of Northern clichés for *When Saturday Comes*. Sean Bean (who else?) plays Jimmy Muir, a gritty, Sheffield United-daft brewery worker with a talent for banging in the goals for his local pub team. With a gritty, unsupportive father and a gritty, simple brother grafting down t'pit (there aren't actually any in Sheffield, but artistic truth demanded it) life's a struggle for the Muirs, and Jimmy's drunken ways suggest it's unlikely that he'll ever excel. Cue gritty local scout Pete Postlethwaite, who says "bugger" a lot and gets Jimmy a trial for the Blades. Our irresponsible hero responds by getting leathered the night before his trial and is unsurprisingly hopeless. A series of gritty events (accident down t'pit, unwanted pregnancy) leads Jimmy to a long dark night of the soul. The outcome is inevitable: after ten minutes of *Rocky*-style jogging through the snow and fancy keepy-uppy, Jimmy lands a place at United. The climax stretches the boundaries of predictability, as Jimmy comes on as sub against Manchester United. Will he be able to hammer home a last-minute penalty, get the girl and reconcile himself with his dad? Have a guess. The football sequences are shoddy too, but overall, *When Saturday Comes* and its dreadful Def Leppard soundtrack just makes it into "so-bad-it's-good" territory. *

***The Cup* (1999)** One to treasure. Bhutan's first ever feature follows Buddhist novice Jamyang Lodro as he tries to persuade his superiors to install a satellite dish in their Himalayan monastery so he can watch his hero Ronaldo in the World Cup. If you prefer your monks to have fancier footwork, try Stephen Chow's *Shaolin Soccer* (2001). ***

***There's Only One Jimmy Grimble* (2000)** A blatant rip-off of two Billys: ballet-dancing film hit *Billy Elliott* and classic comic strip Billy's Boots. Young Northern lad finds ancient boots belonging to pre-war goalscoring legend and is instantly transformed into a superstar. The football scenes are reasonably done, but it's hard to feel much sympathy for the key characters, unlike the Geordie scallies in *Purely Belter* (2000), who nick Alan Shearer's car while trying to score season tickets for St James' Park. **

***Air Bud: World Pup* (2000)** It's *Gregory's Girl* meets *101 Dalmatians*, as teen Kevin Zegers falls for co-ed team-mate Brittany Paige Bouck, while snivelling Michael Jeter attempts to dognap ball-playing Golden Retriever Buddy and his new puppies. Less press paws than eject. *

***Mike Bassett: England Manager* (2001)** Ricky Tomlinson plays an inept Norwich City manager who becomes England boss by default when every other candidate is forced out of the running. The football scenes are mercifully brief, but the low-rent feel and generally lacklustre plot are not aided by cameos from Atomic Kitten and alleged comedian Phill Jupitus. There is but one genuinely amusing moment, when Bassett asks a posse of critical fans how they would turn things around; he is met by a detailed and intelligent analysis of the side's shortcomings, to which he responds "Oh, fuck off" before running onto the team coach. *

***Bend It Like Beckham* (2002)** "Who'd want a girl who plays football all day but can't make chapattis?" So runs the central dilemma of likable Brit-flick *Bend It Like Beckham*. Asian teenager Jes (Parminder K. Nagra) doesn't fancy being a solicitor; she wants to emulate her United and England idol. But her family "would have a collective fit" if they found out she was playing for the Hounslow Harriers women's team – they'd rather she was cooking with her mother. There's much clever comedy – and subtle social commentary – milked from the reverse prejudice of the insular Bhamra family, and the clash between traditional Asian values and modern, football-crazy Britain. And while the soccer scenes are occasionally unrealistic, it's also a fine love letter to the sport. ***

The Miracle of Bern* (2003)** Directed by ex-pro Sönke Wortmann, this is one of the few footie films with authentic action. Young Louis Klamroth gets to know returning POW father Peter Lohmeyer as they trek to Switzerland to watch West Germany avenge an 8–3 drubbing in the group stages to beat Hungary 3–2 in the final of the 1954 World Cup. Despite being shown how to do inspiring Mundial movies, Hollywood botched *The Game of Their Lives* (2005), an account of the USA's 1–0 win over England in 1950. *

The Other Final* (2003)** A superb celebration of the underdog, in which FIFA's lowest-ranked nations, Bhutan (No. 202) and Montserrat (No. 203), play an alternative World Cup final on the same day that Brazil beat Germany in Japan. With half the Caribbean side succumbing to a virus on arriving in Thumphu and the referee failing to show, this documentary is a must for park amateurs and millionaire internationals alike. *

***Goal!* (2005)** Hardly on a par with *The Lord of the Rings,* the trilogy chronicling the fortunes of Mexican wünderkind Santiago Muñez (Kuno Becker) is only worth enduring for the excruciating cameos by various Toon idols and Galacticos. The players in the FIFA Soccer computer games are more lifelike. **

***Zidane: A 21st Century Portrait* (2006)** Taking its cue from Hellmuth Costard's George Best profile, *Fußball wie noch nie/Football As Never Before* (1971), this seventeen-camera portrait tracks Zinedine Zidane's every move during Real Madrid's 2005 clash with Villareal (which culiminates in an early bath that anticipates his 2006 World Cup disgrace). For more in-depth Gallic candidness, try Vikash Dhorasoo's Super 8 diary *Substitute.* ***

The star of *Zidane*. No acting required.

Offside* (2006)** Even though you never see a ball being kicked, this ranks among the finest football films. The satire is razor sharp and the amateur cast excels, as some greenhorn Iranian soldiers try to prevent a group of feisty female fans from entering the Azadi Stadium to watch the men-only World Cup qualifier with Bahrain. *

***Maradona by Kusturica* (2008)** With its recurrent references to the Hand of God and the Church of Maradona, there's little wonder this is such a hagiographical portrait of Diego Armando as sporting superstar, political activist and family man. The animated vanquishing of various Anglo-American leaders to the Sex Pistols' "God Save the Queen" is brilliantly bizarre. But it's hard to believe this exercise in egotistical maverickness took three years to make. **

Looking for Eric* (2009)** "I'm still getting over the bloody seagulls", complains depressed Manchester postman, Eric Bishop, as, in a spliff-induced vision, Eric Cantona appears to dispense advice in a series of gnomic philosophical *pensées*. Cantona sends himself up royally as mentor and muse to the suicidal postie, inspiring his namesake to rebuild his life. Using a cast of extras made up from Manchester United and FC United's hardcore support, Loach captures brilliantly what the French maverick came to represent for a particular group of working-class males. As the second part of the film morphs unconvincingly into an examination of inner city gun crime, Eric the postie and his mates become, equally unconvincingly, Cantona-masked activists, staging a raid on a local gangster's house. *

The Damned United* (2009)** The opening montage of the all-conquering Leeds United team of the 1970s fouling and cheating their way to the top illustrates the common theme of David Peace's novels: that Yorkshire, past and present, is a bloody awful place. Michael Sheen, who as a youth attracted interest from Arsenal, gives a bravura performance as tormented iconoclast Brian Clough taking on an impossible job, following Revie at Leeds. His opening address to his new team is absolutely riveting, even though the words have passed into football history: "The first thing you can do for me is chuck all your medals and all your caps and all your pots and all your pans into the biggest fucking dustbin you can find, because you've never won any of them fairly. You've done it all by bloody cheating." Much of the filming took place at Chesterfield's Saltergate stadium, principally because it had barely changed since the 1970s. Though the Clough family were unhappy with the version of Clough offered by both the book and the film, both deserve to become classics. The film's bile is saved for "Dirty Leeds" and Revie. **

WHEN TWO WORLDS COLLIDE: FOOTBALL AND POP

In 1970, pop music catered for the whole family: "Voodoo Chile" and Woodstock for the hip; "Tears of a Clown" and "Band of Gold" for the cool; "Wandrin' Star" for the prematurely aged – and "Back Home" for the football fan. "Back Home" entered the charts on 18 April, clawed its way to the top on 16 May and stayed there for three weeks, finally yielding to "Yellow River". It hung around for another nine weeks and even made a brief reappearance in August, just as the plucky England vocalists who had mimed so unconvincingly on primetime British TV really were on their way back home from the World Cup. It wasn't as big a hit that year as Elvis's "The Wonder of You", or Mungo Jerry's "In the Summertime"; but it was bigger than Dana's "All Kinds of Everything", so at least there's that to be said for it.

Quite why "Back Home" was such a hit is a mystery. The formula was nothing new. Get the lads (and **Elton John** and physio **Les Cocker** on backing vocals) into a studio to sing some inanely patriotic lyrics to a supremely mediocre tune. Give it a hook in the chorus like a kick in the knee, chuck in some crowd sound effects but, most of all, make it easy, make it cheap and make it quick.

> **"... A curious dream/I've never dreamed before/Stan Matthews on the wing for Stoke at the age of 84."**
> **Keele University students, 1964**

Football records fall into three categories. There's the team anthem (with or without professional help) invariably timed for the FA or World Cup; then there's the footballer as "serious" solo artiste; and finally, there are songs about football by professional performers. The first (and by far the most numerous) category is, it must be said, largely composed of the most God-awful "music" that the human ear has ever been subjected to.

No one really knows when it all started. Jim Phelan, a record sleeve designer, has done more than anyone in this country to bring together the crap and curiosities of footie records. His Exotica label has produced several compilation albums and CDs, on which you can find soccer songs performed by the Nolan Sisters, **Terry Venables**, **Jimmy Greaves**, **Jack Charlton**, the Victor Sylvester Orchestra, and **Franz Beckenbauer**. West Germany did a World Cup song in 1954, which appeared on an album of commentary on the final, but it's by no means certain this was the first World Cup promotional song.

To celebrate Spurs' 1960–61 Double, a bunch of session singers called The Totnamites sang a catchy little number in a chirpy, washing powder commercial sort of way called "Tip-Top Tottenham Hotspur". It went something like this: "Tip-top Tottenham Hotspur, the greatest team of the year/Tip-top Tottenham Hotspur, raise your glasses and give them a cheer/Hooray for the Double and let's live it up/ One drink for the league and one for the cup." It rose without trace.

Neither the ghastly Highland reel of "Men of Scotland", nor the Victor Sylvester "World Cup Cha-Cha-Cha" made it into the charts. Much better, but just as slow-selling, was "Stan Matthews" by Keele Row, one track of a flexi-disc EP produced by Keele University students for the 1964 rag week. This folk song about the Wizard of Dribble starts: "You've heard of Greaves and Puskás, and Pelé from Brazil/But Stanley Matthews from the Potts is the greatest of them all." Dodgy rhyme, but the second verse is better: "Last night I had a curious dream I've never dreamed before/Stan Matthews on the wing for Stoke at the age of 84."

Throughout the 1960s, more and more teams made records (or 45s as they were called back then) but it wasn't until 1970 and "Back Home" that the national side made it onto *Top of the Pops*. Even **Lonnie Donegan**'s 1966 theme "World Cup Willie" missed the charts completely. The success of "Back Home" spawned a host of imitators and something even worse – the spin-off album. As Phelan explains: "One of the pioneers in this area was Larry Page. He managed The Troggs and ran a record company called Page One. He was looking for a way to exploit the Larry Page Orchestra and so he went to Liverpool, Manchester United and Chelsea, and did these singalong records."

A Compilation Album of Hit Football Singles

Song	Artists	Year	Highest chart position	Wks in chart
Back Home	England World Cup Squad	1970	1	16
Please Don't Go	KWS	1992	1	16*
Three Lions	Baddiel and Skinner and The Lightning Seeds	1996	1	15
Come On You Reds	Manchester United	1994	1	15
World in Motion	England/New Order	1990	1	12
Nessun Dorma	Luciano Pavarotti	1990	2	11
Fog on the Tyne	Gazza/Lindisfarne	1990	2	9
Anfield Rap	Liverpool FC	1988	3	6
Ole Ola	Scotland World Cup Squad	1978	4	6
We Have a Dream	Scotland World Cup Squad	1982	5	9
Blue Is the Colour	Chelsea FC	1972	5	12
Ossie's Dream	Tottenham FA Cup Final Squad	1981	5	8
Hot Stuff	Arsenal FC	1998	9	5
Leeds United	Leeds United FC	1972	10	10
Diamond Lights	Glenn and Chris	1987	12	8
Here We Go	Everton FC	1985	14	5
Don't Come Home Too Soon	Del Amitri	1998	15	4

Invariably this meant professional footballers, who should have known better, performing ghastly early 1970s schlock and doing it very badly. The *Back Home* album contained such treasures as **Bobby Moore** and **Francis Lee** singing "Sugar Sugar"; **Geoff Hurst**, **Jeff Astle** and **Peter Bonetti** warbling "Lily The Pink"; and the whole England team attempting to croon their way through "Puppet On A String", and "Ob-la-di Ob-la-da". You have to hear it to believe it.

But who on earth actually bought this stuff? "Mums and grandmas were probably responsible," says Phelan. "They saw these things in shops, said 'That's just right for little Johnny, he likes football', and they bought them as birthday and Christmas presents." As Mari Wilson might say, "just what I always wanted." First on the bandwagon were Chelsea. A bunch of blokes called Stamford Bridge had a No. 47 hit (if there's such a thing) with "Chelsea" in May 1970. It was the first FA Cup final promotional hit record and seemed to do the trick as the London club beat Leeds United 2–1 in the replay. This was just a trial run for 1972 when Chelsea and the Larry Page Orchestra produced the ever-popular "Blue Is The Colour". The album spin-off featured **Peter Osgood** singing "Chirpy-Chirpy Cheep Cheep", an act of musical homicide.

The one exception to this trend in the early 1970s was **Don Fardon**'s "Belfast Boy", a remarkably prescient warning to George Best. "Just play the way the ball bounces/ And bounce the way the ball plays," it starts mysteriously. "Cos you won't have long

We've Got the Whole World in Our Hands	Nottingham Forest with Paper Lace	1978	24	6
Black & White Army	Black and White Army	1998	26	2**
Head Over Heels	Kevin Keegan	1979	31	6
I'm Forever Blowing Bubbles	West Ham FC	1975	31	2
We'll Be With You	The Potters	1972	34	2†
Do the Right Thing	Ian Wright	1993	43	2
Let's Dance	Middlesbrough FC	1997	44	1††
Viva El Fulham	Tony Rees and the Cottagers	1975	46	1
Glad All Over/ Where Eagles Fly	Crystal Palace	1990	50	2
Nine in a Row	Rangers FC	1997	54	2
Niall Quinn's Disco Pants	A Love Supreme	1999	59	2
Go For It!	Coventry City Cup Final Squad	1987	61	2
The Boys In The Old Brighton Blue	Brighton & Hove Albion FC	1983	65	2
Outstanding	Andy Cole	1999	68	1‡

* "Please Don't Go" was Nottingham band KWS's desperate plea to Forest and England centre back Des Walker not to go to Sampdoria. The song was a No.1 smash but failed to persuade Des to stay, though he has since returned to the City Ground.

** Newcastle United fan vocalists

† The Potters were also known as "Stoke City Football Supporters' Vocal Group".

†† With Chris Rea and Bob Mortimer.

‡ An Amazon customer review of this single, by "a music fan from Paris" says: "My advice to you – don your leather jacket and gold jewellery and choose 'Outstanding' as your soundtrack to a night's cruisin' around town".

in the limelight/No you won't have many days/Georgie, Georgie, they call you the Belfast joy." This entered what your parents still embarrassingly referred to as the "hit parade" the same week as "Back Home", but never soared higher than No. 32.

But the die was cast. It was possible to have a hit record with a football song, even one sung by footballers, and everyone had to have a go. Some songs were specifically written (generally by someone's agent on the back of an envelope) but many used new words grafted on to familiar pop themes. While most are utterly unmemorable, a few do stand out. Millwall's 1972 "The Ballad of Harry Cripps", a tribute to their hard-tackling left back, contains some of the best lyrics. "Divisions Four, Three, Two and One, 'Arry has played in every one/He is a man who time will never age/'Arry Cripps is his name/Right up to the last minute/He always gets stuck in it."

However, that's nothing compared to the poetry of Wealdstone's "We Are the Stones", which contains the following imperishable lines: "We go to places as far away as Barrow/One place we always try to win and that's Harrow/If you like a drink go to the players' bar/Oh no, let me think, we haven't built it so far." They don't write them like that any more.

"'Arry Cripps is his name/ Right up to the last minute/ He always gets stuck in it."

From Millwall's "The Ballad of Harry Cripps", 1972

The big football hit of 1973 was "Nice One, Cyril" by **The Cockerel Chorus**, which took the punchline from a TV commercial for bread and applied it to Spurs full back **Cyril Knowles**. It reached No. 14. The spin-off album spun off.

The Scotland World Cup squad's "Easy Easy" was a No. 20 hit in 1974, while Manchester United had their first hit in 1976 with, oddly, "Manchester United". It wasn't until 1979 that anything vaguely different emerged. In October that year **B.A. Robertson** produced the No. 8 hit "Knocked It Off". "I knocked it off, yeah I knocked it off/I was standing in the corner when the ball came across/I thought I'd had another go/But I never thought I'd put it away", he explained. Robertson revealed his football-loving credentials with various contributions to Scotland World Cup records alongside other such Tartan titans as the Bay City Rollers and Lulu. Incidentally, until you've heard **Denis Law** accompanying Rod Stewart on Jimi Hendrix's "Angel" you can't claim to have lived a full life.

The other big football hit of the year was **Kevin Keegan**'s "Head Over Heels in Love" which plateaued at No. 31. The follow-up, "It Ain't Easy", was much less successful but much funnier, revealing just how hard life was for the soccer superstar. "But I come home too tired for loving/Something a girl finds hard to understand/ Believe me, it ain't easy to live this life with me."

Keegan was not the first player to heed bad advice about the quality of his voice and be lured into the studio. **John Charles** teamed up with the William Galassini Orchestra while in Italy and recorded Welsh/Italian hybrid ballads. **Franz Beckenbauer** has been recorded whispering his way – Julio Iglesias style – through "1–0 für deine Liebe" ("1–0 for your Love"). Even worse are **Terry Venables**' Frank Sinatra impersonation as he murders Cole Porter's "I've Got You Under My Skin" and his Cockney knees-up rendition of "Bye-Bye Blackbird".

By the early 1980s, the traditional football song was on its way out. Scotland, with comic actor **John Gordon Sinclair** fronting the squad, tried to inject some humour into "We Have a Dream". England, though, having been out of the World Cup for twelve years, were completely unhip and produced "This Time", a stereotypically jaunty effort which went all the way to No. 2. Again it's the album, produced by K-Tel – buy-one-and-get-the-warehouse-free – that takes the breath away. Not only do you get **Glenn Hoddle** shrieking his way through Queen's "We Are the Champions", but there's also an instrumental rendition of "This Time" performed by the Leyland Vehicles Brass Band. In addition to the K-Tel Klassic, there was another 1982 England album, the "Officially Approved Souvenir LP" with the sleeve bearing a strangely ominous "Football Association Approved" stamp. What's strange about this record is that it's a rip-off of the K-Tel disc, featuring many of the same songs performed by completely different people, including members of the 1966 squad.

By far the best football songs of 1982 were on *The Revolution Starts at Closing Time*, the debut (and probably the only) album of a London band called **Serious Drinking**. Their "Spirit of 1966" made the same mistake as "This Time" with a cheerful chorus – "We're gonna win the World Cup in Spain/We're gonna hoist that World Cup again" – but the verses consisted of the names of the 1966 players yelled at top volume. A surreal touch was added by referring to England's left back as Leonard (not George) Cohen throughout. Also on the album was a reflection on 1970's off-pitch shenanigans entitled "Bobby Moore Is Innocent".

Before all that we'd had the familiar fare. Nottingham Forest teaming up with Paper "Billy Don't Be a Hero" Lace for "We've Got the Whole World at Our Feet", and Spurs with Chas 'n' Dave for "Ossie's Dream" and that truly dreadful trembly-Wembley rhyme. The **Nolan Sisters** had recorded "Blackpool, Blackpool", and 10CC (under the pseudonym Tristar Airbus) had made "Willy Morgan on the Wing", but the big hits were drying up. Brighton's "The Boys in the Old Brighton Blue" peaked at No. 65 in 1983, although Manchester United's "Glory, Glory Man Utd" reached No. 13 the same year.

It took footballers of quality and vision to break the mould: **Hoddle** and **Waddle**. Despite suffering a sense of humour bypass that prompted them to use their first names, they had a No. 12 hit in 1987 with the smoochy ballad "Diamond Lights", the first for singing footballers (rather than a squad press-ganged into the studio) since Keegan. Their follow-up, "It's Goodbye", flopped. Hoddle didn't hit the charts again until Chelsea's "No-one Can Stop Us Now" in 1993.

In fact, the only British footballer to have more than one chart hit is, almost unbelievably, Gazza. Having played a significant part in the ground-breaking "World in Motion" World Cup song (the biggest football hit since "Back Home", and unlike all the others, one that almost bears repeated listening), Gascoigne reached No. 2 in 1990 with a funked-up "Fog on the Tyne". The follow-up, "Geordie Boys (Gazza Rap)" hovered just outside the top thirty.

Rap seemed the only way forward. **Ian Wright** made a brief appearance (two weeks, No. 43) in the charts in August 1993, rapping out "Do The Right Thing", which was better than Vinnie Jones' spirited rendering of "Wooly Bully". **Andy Cole** was perhaps ill-advised to title his solitary foray into music "Outstanding", as it was anything but. Enter Baddiel, Skinner and Ian Broudie (the bloke from Lightning Seeds who looks like a long-lost Baddiel sibling) with the omnipresent "Three Lions" – a pleasant singalong which tends nonetheless to induce psychotic rage on repeated listening. The tune emerged for Euro '96 and was resurrected by popular demand for the World Cup two years later. (Scotland opted for the Del Amitri-backed "Don't Come Home Too Soon". They did.) In the absence of any other presentable song – Bell & Spurling's "Sven Sven Sven" in 2002 was a particular low.

No less than a staggering 29 singles were released to accompany England's 2006 World Cup campaign. The official single, by Yorkshire indie miserabilists Embrace was the FA's failed attempt to spawn another "World in Motion" with an "uplifting, anthemic appeal", though the resulting spacey "World at Your Feet" was too limp and Coldplayesque to stir the terraces. Fey, fragile punk romantic Wreckless Eric unwisely pillaged his own classic, "Whole Wide World" ("There's only one girl in the world for me, she probably lives in Tahiti") as "Whole Wide World 4 England". Post-feminist Yorkshire girl band Branded helpfully provided English womanhood with a means to get behind, or rather in front of the team, with "Tits Out for the Lads". As singer JoBabe commented, "Let's face it, you can't take life too serious all of the time." Despite an endorsement by Mrs Pankhurst, widespread boob/moob flashing didn't take off as the band urged, "Tits Out for John Terry". Dutch band Lopend Vuur recorded their song in German, "Es ist vorbei (Marco ist zurück)" [It's Over. (Marco is Back)], "so those wankers could understand it".

The supremely focused Fabio Capello caused minor outrage and major relief by deciding that there should be no official 2010 anthem to distract England the team from their job of going out in the quarter-finals as usual.

For the aficionado, the best music in this genre is probably by Half Man Half Biscuit who aside from penning songs with such inspired titles as **"I Was a Teenage Honved Fan"** and "All I Want for Christmas Is A Dukla Prague Away Kit" also gave us the immortal spoof of Abba's "Dancing Queen": "Friday night and the gates are low ..." Just as exhilarating, in its way, is *Música De Futebol* (on the Mr Bongo label), a CD of the best Brazilian music inspired by football, interspersed with commentaries highlighting the great moments in the game's history in Brazil. If your idea of a perfect start to the day is a burst of commentary describing the Carlos Alberto goal against Italy in 1970, this is for you.

"YOU FILL UP MY SENSES, LIKE A GREASY CHIP BUTTIE"

Ever since football started (long before **John Denver**'s hit "Annie's Song" was adapted by Sheffield United fans), fans have sung. The oldest known football song still used today is Norwich City's "On The Ball, City", written by Albert T. Smith, a City director, around 1890 as a music hall song. A Blackburn Rovers song sung at the FA Cup final against Old Etonians in 1882 shows that the words may change but the sentiments remain the same. "All hail, ye gallant Rover Lads, Etonians thought you were cads, they've found a football game their dads, By meeting Blackburn Rovers." Rovers lost 1–0.

The West Ham United classic "I'm Forever Blowing Bubbles" is also getting on a bit. It was first heard in 1923 at the White Horse final at Wembley which West Ham lost. In 1975 it was released as a single and got to No. 31 in the charts. The team did rather better that year, winning their second FA Cup.

And who invented the "Ooh, aah, [Cantona]!" chant anyway? Arsenal fans claim to be one of the first to sing it when **Anders Limpar** made his debut for Arsenal in Sweden in 1990. Unfortunately, Anders did not react in quite the way the Gunners fans had hoped. They were as bewildered at his expressions as he was by their chant – until a Swedish fan pointed out that "Ooh aah" means "Who is" in Swedish.

Paul McGrath claims to have been the first target of such affectionate chants. And there are many more. Songs have incredible power sometimes: you just need to listen to a Barça fan singing of Catalan blood. Or Liverpool supporters away from home singing "Poor Scouser Tommy". Home fans are often stunned into silence, as their initial attempts to drown out the words are thwarted by the sheer determination of the Reds to finish the whole bloody song.

The passing of the terraces may mean an end to some of the wit and wisdom as it becomes harder to get chants and songs taken up. But then songs didn't always come into being via the gallows humour of the terraces; sometimes they came through less obvious routes. **Jimmy Hill**, for example, was responsible for two songs still heard today. When manager of Coventry City in the 1960s he and chairman Derrick Robins thought they should devise a club song for the terraces to sing. "I sat down one Sunday night with John Camkin – a board member and commentator for Anglia TV – and we had a few gins, well we had a whole bottle actually, and he'd heard the 'Eton Boating Song' on the radio and said 'Why don't we build it around that?'"

Hill then came up with the words for the "Sky Blue Song" and somehow persuaded Ted Heath (the bandleader, not the former prime minister) to record an "upbeat" version of the song which sold "quite well" – in parts of Coventry at least. The Sky Blues were 2–0 up in a match against Barnsley when fog descended and the match was temporarily abandoned. Hill and Robins, who had sung in amateur opera, seized their chance for stardom: Robins on the mike and Hill conducting the crowd through the mist. To ensure all the Coventry fans sang, the words were printed in the programme.

The other song Hill wrote was when he was Head of Sport at LWT. In 1971, the big match was Arsenal against Liverpool in the FA Cup final and Hill asked TV viewers to write a song for Arsenal to the tune of "Land of Hope and Glory". However the Elgar Society, which owned the copyright to the tune, complained about the trivialization of one of England's greatest anthems and Hill was left with the embarrassment of having to change his tune (all good practice for *Match of the Day* reporting).

In a flash of inspiration befitting one who had been the first-ever manager to face the *Match of the Day* cameras at half-time, Hill asked **Bertie Mee**, Arsenal's manager, if he would accept "Rule Britannia", with Hill's words, as Arsenal's song for the Cup final. Mee accepted, the band played it at the next home match and the Gunners' favourite "Good Old Arsenal" was born. "I still get royalties for that song", says The Chin. "It's a long way from Phil Collins, but it's still nice."

LOOK AND LISTEN

The first match to be broadcast on British television was Arsenal v. Everton on 29 August 1936, so the traditional cry of "Not Arsenal again!" is older than you thought. Football on television has come a long way since then, although as late as the 1950s it largely amounted to friendlies involving Wolves against "crack" continental opposition. It wasn't until 1964 that *Match of the Day* was launched on the new minority-interest TV channel BBC2, with Kenneth Wolstenholme journeying to Beatleville to commentate on Liverpool against, yes, Arsenal. The programme was not supposed to run and run: it was really a dry run for the BBC's 1966 World Cup coverage.

The fact that lots of people actually wanted to watch football on TV evidently took the academics at the Beeb by surprise, but *Match of the Day*'s continuing success saw it moved to BBC1 in 1966. David "One-nil!" Coleman took over as commentator-in-chief three years later.

By then ITV had launched *The Big Match* on LWT in 1968, introducing revolutionary new devices like the slow-motion replay under the stewardship of **Brian Moore** and **Jimmy Hill**. The duo also headed up ITV's innovative pundit panel for Mexico '70, with Malcolm Allison, **Derek Dougan** et al. opinionating in a kaleidoscope of lurid shirts, kipper ties and cravats. By now most ITV regions were running their own Sunday afternoon highlights package, but Hill, it was said, was lured to the nationwide stage of the BBC in 1973 because he'd outgrown performing only to the London gallery and was tired of Northern cabbies asking him what he was up to.

Meanwhile the battlefront had extended to Saturday lunchtimes. **Sam Leitch** and later **Bob Wilson** fronted the Beeb's *Football Focus* (title devised by Motty, fact fans), while Brian Moore hosted ITV's *On the Ball*, and the two sides entered into head-to-head competition every FA Cup final Saturday. The natural order was shattered in 1978, however, when in a "Snatch of the Day", ITV bought up exclusive coverage of the Football League. The BBC complained to the Office of Fair Trading and got their rights back, but had to cede the Saturday night slot to ITV every other season. Jimmy Hill over the roast spuds was just all wrong.

Ratings then went into decline, and by 1985 things were in such a mess that when contract talks broke down, television walked away, leaving the screens football-free for months – much to the delight of wives and girlfriends everywhere.

Their joy was short-lived, however, as normal service was resumed in time for Mexico '86. In 1988, upstart satellite newcomers BSB tried to poke their nose in but were beaten to the Football League contract by ITV. With the accent on live matches, ITV's "live and exclusive" coverage (fronted by the oleaginous **Elton Welsby**, who made Jim Rosenthal look like Des Lynam) concentrated firmly on the Big Five (unlikely as it may seem, younger readers, Everton and Spurs were the other two). The first campaign ended in a breathtaking climax, Arsenal beating Liverpool in the final seconds of the season.

The looming threat of satellite intervention finally materialized in 1992, when the rights for the new Premiership were bought up by the riches of Rupert Murdoch's Sky Sports, who had already eaten up BSB. Their "revolution" promised a Whole New Ball Game of wall-to-wall coverage, Monday night matches, cheerleaders, **Andy Gray**'s incisive analysis and imperfect mastery of the video machine, and Richard Keys' blazers (furnished by Yves St Laurent). A deal was also done to allow the return of *MOTD* on terrestrial TV, now with Des Lynam behind the desk. Euro '96 indicated that football was a primetime attraction once more, and the cost escalated to a price the BBC couldn't pay. In 1999, the unthinkable happened: Lynam defected to ITV, and the Premiership highlights followed. The BBC consoled themselves with the FA Cup and the emergence of **Gary Lineker** as anchorman, while OnDigital (later ITV Digital) bought the Nationwide League rights for a fee that would bankrupt the network. Along with the failure of ITV's Saturday evening Premiership highlights package in 2001, it was a warning to others that televised football was not necessarily a crock of gold. This didn't stop Irish broadcasters Setanta taking on the might of Sky, launching their own rival news channel and bidding for the two English Premier League packages. But the rights to show 46 matches annually for three seasons until 2010 were not enough to keep the channel from financial meltdown. Setanta's innovative "no frills", realistic coverage of the Blue Square Premier League had its fans and was certainly different. Coaches could be heard shouting from the touchline, and players shouting to each other. Dressing room cameras relayed the half-time team talks. Commentators Steve Bower and Paul Parker (Parker earned a Facebook page, "Paul Parker is a babbling fool, get him off my TV!"), with no cosy studio to shelter in, frequently delivered their summaries lashed by wind and rain. Setanta went belly up in 2009, to be replaced by US network ESPN, with ex-BBC presenter Ray Stubbs, supposedly hacked off by being replaced by Gabby Yorath on *Final Score*.

Honourable mention must also go to Channel 4's *Gazzetta Football Italia*, especially to the Sunday when, due to the vagaries of the Italian weather and broadcasting technology, a long pass soared into the air in one stadium to land in another fifty miles away. Commentator Peter Brackley was, as ever, unflappable.

Football drama has been less of a success. *Those Glory, Glory Days*, about a girl's obsession with Spurs' Double-winning side of 1960–61, was made by Channel 4 in 1983 and had a limited cinema release. Tyne Tees made *The World Cup – A Captain's Tale*, based on the true story of a team of Durham miners who represented England in the first ever "World Cup", played in 1910, and won it, beating Juventus in the final. Dennis Waterman played **Bob Jones**, the West Auckland centre half and captain. The whole project was Waterman's idea. He stumbled across the story while reading a book about football on the loo.

The theme of women breaking into the board and changing rooms has been explored with **Cherie Lunghi** in *The Manageress*, and in the BBC play *Born Kicking*. Both tackled wider issues (sexism, racism, violence etc) but were let down by their action scenes. In *Born Kicking*, the ponytailed Roxy scores a remarkable number of headed goals without a challenge in sight. The highlight of the action is her Vinnie Jones-inspired gonad grab on a rather-too-close marking defender, but the play fails to avoid the cliché of Roxy coming off the bench to score the winning penalty in the dying seconds.

The single best television programme about football still has to be the fly-on-the-wall Graham Taylor documentary, available on video as *Do I Not Like That*. Among the many classic moments are Nigel Clough struggling to understand Taylor's instructions when he comes on as sub, Gazza shaming Taylor's amateurish training by showing the manager how to plot a set piece, and the famous badgering of the officials: "He's cost me my job ..." As Taylor himself said many times during this Channel 4 programme: "what sort of thing is happening here?" You tell us, Graham. It certainly wasn't football.

Television has undoubtedly had a profound effect on the sport it is covering. In the Premiership, the huge sums from screening rights have brought about spiralling wage demands from imported (and domestic) star attractions, to say nothing of fixtures disruption for the non-armchair fan. At a lower level, however, the failure of ITV Digital imperilled the future of several Nationwide League clubs who were supposed to be benefiting from its income and spent the money before it came in. But in an era when a mini-dish can bring you action from around the planet 24 hours a day, and delivered such innovations (or irritations) as pick-your-own camera angles, tactics trucks and **Peter Drury**, it seems impossible now to conceive of professional football without it.

Before vision, there was only sound. The first match to be broadcast on the radio was the 1926 Cup final between Bolton and Manchester City, which was relayed back to Manchester to be heard in large public halls. The BBC broadcast the Arsenal–Sheffield United game at Highbury a year later, introducing a unique system in which the pitch was printed in the *Radio Times*, divided into eight numbered squares. While the commentary went on, an announcer in the background called out the squares' numbers as the ball passed them, thereby allowing listeners to visualize where the action was taking place and giving rise to the phrase "back to square one". The system died out after the war.

Radio commentaries were massively popular, but the Football League took a dim view, fearing attendances would plummet. A ban on broadcasting live matches was imposed in 1951, but rescinded later in the decade.

The arrival of Radio 5 in the 1990s was a Sky-style revolution, but wall-to-wall coverage on the box is slowly killing the medium, with inane banter of the my-team's-better-than-yours variety now standard fare for an entire station (former *Sun* editor Kelvin MacKenzie's talkSPORT with its undoubted star ex-Celtic and Manchester United player **Alan Brazil**, the man who once referred to the Japanese as "nips" during a "light-hearted" discussion about whaling.) And that's without even mentioning David "Mellorphant" Mellor or Jonathan Pearce, whose breathless account of **Eric Cantona**'s kung-fu attack ("And I care not one jot for his talent …") is a classic of its kind and was circulated as a promotional tool by Capital Gold. It's a rare privilege to hear a man almost have an aneurysm live on air. Relentlessly perky Norn Ireland enthusiast **Colin Murray** is the latest frontman for the revamped Five Live's weekend sports coverage before he moved to fill the boots of **Adrian Chiles** on *MOTD2*.

NINE GREAT FOOTBALL TV COMEDY MOMENTS

1 ***Whatever Happened to the Likely Lads?*** Bulgaria v. England, "it's on the box tonight", "Malcolm Macdonald uses the same conditioner as me", **Brian Glover**, "people don't go around saying nil–two", heavy pitch, "Koreans – not to be trusted … Danes – pornographic!", "the crowd will have streamed back to their collective farms", "the gospel according to Sir Alf", "England … flooded out!"

2 *Monty Python's Flying Circus* The sketch where Greek philosophers take on their German counterparts captained by "Nobby" Hegel. Referee Confucius sends of Nietzsche for accusing him of having no "free will" and Kant disputes Socrates, winning goal "via the categorical imperative ... holding that ontologically it exists only in the imagination" and so on.

3 *Porridge* The episode where Spurs fan Fletch hoodwinks Norris, a fellow *HMP Slade* inmate due for release, into buying a treasure map, only to dig for the hidden contraband in the middle of Elland Road. Also the episode when Fletch and co. attempt escape under cover of a celebrities versus cons football match.

4 *Steptoe and Son* In the episode "Divided We Stand", Harold and Albert end up partitioning their bijou Oildrum Lane abode, a decision which extends to dividing the TV set in half, only for father and son to argue over whether to watch ballet or the European Cup. "Was that a goal?" "No, he saved it!" "Oh gawd!"

5 *Rising Damp* Leeds United fan and sleazy landlord Rigsby recalls the 1975 European Cup final. "When Bayern Munich scored that second goal, I thought they were going to break out into the goosestep …"

6 Paul Whitehouse and Harry Enfield Ron Manager and to a lesser extent Jose Arrogantio may have been done to death but the comedy sketch duo's finest figure of fun was Colombian footballer and language-mangler Julio Geordio.

7 *Father Ted* Father Ted tests his managerial skills in the annual All-Priests Over-75s Five-a-Side challenge match – except that his best player is dead, Father Jack has overdosed on Dreamy Sleepy Nighty Snoozy Snooze, and rival Father Dick Byrne has signed a crack Italian star (Dougal: "The Italians know about football all right. And fashion. Ted, do you remember that fella that was so good at fashion they had to shoot him?") Alas, Ted's plan to snatch victory using rubber arms and an electric wheelchair is thwarted.

8 Peter Cook Part of a swansong series of comedy character interviews from the comic legend in a slot on *Clive Anderson Talks Back*. Cook plays Scunthorpe-bred Graham Taylor era football manager Alan Latchley. The secret of his success? The three Ms: "motivation, motivation and motivation". Cook's eight-minute stint explains why most of our biggest clubs are now run by continentals. Brilliant.

9 *Phoenix Nights* Chanting midget Bolton fans beat up doormen Max and Paddy at the nightclub when refused entry. It's not exactly a football-filled episode but it's a good excuse to salute *Nights* creator Peter Kay's no-nonsense beer advert, John Smith "Ave It", that perfectly expresses the sublime joy of the hefty hoof. "O yes."

FIVE BEST FOOTBALL PROGRAMMES

1 *Soccer AM* (Sky Sports) Sky's Saturday morning pre-match fry-up, masterminded until 2007 by preening Chelsea boy **Tim Lovejoy,** assisted by fire-eating Torquay überfan **Helen Chamberlain**, plus highly attractive women in replica shirts and rock stars shakily professing their love of football. Essentially three hours of *Tiswas*-but-with-football, it's given the world the majestic "Third Eye" (amusing happenings at matches caught on camera), not to mention the virus-like cult of the "Save Chip" banner.

2 *Soccer Saturday* (Sky Sports) Then, if you want to waste your Saturday completely, spend the next five and a half hours in front of this compelling nonstop football chat and results programme, anchored by the unruffled cult hero **Jeff Stelling**. **Paul Merson** ("Ronaldo – about eight legovers there"), **Phil Thompson, Charlie Nicholas** et al sit behind a desk watching matches on television and describe the action in their own unique style – in Phil Thompson's case this involves becoming increasingly Scouse as the action hots up, "Den dey get de ball." BBC's attempt to do the same on its digital *Score* programme doesn't come close, even despite the labyrinthine comments of Garth Crooks.

3 *Sgorio* (S4C) Years before James Richardson ordered his first cappuccino and skimmed through the latest *Gazzetta Dello Sport*, or made his brief foray onto Setanta, Welsh-language channel S4C presented the finest action from Serie A and La Liga every Monday night. The programme acquired cult status on Merseyside, where S4C transmissions could be picked up.

4 *Fantasy Football League* (BBC2/ITV) David Baddiel and **Frank Skinner** sat on a battered sofa, bunged on funny football clips old and new, nattered with guest "managers" (Peter Cook, Bob Mortimer and Basil Brush to name three), abused Angus "Statto" Loughran, appeared in vaguely satirical sketches ("Saint and Greavsie Talk about the Endsleigh League As if it's Important"), recreated classic moments in someone's back garden in Phoenix from the Flames ("Play David Coleman!") and Jeff Astle sang. Badly. Fantastic stuff in its pomp, less so for the live France '98 revival on ITV, when the jokes were wearing thin.

5 *Kick-Off* (Granada) Essential viewing for any northwest fan in the 1970s, this Friday-teatime preview was fronted by **Gerald Sinstadt**, who would sometimes take an unusually uncompromising line ("We'll be asking Lawrie McMenemy why his Southampton team were so boring at Old Trafford last week"). Light relief came in the form of the "Who's My Daddy" quiz, where viewers had to guess the identity of a famed footballer from his offspring's clues, more original than the mystery sportsman on *A Question of Sport* and, to be fair, more naff. Brilliant theme tune as well. Briefly revived in the late 1980s with the omnipresent Elton Welsby.

FIVE WORST FOOTBALL PROGRAMMES

1 *Poland v. England*, 1997 (Channel Five) Perhaps a contender for the worst programme of all time, full stop. The nascent C5 bought up the World Cup qualifier to raise its profile, but for some inexplicable reason they hired racing commentator **Brough Scott** (in a plaid jacket that sent the cameras funny), professionally unfunny Scot Dominik Diamond and page-three stunna **Gail McKenna** to present three interminable hours of "build-up" from a noisy "football café" peopled by ex-Gladiators and the "stars" of lacklustre soap *Family Affairs*, before **Jonathan Pearce** bawled his TV debut in the commentary box. Tragic.

2 *The Match* (ITV) Live and exclusive, only on ITV! Sunday afternoons around the start of the 1990s meant **Elton Welsby** and co presenting a live match, although as someone once pointed out, ITV's season started in November and ended halfway through a Howard Wilkinson interview. The two highlights were Arsenal's *Fever Pitch*-inspiring last-gasp clincher in 1989, and live coverage from **Lee Chapman**'s front room in 1992 as Leeds United discovered they were champions after rivals Manchester United slipped up.

3 *Jimmy Hill's Sunday Supplement* (Sky Sports) Jim was assisted by Brian "The Bison" Woolnough and two other hacks, who convened in a fake MFI kitchen in Isleworth. They chewed the fat, mulled over the back pages and settled old scores while Jimmy attempted in vain to convince viewers that the set was real ("I'm just off to baste the meat and my spuds"). When he retired the show was renamed *Sunday Supplement* and is now the sole preserve of journalists who no longer have to hear Hill reminding them that they don't know what they are talking about because they have never played professional football.

4 *The Premiership* (ITV) ITV's bid to make football highlights a Saturday evening attraction rapidly became the biggest TV primetime failure in recent years, thanks to such misguided innovations as the Tactics Truck (inside which **Andy Townsend** helpfully explained to a nonplussed **Ugo Ehiogu** why his team had lost) and ProZone, a load of numbers on a computer screen which Terry Venables attempted to get enthusiastic about. Tel, Des and **Ally McCoist** bantered for all they were worth, but the programme was soon shunted back to 10.30pm.

> **"I've always supported the Lilywhites. Do they still call them the Lilywhites?"**
> **Bruce Forsyth, *Cup Final Saturday***

5 *Monday Night Football* (Sky Sports) It's all very respectable these days, but in the early days of *Monday Night Football*, pre-match entertainment was provided by the Sky Strikers dancing troupe, who were intended to bring a bit of all-American razzmatazz to Boundary Park or Carrow Road on a damp November night. Memorably, they once danced out of a huge Christmas cracker before a festive fixture at Ayresome Park. Other notable moments included "half-time musical guests" technopop outfit The Shamen being greeted by the North Bank with a full-throated "Oo the f***in' 'ell are you?"

SEVEN FICTIONAL TV FOOTBALL FOLK

1 Gabriella Benson Played by Cherie Lunghi (the kind of actress always described as "delectable"), Benson was The Manageress in C4's 1989 series about professional football's first female boss. Despite the decried "it'll never happen" premise, it was a decent stab at a realistic football drama, with Warren Clarke as the dodgy chairman and a team featuring Stephen Tompkinson and Mark McGann. Lunghi soon legged it to run some coffee company, mind.

2 Jossie Blair Written by Sid Waddell, the drinking man's Alan Bennett, *Jossie's Giants* (BBC1, 1986) depicted the travails of former Newcastle United star Joswell "Jossie" Blair, aka Jim Barclay, in his comic attempts to coach a hopeless kids team, the Glipton Grasshoppers. The theme song claimed that football was just a branch of science, but Jossie's coaching methods suggested that the writers were simply desperate to find a rhyme for "giants".

3 Mac Murphy In slightly grittier vein, ITV's *Murphy's Mob* (1985) followed the adventures of Dunmore United's junior supporters' club. Mac Murphy, portrayed by Ken Hutchinson, was the team's phlegmatic Scottish manager, while the club chairman was former rock star Rasputin Jones. Appropriately enough, the series was filmed at Vicarage Road for a time.

4 Darren Matthews The hero of ITV's *All in the Game*, a 1993 drama about a top English striker who makes a big-money move to Barcelona. Clearly a scenario which must have taxed the imagination of co-creator Gary Lineker, who naturally popped up to deliver an MDF cameo offering Matthews some sage advice before his transfer ("Don't forget rule number one – score some goals, you dope!"). Lineker also inspired *An Evening with Gary Lineker* which, as football comedies go, was quite funny and only slightly smug.

5 Franny Scully The creation of Alan Bleasdale, who invented the Liverpool-obsessed teen idler to entertain pupils when he was a teacher. His stories later became a Radio Merseyside series and a BBC play, before C4's 1984 adaptation.

The titles depicted Scully (Andrew Schofield) running out in front of the Kop in his daydreams to the strains of "There's only one Franny Scully!" The series boasted a great theme tune from Elvis Costello and cameos from Kenny Dalglish.

6 Tanya Turner Those who never watched *Footballers' Wives* just associate it with a character called Chardonnay but its heartbeat was really steely vamp Turner played by actress Zöe Lucker. Turner had got through three husbands, numerous lovers and a host of improbable situations (hermaphrodite babies anyone?) when the show was halted, to survive as undisputed Queen WAG.

7 Frankie Ray Winstone in the topical 2006 drama *All in the Game* as the sheep-skin-styled Premier manager connected to dodgy dealings over a star new player signing intended to help bankroll a new house. Winstone's angry effing and blinding style is what you'd expect if not even more over the top, so whilst interesting as a period piece this is no classic. Danny Dyer is his agent son Martin with Dyer's other footie assists including fan comedy *The Other Half* and hooligan flick *The Football Factory.*

TEN GREAT TV COMMENTARY MOMENTS

1 "Rivelino ... watch Pelé now – what a beautiful goal from Pelé – El Rai Pele!" In a career that spanned Molineux and the Maracanã, Hugh Johns erupts as Pelé leaps like John West's finest to put Brazil ahead in the 1970 World Cup final.

2 "Pelé, out to Carlos Alberto on the right ... and it's four! Oh, that was sheer delightful football!" Never mind all that overexposed stuff from 1966, Ken Wolstenholme never bettered his description of the climax four years on. They seemed to take it in turns to give an exhibition.

3 "And the goal by Astle ... and Leeds will go mad! And they've every right to go mad!" Referee Ray Tinkler waves offside West Brom on, Jeff Astle scores, Albion win 2–1, fans spill on to the pitch, Leeds lose the 1971 title by a point (don't laugh – oh, all right then, if you must), **Barry Davies** almost seems to encourage a riot.

4 "Radford again ... oh, what a goal! Radford the scorer, Ronnie Radford! And the crowd are invading the pitch!" Easily the most repeated clip after 1966, but one you never tire of seeing. Non-leaguers Hereford slay the Mags in 1972 as a youthful John Motson gets his big break. Small boys, parkas for goal-posts, enduring image, isn't it?

5 "Lee ... interesting ... very interesting! Look at his face ... just LOOK at his face!" Two great lines in one. Derby's Frannie Lee belts a screamer into the

Man City net in 1974. Barry Davies gets all ecstatic, and a little Aled Jones halfway through.

6 "Goals pay the rent, and Keegan does his share!" David Coleman raves over Liverpool's 1974 FA Cup final triumph, exclaiming at one point that "Newcastle were undressed!", conjuring a terrifying image of **Frank Clark** and **Bob Moncur**. Keegan two, Heighway one, Liverpool three, Newcastle none!

7 "Thomas, charging through the midfield ... it's up for grabs now!" It's just after 10pm on Friday 26 May 1989, and Brian Moore is on the mic as **Michael Thomas** wins the title for the Gunners in injury time. Recounted to Mooro by Arsenal-supporting cabbies until his dying day.

8 "Barnes, Rush, Barnes ... still John Barnes ... Collymore closing iiiiiiinnn! Liverpool lead in stoppage time!" Martin Tyler gives the Sky Sports lip-mic a real bashing as Stan the Man seals an extraordinary last-gasp 4–3 victory for Liverpool over Newcastle in 1996. Kevin Keegan slumps over a Carlsberg hoarding. He didn't love it.

9 "Can Manchester United score? They always score ..." Uttered by Clive Tyldesley spookily just before **Sheringham**'s equalizer ("Name on the trophy!") in the 1999 Champions League final in the Nou Camp, before **Ole Gunnar** put the ball in the Bayern net seconds later ("and Solskjaer has won it!") Mercifully, Clive has rarely referred to that night in the Nou Camp since.

10 "And Urzaiz is there, and here's a chance for the goal. And it's in! It's Alfonsoooooo! It ... it's unbelievable!" The European Championships always seem to bring out something special from Motty – like his throaty "Tigana! Platini! In the last minute!" in 1984 and "It's dramatic, it's delightful, it's Denmark!" in 1992. Here, Spain come back from 3–2 down in injury time to win 4–3 during Euro 2000, sending Motson into orbit.

NETBUSTERS

Given the way the Internet has fundamentally changed the nature of buying, say, music, you might have thought football had escaped the digital revolution largely unscathed. You'd be wrong. Although it'll probably be quite a while before players are bought and sold on eBay (which hasn't stopped some sarcastic fans from trying), the Internet has fundamentally changed the way that clubs communicate with their fans. It allows immediate dissemination of official information, which then travels at the speed of light across the net via message boards and mailing lists. Supporters, too, have organized mass protests and launched campaigns online. It has allowed a stake in Ebbsfleet United in the Blue Square Premier to be purchased by fans online at myfootballclub.co.uk and for those who pay their subscription to have a say in the club's affairs, leading one newspaper to describe it as a "magnificently chaotic democracy".

Today, every professional club must have its own site, yet for some that's a relatively new development. When the net was in its infancy during the mid- to late 1990s, fans' sites ruled the roost, trading in gossip and often highly critical of clubs. Chelsea liked one fan site so much they gave its web editor a full-time job. Slowly but surely, however, clubs woke up to the pressing commercial need for an online presence, and by the height of the dotcom boom, the Premiership was awash with official sites.

At one point Fulham's was valued at several million pounds, although the daily number of hits (and hence its perceived value) was distorted by fans desperate for news about their club's uncertain future. There was even a spot of dotcom fever – with start-up news site Soccernet sold to US giant ESPN for around £80 million.

Most official sites are now run by a handful of companies and tend to offer fairly standard information and added extras, the latest of which is goals and highlights packages. Email has allowed rumours to spread like wildfire, even forcing Arsène Wenger to officially deny one baseless allegation. The **League Managers Association** gave top managers laptops so they could enter the twenty-first century and email each other to transfer players, swap gossip about referees and complain about how slimy they feel after being "interviewed" by Garth Crooks.

Blogs became *de rigueur* post-millennium, and some professional footballers even embraced Twitter, with interesting results. In January 2010 a number of Premier League clubs strongly advised their players to give up their use of social networking sites as they had become another means of "embarrassing themselves" (along with camcorders and cameraphones, presumably). Sunderland striker Darren Bent was one of football's most enthusiastic tweeters, with thirty thousand followers. He stirred up controversy by using tweets to supposedly engineer his transfer to the club from Spurs. West Ham's **Danny Gabbidon** had to apologize to fans for appearing to criticize them in a tweet.

BEST FOOTBALL SITES

Football 365 (www.football365.com) Combines admirable irreverence with selected news coverage of the British game and entertaining fans' feedback.

Soccerbase (www.soccerbase.com) An online football encyclopedia to rival the mighty Rothmans – details of every player and every match can be found here.

E-soccer (www.e-soccer.com) The best repository of links, covering every UK club and more general sites.

Footballtransfers.co.uk (www.footballtransfers.co.uk) Does what it says on the tin: a repository of information about transfers, records and rumours. Not the most up-to-date site, but we love the speculation section – divided into confirmed and unconfirmed. Unconfirmed speculation?

The Rec.Sport.Soccer Statistics Foundation (www.rsssf.com) Statto's heaven – a massive archive of international and domestic football scores and scorers, rankings, various trivia and the odd argument about the merits of South American versus European football. Not a site to be visited if you have to get somewhere in a hurry.

TUBEWAY ARMY: FIVE FOOTBALL YOUTUBE ODDITIES

Since 2005, a YouTube search has become the first port of call for anyone wanting to find a clip of anything that has happened in football and is recent enough to have been captured on camera. It also offers limitless possibilities for those who fancy themselves as keepy-uppy kings or undiscovered talents to expose themselves to the ridicule of millions. Budding Spielbergs produce hundreds of slavish tributes to football stars with cheesy soundtracks, frequently blocked for copyright infringements, as well as endless "blooper" compilations compiled from bleached-out ancient VHS copies.

Worst Miss Ever YouTube is awash with worst misses but you have to look long and hard to find anything quite so disastrous as this effort from Kei Kamara of the Kansas Wizards against LA Galaxy. All he has to do is touch a goal line ball to score. Instead he manages to handle the ball he should be dispatching as he falls on his backside into the net. To be fair the ball was spinning but it is difficult to imagine how you could made a bigger mess of the chance. A priceless gift to rubbish players everywhere. **tinyurl.com/worstmissever**

Both Ends Burning Fifty seconds of sheer bathos, as Hans Jörg Butt, Bayer Leverkusen's goalie and penalty specialist, scores a spot kick against Schalke 04 in a 2004 Bundesliga match and makes his triumphant progress the length of the pitch. He reaches his goal just as the ball loops into the net, the referee, obviously tiring of watching Butt high-fiving every team-mate, quietly allowing the other side to kick off. **tinyurl.com/bothendsburning**

Off the Menu The TV documentary *Leyton Orient: Club for a Fiver*, deserves to be better known. John Sitton, embattled and increasingly unhinged manager, offloads his angst onto his baffled players in a series of deranged but strangely poetic rants. His rambling half-time team talk (also available) in which he refers hauntingly to "a man with a face like mine", squeezes in more f-words than

A Whole New Ball Game

There's nothing in the rules of the game to say that you have to wear shorts. It's a loophole that Brazilian team Roza FC are particularly grateful for. Roza are Brazil's leading – and possibly only – transvestite football team. Based on a dirt pitch just outside Rio, Roza play their derby game every year against a local team of married men. Why the other team should all be married isn't made entirely clear, but when their opposition consists of drag queens and the referee is dressed in red PVC, it'd obviously be churlish to ask.

It's taken Brazilian journalist Alex Bellos' description of the side in his book, *Futebol: The Brazilian Way of Life*, to bring Roza to a wider audience. Naming the referee as "Laura de Vision … a 20-stone silicone-enhanced club performer whose star trick usually involves lollipops, not whistles", Bellos describes some of de Vision's more dubious decisions, including the award of a penalty for "chatting up the centre forward". Even if his book also includes what must be the most surreal action photograph ever, depicting a svelte player in a blue mini-skirt dribbling past a significantly less svelte figure squeezed into an unforgiving sequinned dress, Bellos does have the good grace to take Roza seriously. Team captain Kaika Sabatela, a 36-year-old in a shocking pink catsuit, tells Bellos: "We work, we pay our taxes and we like watching football – why shouldn't we be allowed to play the game?"

Graham Taylor managed in two years. This clip contains the disintegrating Sitton's most cryptic outburst, in which he offers out two players and tells them to "bring your dinner". **tinyurl.com/clubforafiver**

Farley Good One of Darren Farley's spot-on impersonations of Benitez, Gerrard, Carragher, Owen and Crouch. Shot in a corner shop against a backdrop of cornflake packets, spaghetti and tinned veg by a mate who can't hold the camera still he's laughing so much. Farley's Michael Owen is uncanny. **tinyurl.com/farleyimpersonations**

Dirty Play Nine minutes fifty-six seconds of women and men playing football in Iceland in a muddy bog just slightly worse than most First Division pitches in the 1960s and 70s. One of the female teams appear to be dressed as brides; one lot of blokes might be moving towards cross-dressing with denim shorts and crop tops. Worth it if only for the inconsequential details: the goalkeeper trying to get up after making a save, the breathtaking scenery and a lengthy futile attempt to create a penalty spot. Claims to be a reply to "mud soccer in Finland and Russia". **tinyurl.com/icelandicmud**

IN THE BOOK

Blame **Billy Wright**. Merchandising and off-field activities were rare among footballers in the sedate 1950s, so the then-captain of England hit on a nice little earner by writing about his life and career in such tomes as *Football Is My Passport*, *Captain of England* and *One Hundred Caps and All That*. Wright's writings – and those of fellow stars like **Neil Franklin** and **Bert Trautmann** – were acceptable enough and sold well. Unfortunately, this gave rise to the regrettable idea that all players could, and should, put pen to paper. Some of these autobiographies even proved prophetic. Maybe the FA should have looked at Don Revie's autobiography as a player and wondered why it was called *The Happy Wanderer* before they gave him the England job and before he happily wandered off to the Middle East. **Malcolm Macdonald**'s effort *Not Afraid to Miss* is worth noting just for the honesty of the title; presumably Vladimir Smicer's memoirs would be called *Afraid to Shoot*.

The nadir was probably reached around 1998 with the publication of *My Story So Far* by **Alan Shearer**, a tome so devoid of character you could almost see it turning back into plant life. Chillingly, it's also available on audio cassette, read by Shearer lookalike Robson Green. Sample anecdote: "I was paying my extras bill at the hotel before we left for Highfield Road when a woman asked for my signature. I asked her if she would give me a minute while I settled my account. There was a query on the bill so it took a little longer than I expected. By the time I had finished, I had completely forgotten about the autograph-hunter and I left the hotel lobby without signing her book." Riveting stuff.

But if the old pros were bland, their books at least offered fans a glimpse into a private world rarely explored by the media. Tales of dressing-room camaraderie, lists of favourite opponents and such startling revelations as "I can't complain really, it's a smashing way to make a living" were what the public wanted.

Special mention should go to **Fred Eyre**, whose autobiography *Kicked Into Touch* (1981) became a surprise bestseller by virtue of its glamour-free grittiness. Eyre was a lower-division and non-league journeyman whose career was characterized by under-achievement, yet his very persistence and good humour endeared him to readers (although the two follow-ups detailing his career as a radio pundit and after-dinner speaker may have been pushing it a bit). **Len Shackleton** also entertained, entitling a chapter of his autobiography "What your average club director knows about football". The next page was blank.

> **"I have had the finger of blame pointed at me when the toes have been cut out of socks."**
> **Laugh-a-minute Alan Shearer**

Come the 1990s, however, newspapers had woken up to the fact that autobiographies were potentially a rich source of scandal, particularly among players coming to the end of their careers. A serialization became almost as important to publishers as sales of the book itself, and revelations came thick and fast. In *Rock Bottom* (1996), **Paul Merson** confessed the extent of his addictions, as did **Tony Adams** in the aptly named Addicted (1999).

Others have trashed managers or fellow pros, or even both (see Vinnie: *The Autobiography*). Some really overstepped the mark – Glenn Hoddle's notorious 1998 World Cup diary and David O'Leary's *Leeds United On Trial* were ill-advised, badly timed and almost certainly contributed to both men losing their jobs.

When real writers have done the writing and left the footballers to the, er, footballing, however, things have turned out rather better. The surge in middle-class interest in the game created a range of coffee table titles of dubious quality but has also contributed some modern classics to add to a burgeoning library.

FOOTBALL BOOKS – THE TOP TWENTY

1 *All Played Out*, Pete Davies (Jonathan Cape, 1990) Davies' journey to the World Cup in Italy saw him follow, and interview, the England team, pondering the nature of football, the savagery of the media and the pointlessness of John Barnes. He also came closer than any other author to pinpointing what makes being a fan so important. Davies' compelling prose betrays his love for the game, yet he also places it, subtly, in a wider sociological context, mingling with supporters as they run the gauntlet of the Italian police and experiencing the lows of semi-final defeat.

2 *Keane: The Autobiography* (Michael Joseph, 2002) Writer (Eamon Dunphy) and subject (the "driven bastard" Roy Keane) were a marriage made in heaven, both malcontents and mavericks, respecters of no reputations. Keane's exposure of the shambolic Irish 2002 World Cup campaign he walked out of, in his eyes amateurish and parochial (cheese sandwiches and potholed training pitches), caused enormous controversy and cranked up his feud with Mick McCarthy, whom he told to stick the World Cup "up his arse". His denunciation of his United teammates as "bluffers and bullshitters" resting on their laurels shattered the code of dressing room, though he didn't go as far as naming names.

3 *Only A Game?* Eamon Dunphy (Penguin, 1973) Reaching the end of his career and desperate for a first taste of genuine glory, Irish-born journeyman Dunphy charted a season with Millwall and the personalities, issues and disappointments that ensued. It could have been standard fare, but it became a classic, with Dunphy's ruminations on the nature of the game giving the average professional footballer an articulate voice for perhaps the first time.

4 *The Story of the World Cup*, Brian Glanville (Faber & Faber, 2001) Glanville is rightly revered as one of Britain's finest football journalists, and his regularly updated history is a chronicle of all that's right in the game, balancing an eye for detail with magical descriptions of stars and teams. Best bit: calling former Tory sports minister Colin Moynihan "small but imperfectly informed". His *Football Memories* ain't bad either – if you skip all the bits about his own literary efforts.

5 *Full Time: The Secret Life of Tony Cascarino*, Paul Kimmage (Scribner, 2000) A ghosted autobiography of beanpole striker Tony Cascarino should have been pretty uninspiring stuff, but the result was astonishing. The former Millwall journeyman reveals his failings as a husband, friend and footballer (despite winning sixty caps for Ireland, he wasn't Irish) with such candid detail that it's often almost too much to bear. Yet he also recounts the vices that stalk the game with a real intelligence and eloquence.

6 *Manchester Unlimited*, Mihir Bose (Texere, 1999) *Telegraph* journalist Bose has a nose for the cloudy world of football finance, and here he tells of the in-fighting and behind-the-scenes intrigue surrounding Manchester United's rise from mid-table mediocrity to richest club in the world. The best bit, however, deals with United lawyer Maurice Watkins' handling of Eric Cantona's FA disciplinary hearing following his infamous kung-fu kick: "Watkins heard Cantona, after apologizing to the FA, his fans, his team-mates and the club, say 'And I want to apologize to the prostitute who shared my bed last evening'. Maurice turned, his mouth fell open and he almost fell off his chair. Gordon McKeag, one of the three-man tribunal, turned to Geoff Thomson, the FA chairman and said 'What did he say? He prostrates himself before the FA?' 'Yes', said Thomson, eager to get away from the subject."

7 *Cantona: The Rebel Who Would Be King*, Philippe Auclair (Macmillan, 2009) At times bordering on pretension, always elegant and often provocative, this meticulously researched book comes closer to understanding the enigma of Cantona than any of his previous biographies. Written by an anglophile French singer and journalist (Auclair has been described as "the elder statesman of indie-pop" and is London correspondent for *France Football*), it references Velazquez, Derrida and "the absolute nothingness that lies beyond the pitch" in its analysis of Cantona's psychology and style. Auclair argues that Cantona has always been seeking a father figure and found him for a time in Alex Ferguson. And that the Frenchman invented the position of 9½, not an out-and-out forward, but more involved than a number 10, changing the shape of English football.

8 *The Rothmans Football Yearbook* (Headline) Not a novel, nor a warts-and-all autobiography, but the football fan's Bible (or, more accurately, their answer to *Wisden*). Since 1969, this fat volume has been compiling statistics, results, player details and fixtures from every echelon of the British game in a way that slimmer, less prestigious rivals could only dream of. A Great British institution. Now called *Sky Sports Football Yearbook*. Shame.

9 *Why England Lose: And Other Curious Phenomena Explained,* Simon Kuper and Stefan Szymanski (Harper Collins, 2009) In which it is proved it is player wages not big transfers that win trophies, that football makes fans happier (win or lose) and that England actually do perform to reasonable economists' expectations. Stimulating and well-written stuff marred only by the occasional smug pomposity beloved of pop economists. Called *Soccernomics* in the US, a better and more accurate title.

10 *The Ball is Round: A Global History of Football,* David Goldblatt (Penguin, 2006) The best one-volume history of global football and the spread of the game. Serious and seriously comprehensive at close to a thousand pages it is not without its quirky moments, but the emphasis on underlying economics from the get-go is generally sobering. You don't know football if you haven't read it.

11 *A Season with Verona: Travels Around Italy in Search of Illusion, National Character and Goals,* Tim Parks (Vintage, 2003) Literature professor and novelist Parks embeds himself with diehard travelling Verona fans to follow the unfashionable La Liga side for a year in their battle against relegation. A great book about international football fandom that does translate.

12 *Inverting the Pyramid: A History of Football Tactics,* Jonathan Wilson (Orion 2008) This story of tactics and formations is hugely revealing. Discover how the Scots invented the passing game, why modern play has made poachers like Michael Owen near redundant and how Europe responded to the innovation of Graham Taylor's pressing game.

13 *Futebol: The Brazilian Way of Life,* Alex Bellos (Bloomsbury, 2003) Great book on Brazilian football that is part travelogue, part history but always revealing about the world's greatest football nation. Could do with an update though.

14 *Brilliant Orange: The Neurotic Genius of Dutch Football,* David Winner (Bloomsbury, 2000) A real eye-opener about one of the great revolutions of the modern game: total football. Apparently (we kid you not) it was influenced by such things as architecture.

15 *The Keeper of Dreams,* Ronald Reng (Yellow Jersey Press, 2003) Strangely affecting story of nice-guy German goalkeeper Lars Leese's journey from footie obscurity to Anfield hero and back again in double-quick time. Barnsley fans will need no reminding of their former goalkeeper and their team's time in the spotlight – though the anecdotes about the local would-be WAGS photographing their genitalia to get his attention won't make it into the movie adaptation that should be made from it.

16 *When Friday Comes: Football in the War Zone*, James Montague (Mainstream, 2008) Egyptian derbies, Israeli hardcore hooligans and Syrian stars are all here in one of the world's most undereported soccer regions. One of the best of the genre of football travelogue which mixes the inevitable politics with local detail with aplomb.

17 *You'll Win Nothing with Kids: Fathers' Sons and Football*, Jim White (Little Brown, 2007) In Russia the expression to support a football team roughly translates as "I suffer for …". Parents on the touchline on a wet Sunday morning watching their offspring and mates trail 8–0 to the local bully boys may be able to relate to that way of putting things. Jim White's well-written and amusing misery memoir reflects all the ups and downs of the game at its lowest levels. Deserves to kick off a whole new genre.

18 *Feet of the Chameleon: The Story of African Football*, Ian Hawkey (Portico, 2009) Pelé's prediction may have hexed an African team's chances of winning a World Cup but the presence of its footballers on the world stage continues to grow from strength to strength. Touching on tragic air crashes and crazy fans, apartheid and voodoo, journalist Hawkey travels the continent uncovering what makes its football heart tick and the sad, inspiring reality behind the export of African players.

19 *My Father and Other Working Class Football Heroes*, Gary Imlach (Yellow Jersey Press, 2006) Biography of Scottish winger and professional footballer of modest renown written by his son. Back in the 1950s and 1960s players did not call the shots and the going was not so good. Or was it? Probably the best and most heartfelt of a new wave of disenchanted but openly nostalgic football books.

20 *Provided You Don't Kiss Me: 20 Years with Brian Clough*, Duncan Hamilton (Fourth Estate, 2007) The necessary antidote to David Peace's cod hard-boiled mutation of the Cloughie legend *The Damned United*, subsequently made into a rather better film (see p. 180). Hamilton displays the "warts and all" of the original special one whilst crediting the complementary genius of Peter Taylor.

FIVE OF THE WORST

1 *David Beckham: My Story/My World* (1998/2001, Hodder & Stoughton) Ah yes, the snipers are already saying, but young David is a footballer, not an author, so leave him alone. In which case, thc reply must come, don't write books then. These two volumes reduce every high and low in the footballing oeuvre to the most bland and easily digestible of emotions. When Glenn Hoddle has lambasted our hero in the World Cup, for example, he tells us: "You just have to get on with it", while winning the title is "great". Most of the dust-jacket quotes praise the photos without mentioning the prose – wonder why?

2 *Sweeper!/Striker!/Defender!*, Steve Bruce (Paragon Press) While on holiday during his brief tenure as Huddersfield Town boss, Bruce put pen to paper to create the first of three seminal tales of intrigue and mystery at, ahem, Leddersfield Town. In them, manager Steve Barnes (formerly of Mulcaster United) must clear up a calamitous series of deaths and disasters, while also writing alarmingly short sentences: "A shiver ran down the length of my spine. And I'll tell you what. It wasn't because of the influenza virus." Sadly, Bruce is too busy keeping Sunderland in the Premiership to pen the follow-ups, *Midfielder*!, *Winger*! and *Utility Man*! Still, literature's loss is football's gain.

3 *Lovejoy on Football: One Man's Passion for the Most Important Subject in the World*, Tim Lovejoy (Century, 2007) Self-regarding, self-indulgent drivel from Lovejoy, who decided to write a book to commemorate leaving the *Soccer AM* show. There are no less than 38 photographs of Lovejoy, memorably described by one critic (Taylor Parkes, in a brilliant review for *When Saturday Comes*) as sporting "fashionably receding hair and a voice oddly reminiscent of Rod Hull". In it he manages to defend the indefensible throughout: the Glazers, "that Thai bloke at Man City" while revealing his woeful ignorance about football. As Parkes said, this book is the illustration of "a startlingly small mind".

4 *My Story So Far*, Alan Shearer (Hodder & Stoughton, 1998) Let's just remind ourselves again: "I have been described as England's Captain Clean but I hate the public image that I am too good to be true. My team-mates will tell you I love a laugh and a joke the same as everyone. I've been known to take part in a few dressing-room pranks. I have had the finger of blame pointed at me when the toes have been cut out of team-mates' socks."

5 Any book on football violence One of the worst excesses of the rise in football "literature" was the money suddenly thrown at reformed hooligans to tell all about their time on the wrong side of the law. Dougie and Eddy Brimson, who have now stretched their collective oeuvre to over a dozen titles, are the worst, but they're far from being the only offenders.

FANZINES, MAGAZINES ... STUFF LIKE THAT

Ever since the first footballing pioneers started kicking a pig's bladder around, fans have had an overwhelming urge to read about the thrilling heroics of their idols. The earliest publication in the British Library's football collection is *The Goal: The*

Chronicle of Football, from 1873, which lasted just 22 issues. For the next 75 years or so, titles came and went, like 1882's imaginatively named *Football*, which managed 28 editions before being merged with the equally excitingly titled *Pastime*, as well as *Football Bits* in 1919 and *The Football Favourite* in 1920.

But football magazines didn't really take off until after World War II, and the arrival on the bookstands of Charles Buchan's *Football Monthly*, masterminded by the eponymous former England international-turned-journalist. The first issue in September 1951 cost 1/6 and featured a hand-tinted Stanley Matthews on the cover. At its peak, in the early 1960s, the magazine was selling 130,000 copies a month.

By the turn of the decade, however, the magazine, with its whiff of liniment and baggy-shorted ethos, suddenly found itself up against tricky new rivals more in tune with the era of George Best and the King's Road. *Goal* launched in August 1968, promising pages of colour, personalities and revealing, hard-hitting exclusives ("'No, I'll Never Start Playing Like A Fairy', says **Tommy Smith**"). And decades before *Footballers' Wives*, *Goal* trained the spotlight on our heroes' other halves in a series of weekly portraits ("Life can be hectic for a soccer star but that doesn't worry Marilyn, 20-year-old wife of **Billy Bonds**").

Shoot! hit the newsagents in 1969, yours for one shilling, with founding columnist Bobby Moore starring on the first cover. That premiere issue featured the debut of a perennial *Shoot!* free gift, the League Ladders – a cardboard ready-reckoner enabling fans to keep track of the League ups and downs via the medium of fiddly cardboard tabs. Inside, *Shoot!*'s big attractions were the star columnists. Back then, you knew you'd really made it when you were snapped up to put your name to a ghosted *Shoot!* column. Sales leaped tody fifty thousand when George Best signed on the line, and **Keegan**, **Dalglish**, **Shilton**, **Gray**, **Rush**, **Nicholas**, **Barnes** and **Gascoigne**, among others, followed in his wake. Meanwhile, "You Are the Ref" tested readers' grasp of the laws of the game ("or (c) an indirect free-kick?").

And there was the legendary "Focus" page, probing the likes and dislikes of the stars, and prompting a generation of impressionable young fans to yearn for the footballer's lager-and-lime lifestyle of *The Sweeney*, scampi, George Benson and Bo Derek. **Frank Worthington** declared his Most Difficult Opponent to be "my ex-wife" while the person **Uli Stielike** most wanted to meet was "the late President Sadat of Egypt". Oh, and commiserations to self-confessed *Daily Star* reader Gary Lineker, who never quite fulfiled his post-career ambition to be "a bookmaker, hopefully".

Other titles from the 1960s and 1970s included *World Soccer*, launched in 1960 and still frighteningly comprehensive today, the dour *Soccer Star*, *Jimmy Hill's Football Weekly*, *Inside Football* and *Striker*. *Football Monthly* responded to the competition by dropping the Buchan name from the cover and campaigning for "Champagne Soccer", rewarding teams who scored six goals with a magnum of bubbly for the supporters' club – not much incentive for the players, surely? In 1974, the magazine adopted a *Reader's Digest*-style A5 look, but the game was up, although the title managed to limp into the 1990s under a succession of titles, owners and formats.

> **"He's nice, who's he? David Beckham? I'll go up to Manchester then, we can have dinner afterwards."**
> **Victoria Beckham opens her heart to *90 Minutes* magazine**

The late 1970s brought the Marshall Cavendish partwork *Football Handbook*, edited by Martin Tyler with "consultant" **Graham Taylor** and building up over 63 weeks into a big pile of magazines. In 1979, *Shoot!* gained a rival in the shape of clone *Match Weekly*, but the football recession of the 1980s meant that there were few launches, save for the weighty-but-pretentious *Soccer International*, and *Football Today* for the parka and Thermos brigade. But in the wake of Heysel, Hillsborough and the spectre of membership cards, the rise of the fanzine at last gave supporters a more readable alternative to the glossies.

The first fanzine was probably *Foul*, a sort of footballing *Private Eye* published by Cambridge undergraduates between 1972 and 1976. The torch was rekindled in the mid-1980s by the Midlands-based *Off the Ball*, *The Absolute Game* in Scotland and the best-known of the lot, *When Saturday Comes*. In their wake came an avalanche of inky bedroom-published 'zines devoted to clubs from top flight to non-league, spearheaded by Bradford City's *City Gent*.

Even if the content wasn't always particularly original, it was passionate, and at its height the movement boasted a magnificent array of titles: Gillingham's *Brian Moore's Head Looks Uncannily Like The London Planetarium*, Crewe's *Super Dario Land*, WBA's *Grorty Dick*, Blackburn's *Four Thousand Holes* and the *Leyton Orienteer*. Since their heyday in the 1990s, many fanzines have disappeared, while some survivors have their own websites, where subscribers can post on message boards. Football message boards proliferated. A lack of editorial control meant anyone with a keyboard was free to post what they wished. This was democracy gone wild. The 2000s was the decade of the self-appointed cyber warrior, the internet know-it-all hiding behind a pseudonym and dispensing abuse and caustic – usually appallingly spelt – views. With knee-jerk reactions aplenty, players were heroes or zeroes according to their last game and no reputations were spared. One thread entitled "Fuck off Giggs, you wage thief. If you never pull the shirt on again I won't be upset", appeared on a Manchester United website in November 2007.

Giggs won the Premiership and Champions League Cup later that season. And, given his excellence in his maturing years, the Sports Personality of the Year in 2009.

This was mild compared with the message boards for some clubs, with directors requesting that their detractors revealed themselves. Sheffield Wednesday's board went further by instigating legal action against one ultra-critical website

The influence of the fanzines inevitably filtered into the mainstream, exemplified by *90 Minutes*, launched a few weeks before Italia '90 and finding a niche as a sort of fanzine-equivalent of *Shoot!* that kids and *NME* readers alike could read. Highlights included a prescient **Gordon Grenville** interview with the **Spice Girls**. (Victoria: "Ooh, he's nice, who's he? David Beckham? Oh, I'll go up to Manchester then, we can go out for dinner afterwards!")

FourFourTwo arrived in 1994, somehow surviving showing Jimmy Hill in a football kit on the cover, followed the following year by *Total Football* and a relaunched *Goal* from the *90 Minutes* stable, and in 1997 the BBC weighed in with *Match of the Day* magazine. But even though football was more popular than ever, the rise of the Internet, wall-to-wall TV coverage and countless newspaper supplements sated the appetite of potential readers, and all the adult titles bar *FourFourTwo* and the nichier monthly *When Saturday Comes* went to the wall. Even *Shoot!* ceased popping through the letterbox as a weekly in 2001, lingering on only as a monthly.

COMICS

"Oh I say … that is *Schoolboy's Own* stuff!" Barry Davies had it right when he exploded with delight at Paul Gascoigne's extraordinary free kick for Spurs in the 1991 FA Cup semi-final. But for the best part of five decades, improbable feats like Gazza's were performed week in, week out in the pages of the comics, in an alternative footballing universe where scrap metal dealers kept goal, magic boots made kids play like Johan Cruyff and Melchester Rovers never, ever lost …

Billy's Boots (*Scorcher/Tiger/Roy of The Rovers*) "Is this me or is this Dead Shot Keen?" was the catchphrase of Billy Dane as he bore down on goal – a fact noted by Half Man Half Biscuit on the album *MacIntyre, Treadmore and Davitt* (named after Michael Palin's Barnstoneworth United team in *Ripping Yarns*, natch). Dane had somehow acquired the boots that had belonged to 1920s hotshot Keen, which magically enabled the otherwise talentless adolescent to play like him. Naturally the boots were discarded with frustrating regularity by Billy's gran (like all comic teens, he was an orphan) who kept giving them to jumble sales or tossing them onto bonfires. The inspiration for rubbish footyflick *There's Only One Jimmy Grimble.*

Billy The Fish (*Viz*) Fittingly, in these post-modernist times, this strip in adult comic *Viz* was a send-up of the more ludicrous elements of "Roy of The Rovers". Billy the Fish, half man, half fish, sporting a mullet (naturally), kept goal for Fulchester Rovers, who boasted invisible striker Johnny X, a scantily dressed Native American female winger, Brown Fox, and had a Martian as chairman. When Billy is killed saving a penalty in the FA Cup final, even though he knows the ball has been booby-trapped with a forty-pound bomb, no-nonsense managerial buffoon Tommy Brown, later revealed to be a woman in drag, declares, "Whenever man may gather to talk of football or fish, they will toast the name of Billy Johnson". "Thomson, boss", corrects trainer Syd Preston. Billy is later replaced by his identical son, also named Billy who in one memorable episode, has to choose between flying to Australia to have sex with an unfeasibly large-breasted Kylie Minogue or playing against Maradona, new signing of rivals Rossdale Rovers.

Gorgeous Gus (*Wizard/Victor*) Our aristocratic hero in this 1960s strip was the, er, Earl of Boote, who bought the ailing Redburn Rovers after they failed to score in their first four games of the season. He was christened Gorgeous Gus by the fans because of his distaste for tackling and running – he simply expected his team-mates to set him up with chances which he'd blast into the net. Once Rovers had established a commanding lead, Gus would retire to a special area on the touch-line, where he would be attended to by his butler Jenkins.

The Hard Man (*Roy of The Rovers*) This told tough-tackling tales of Johnny Dexter, a sort of **Terry Butcher** figure forever in trouble with the footballing authorities and blessed with the ability to perform perfect headlong diving headers, as only comic footballers can. Dexter's gaffer at Danefield United was Viktor Boskovic, an Eastern European of uncertain origin who predated the current vogue for foreign coaches by at least a decade and looked a bit like Fred Elliott off Corrie. Dexter later spun off into a new story, "Dexter's Dozen", before winding up at the mighty Melchester Rovers.

Hot Shot Hamish (*Tiger/Roy of The Rovers*) Hamish Balfour, a Herculean striker with a blond mullet, was brought from a tiny Hebridean island to play for Princes Park in the Scottish League by manager Mr McWhacker. He had a pet sheep called McMutton. In later seasons, when *Tiger* merged with *Roy of The Rovers*, he teamed up in a Butch-and-Sundance-style double act with rotund footballing hospital porter Mighty Mouse.

Iron Barr (*Spike/Champ*) The star of this was giant Charlie "Iron" Barr who, you'll be amazed to learn, worked as a scrap metal dealer when he wasn't playing in goal for Darbury Rangers for free (he preferred to remain amateur for some bizarre reason). He once scored from his own line, and on another occasion dribbled the length of the field to put the ball in the net. Later handily signed for United when *Spike* merged with *Champ*. He also had his own column, "Iron Barr's Sports Round-up".

Jack of United and **Jimmy of City (*Score and Roar/Scorcher*)** The adventures of two brothers playing for rival clubs in the same city provides the storyline here. The square-jawed Jack was the more reliable **Bobby Charlton** figure of the two, while Jimmy was the glamorous maverick **Stan Bowles** type. Each had their own strip every week, with a neat "crossover" element.

Limp Along Leslie (*Wizard/Hotspur*) Talented youngster Leslie Thomson was involved in a car accident as a child which, naturally, killed both his parents, and rendered his left leg shorter than the right. Now he lived on Low Dyke Farm with his Aunt Lucy and Uncle Arnold, and was torn between his two ambitions – to play for the mighty Darbury Rangers or to train his sheepdog Pal into a champion. Scored brilliant curling free kicks.

Mike's Mini Men (*Roy of The Rovers*) Teenager Mike Dailey owns a Subbuteo team called Redstone Rovers. Er, that's it. On the "Billy's Boots" principle, they got nicked or lost every three weeks.

Mi££ionaire Villa (*Roy of The Rovers*) This one's a bit of a rip-off of "Gorgeous Gus", with millionaire David Bradley giving Division One club Selby Villa £2 million on condition he plays in the first team. Possibly the inspiration for Michael Knighton's takeover bid and keepy-uppy exploits at Old Trafford.

Nipper (*Scorcher/Tiger/Roy of The Rovers*) The enduring story of Nipper Lawrence – you've guessed it, a young orphan who played for Blackport Rovers – outlasted the rest because Nipper was just that bit more human than his rivals, cursed as he had a quick temper. Had a dog called Stumpy.

Roy of The Rovers (*Tiger/Roy of The Rovers*) Far and away the most celebrated football strip ever, "Roy of The Rovers" was conceived for the launch of *Tiger* in 1954 as a more down-to-earth hero than Dan Dare, star of *Tiger*'s sister comic *Eagle*. Devised by Frank Pepper, the story originally focused on the teenage Roy Race's battle to make the big time. Established in the Melchester Rovers front line alongside Blackie Gray, Roy set about winning everything in the game, invariably bringing him into conflict with nasty cheating foreigners and the odd jealous team-mate.

The late 1970s and 1980s brought a touch more realism, with Roy no longer scoring a hat-trick with his left-foot rocket every week. He even married secretary Penny in 1976, the year Roy's own comic was launched. In 1981 Rovers were relegated, and Roy was shot by actor Elton Blake. Two years later, a restless Roy resigned to manage Walford Rovers, but returned within months. Bizarrely, in 1985 Martin Kemp and Steve Norman of Spandau Ballet were briefly recruited to the Rovers squad after impressing in a charity match, a move which coincided with the beginning of the end. Despite (or perhaps because of) storylines which included half the team being blown up by terrorists, the comic's popularity waned; it closed in 1993 as Roy lost his left foot in a helicopter crash. In four decades, Roy had won the League 10 times, the FA Cup six times, the European Cup three times, scored 436 goals and even briefly managed England.

The Safest Hands in Soccer/Goalkeeper (*Roy of The Rovers*) For five years "Safest Hands", beautifully drawn by Osvaldo Torta, followed the daring deeds of No.1 ace Gordon Stewart, who played for Tynefield City and Longford Forest before being killed in a car accident. Twelve months later, "Goalkeeper" picked up the story of his talented teenage son Rick, and his attempts to emulate his dad at rival clubs Tynefield United and Oakhampton.

Tommy's Troubles (*Roy of The Rovers*) Tommy Barnes and his trusty best pal Ginger Collins were just mad about football. But guess what: they only play rugby at Crowhurst Road School! Realizing this might result in a somewhat truncated football story, Tommy sets about assembling his own extracurricular soccer team, Barnes United. Lasted a good ten years, this one.

We Are United (*Champ/Victor*) This was an excellent attempt at putting a more realistic spin on the "Roy of The Rovers" formula. Manager Joe Pearson was the man attempting to revive sleeping giants United, aided and abetted by mohicaned punk winger Hedgehog Jones, mercurial Welsh striker Terry Evans and later, that man Charlie Barr. The story neatly followed the season's actual fixture list, whereas it seemed to take Melchester a month to complete one game. Pretty good, all told, even once dabbling with a hooliganism storyline, when a bunch of Pringled-up casuals affixed themselves to the club.

MEMORABILIA

"For sure, continuations of negative campaigns may well see the club relegated, and one would have thought that nobody or no groups of people would be as futile, self-centred or indignant enough to place themselves in a position where they consider they are more important than the well-being of the establishment" (Brief) extract from the programme notes of Colin Murphy, former Lincoln boss

Before football clubs took memorabilia to the extreme with the mandatory club shops and new strips every few months, ticket stubs, programmes and playing kit were the stuff of the most avid fans' collections. The British are without doubt the biggest spenders on memorabilia. While the French and Italians stick to competition medals and team badges, the Brits are often unconcerned whether they're buying sought-after collectibles or simply junk.

Programmes were once the core memorabilia items. Age and scarcity tend to add to market value, though the passing years are unlikely to add greatly to the desirability of that Raith Rovers v. Brechin City programme you kept from that far-off childhood holiday. Ticket stubs, meanwhile, have recently increased in value. Anyone who went to the 2002 World Cup is advised to put their tickets in a safe place if they want to secure a large payout.

The value of signed items varies widely. An autographed pair of boots used by Beckham or Owen sounds like a dream purchase to a Manchester United or Liverpool fan. Unfortunately, unless they were used in a prestigious event, you're unlikely to reap much in the way of monetary rewards, simply because both are still playing and the market could be flooded with similar items.

Finally, aim for originality when you're putting together your collection. Official mascot postcards issued for the 1966 World Cup, for example, fetch up to £50 today, collectors viewing them as unusual and prestigious enough to warrant that kind of money.

MOST VALUABLE MEMORABILIA

1. **Oldest surviving FA Cup (1896–1910)** Sold for £478,000 in 2005, the world record price for any football memorabilia at auction.
2. **Alan Ball's 1966 World Cup winner's medal** £164,800, also a world record price for a football medal at auction.
3. **Yellow Brazil shirt worn by Pelé in the 1970 World Cup final** The hammer finally fell at £157,750, another world record price for a shirt.
4. **Gordon Banks' World Cup winner's medal** Fetched £124,000 in 2001.
5. **Red England shirt worn by Geoff Hurst in the 1966 World Cup final** Sold for £91,750 in 2000.
6. **England World Cup 1966 international cap** Sold at Christies for £37,600 in 2000.

MOST SOUGHT-AFTER FOOTBALL PROGRAMMES

A 1999 survey claimed that football fans across Britain were hoarding £15 million worth of memorabilia, a figure that would reach over £30 million by 2003. Much of that money was tied up in programmes, for years the preserve of anorak-clad ground-hoppers but more recently the plaything of the richer fan, willing to pay handsomely for that rare collectible, with anything involving Manchester United worth considerably more than average.

The first known programme was produced for a Preston North End v. Derby County fixture in 1893, but no copies remain. As a rule, pre-war programmes are collectors' items, worth the extra expense as an investment. A 1966 World Cup final programme could set you back around £400 and will continue to increase in value, partly because not enough copies were printed and partly because England don't look like repeating that success.

Programmes from the past twenty years are usually worth little more than the cover price, and often less, but those in the know advise that it's always worth looking out for anything slightly unusual. Last-minute postponements are a particular favourite – if a game is called off with just hours to go, the programmes will already have been printed but rarely go into circulation.

1. **Tottenham Hotspur v. Sheffield United, FA Cup final, 1901** At £14,400, it's the dearest programme ever sold at an auction – commanding five times its reserve price.

2. **Scotland v. England, 1897** The oldest international match to come to auction, fetching £6000.
3. **Manchester United v. Wolverhampton Wanderers, 1958** The match that was never played due to the Munich air disaster. Although the programme was printed and then pulped, a few copies got into the hands of fans and now fetch around £1000.
4. **Any pre-war FA Cup final** £500–£2,000
5. **1966 World Cup final programme** £300–£500

WORST PIECES OF OFFICIAL MERCHANDISE

In the pre-*Fever Pitch* days, it was considered shameless corporate exploitation to try and flog your fans a training top. Souvenirs were basic – scarves, photos, badges and rosettes – displayed in cramped, shabby sheds big enough for only five punters at a time. But then football clubs started floating on the Stock Exchange and club directors slowly realized the potential income to be squeezed from the loyal supporter. Car stickers, mugs and pens became pyjamas, slippers and bedspreads. Manchester United opened an Old Trafford Megastore which made Harrods look like a corner shop. They also became one of the first clubs to introduce a branded credit card, so that even the money you spent on the club was owned by the club. Still, it's hard to argue that a nodding-head Ryan Giggs isn't the sort of item any self-respecting car owner would treasure.

Manchester United mortgage Your home may have been at risk if you defaulted, but you did get a free subscription to MUTV. Now it's the club which is struggling to keep up the repayments.
Arsenal dog collar £7.50 & dog coat £18.50 It's a dog's sporting life. Make Fido's misery complete with a Gunners-themed restraint and cover.
Liverpool FC tax disc holder £1.50 Insert your own joke about car ownership and Scousers.
Celtic Huddle Curtains £29.78 For when Rangers are playing at the bottom of your garden.
Rangers Frilly Ladies Garter £6.99 The Ultimate Contraceptive?
Fulham baby bibs £5 Until surprisingly recently, the Fulham club shop sold infant items with a graphic of a smiling house and the embarrassing motto "I'm A Little Cottager"...

GAMES

"So he'd send his doting mother up the stairs
To get Subbuteo out of the loft

He had all the accessories required for that big match atmosphere
The crowd and the dugout and the floodlights too
You'd always get palmed off with a headless centre forward
And a goalkeeper with no arms and a face like his
And he'd managed to get hold of a Dukla Prague away kit
'Cos his uncle owned a sports shop and he'd kept it to one side"

So runs "All I Want for Christmas Is a Dukla Prague Away Kit", a nostalgic tribute to *Subbuteo* by Wirral punks **Half Man Half Biscuit** that will strike a chord with anyone who grew up in the 1970s or 1980s. Young boys have always followed football obsessively, so it's no wonder that board games manufacturers fought tooth and nail to capture a potentially lucrative market.

Striker was a smaller, five-a-side version of *Subbuteo* where you pressed players on the head to activate a kicking mechanism. *Cup Final* consisted of two teams with three players – a goalkeeper who could throw (and score, if you were well practised), a "chipper" with shovel-style feet, and a "shooter", who kicked along the ground. There was also the inexplicable dice game *Wembley*, and *Supercup Football*, with ice-hockey-style twisting players controlled by dials. This led on to standard table football, which has recently enjoyed a renaissance (perhaps due to its urban-cool factor after appearing in the TV *Friends* apartment), but strangely remains more popular in French bars than here.

For the more cerebral, there were basic management games. Terry Venables invented and endorsed his game *The Manager*, a management exercise "for all ages and two to four players". In true El Tel style, the player making the most money – rather than winning the most honours – won. Other efforts like *Emlyn Hughes' Team Tactix* came and went.

But conquering the lot for playability, value for money, a realistic looking set-up and teams to collect and keep, was *Subbuteo*.

The pitch, either original baize or Luton Town-style astroturf, would be laid out on a carpet, or if you were lucky, the kitchen table. Under *Subbuteo*'s surprisingly strict rules, only the nail part of the finger was permitted to make contact for "the flick", but various methods of cheating soon became apparent, from melting down and stretching the goalkeeper's arms to furniture-polishing player bases for extra glide. At least one player would inevitably be trodden or knelt on during every game, and the throw-in men rarely functioned properly, but *Subbuteo* still became an obsession for many, who would log results in their schoolbooks with incredible dedication, even staging *Subbuteo* versions of major tournaments in bedrooms across the land.

Some people never grew out of the fascination, and *Subbuteo* is now a highly collectible alternative for grown men who would really like a train set but are too afraid to ask their partner. One of the best aspects of *Subbuteo* was the massive range of accessories – from stadiums to floodlights, from ball-boys to miniature trophies – that were entirely superfluous to the actual game itself. Having crowd trouble? Simply deploy a policeman, or install crowd-control barriers. There was a cameraman in the stands to catch it all, and at the end even a mini-Her Majesty the Queen to present the tiny FA Cup. The possibilities were endless.

> **"As a boy in the 1960s, Subbuteo was all you had. That and Barbarella ... and here, with a Barbarella-style haircut, comes Ray Parlour."**
>
> Jonathan Pearce in full flow, 2002
> *90 Minutes* magazine

Then there were goalkeepers on plastic control rods, number transfers so you could identify players individually, linesmen, corner flags, athletics tracks to help create a European feel and different tournament balls. One enthusiast even went as far as to manufacture streakers for use in competitions. Don't laugh – if a streaker was on the pitch, play would stop until your opponent flicked a policeman close enough to make an arrest. You could waste vital seconds.

That's even before you get to the different teams. Fancy a crack outfit in the 1970 Haiti kit? It's available – at a price. How about the Boston Minutemen? Landskrona, Antwerp, Hartford Bicentennials, Admira Wacker, Wisla Krakow, the Port Vale away kit ... they're all here, and you'll never own the lot, even if you visit car boot sales daily for the rest of your life. Three black players were belatedly added to all English sides in 1987 to reflect their proliferation in the real-life game (the French national side had boasted coloured stars as early as the 1970s); in 1992, there was a bold, but ultimately unsuccessful, attempt to have *Subbuteo* made an Olympic sport.

Unsurprisingly, there's a big Internet community devoted to *Subbuteo*, and even a magazine called *The Flicker* for the real devotee. The manufacturers branched out into snooker, rugby, baseball, speedway, hockey and – at a particular nadir – even angling, but nothing can top the original and best game. It has seen off many rivals, and remains popular even in the era of PlayStation, X-Box and Nintendo, even though it's no longer being manufactured and exists merely as memorabilia. Up to the loft, mother ...

COMPUTER GAMES

In April 2003, *Championship Manager 4* shattered all video-game sales records by shifting 124,627 copies in its first week after launch alone. The extraordinary popularity of *CM*, a game so addictive it has been cited in three divorce cases, highlights just how far getting your football fix via keyboard or joystick has come since the 1970s, when prehistoric monochrome *Pong*-style TV games were as good as it got.

The 1980s saw the rise of Atari, promoted by Trevor Brooking with the help of Morecambe and Wise, and a tidal wave of affordable home computers like the Spectrum and Commodore 64 washed up a surfeit of soccer games. Footballers and their agents weren't slow to recognize the lucrative potential of a superstar's signature on the box, although for every *Emlyn Hughes' International Soccer*, there was a *Peter Shilton's Handball Maradona!* or a *Gary Lineker's Super Skills*, which involved Leicester's favourite son performing press-ups, weightlifting and squat thrusts. Oh, and let's not forget *Jack Charlton's Fishing*.

In the 1990s, football gaming became a huge industry, with series such as *FIFA* and *International Superstar Soccer* battling for dominance on the new generation of consoles, led by the PlayStation. Ultimately though it was Konami's *Pro Evolution Soccer* and *FIFA* that have become the Apple and Microsoft of football-player-centric computer games with much of the world divided into one of two camps even as the two offerings gradually improved and converged, in terms of quality. *Football Manager* and close relative *Championship Manager* were to rule the roost in terms of manager games. It wasn't always this way, though.

Football Manager The original. Not to be confused with the later game of the same name. It sold a million and made a cult hero of creator Kevin Toms, the bearded boffin who appeared on the box. In this godfather of the management genre, you played the sheepskin-clad boss of a Division Four team, wheeling and dealing your way to the top of the League. It might look primitive now, with its animated matchstick highlights, but its gripping gameplay and the inclusion of authentic teams, cups and players was a revelation in 1982, even if the price tags might have been a touch unrealistic (Kevin Keegan for £5,000?). Toms is still working on new app incarnations of his brainchild for a variety of platforms.

Match Day The first really successful attempt at an arcade-style football sim, *Match Day* hit the shelves in 1985 and sold by the shedload. It offered a 3-D view of the pitch, smooth animation and maximum playability, although you couldn't foul the opposition, much to the frustration of armchair Terry Butchers everywhere. And it played the *Match of the Day* theme at the start. *Match Day 2* arrived in 1988 and managed to be even better.

Peter Shilton's Handball Maradona! File under blatant rip-off. Funnily enough, this appalling game featured neither Peter Shilton nor Diego Maradona. In effect, it was a goalkeeping sim, of all things, and thus proved to be the video-game equivalent of the hopeless kid who always had to go between the sticks down the park every Saturday morning. No cups, no leagues – all you had to do was save four shots in a row to move up a skill level.

Emlyn Hughes' International Soccer It's 1988 and with *A Question of Sport* in its pomp, even Princess Anne can't escape the bejumpered clutches of the perma-chuckling "Crazy Horse". Perfect fodder for a timely cash-in, then, except this one was actually quite good. Neatly combining management and arcade genres, *International Soccer* enabled you to fine-tune your team on the practice pitch before taking on the computer or your mates.

Footballer of the Year Neither a management game nor an action sim, this 1986 release and its sequel allowed you to work your way up from a seventeen-year-old apprentice in the nether regions of the League to become the country's best striker and, well, "Footballer of the Year". You did this by memorizing tactics and hence scoring goals, answering trivia questions and – here's the realistic bit – gambling cash. Not bad, all told.

Microprose Soccer Was based on the American indoor league of the time for its six-a-side variant. Heralded at the time for its swerving shot capacity and a rudimentary action replay feature, it was swiftly superseded by Sensible Soccer.

Brian Clough's Football Fortunes A predictably idiosyncratic effort, this managerial challenge was a bizarre hybrid of computer and board game. Team-building involved the usual ducking and diving, with added obstacles thrown up by the toss of the dice. Fun enough, even if scenarios like your two star strikers being killed in a car crash seemed a little unnecessary. Green sweatshirt optional.

Subbuteo Exactly what the point was, nobody's quite sure, but in 1991 a computer adaptation of the flick-to-kick tabletop perennial was released. Sure, it meant that your precious Dukla Prague star striker no longer faced being flicked under the settee, but the interminable take-it-in-turns gameplay (translated faithfully from the original) undermined the big match atmosphere somewhat.

Sensible Soccer *Sensi*, as its devotees called it, seized the crown from *Match Day 2* in 1992, despite competition from the popular *Kick-Off* and its sequels. Both incorporated a bird's-eye view of the pitch, but while *Kick-Off* might have allowed you to put bend on passes and shots, *Sensi* was the first arcade release to boast those all-important real teams and be fully customizable. More improvements and tweaks throughout the 1990s, including the addition of ear-bashing commentary from Jonathan Pearce, extended its reign. Fans of a retro sensibility had high hopes for a 3-D revival in 2006 but many were disappointed. Can still be found on hand-held, online and iPhone or Xbox live.

Hooligans: Storm Over Europe Basing games on fan experience has not really caught on, with one notorious exception. Presented as a darkly humorous strategy game, reviewers found little comedy in *Hooligan's* weak AI, not to mention the concept of leading a gang of stereotyped soccer thugs through a football season rife with extreme violence, drug and alcohol abuse – and looting. Maybe it should have been called *Senseless Soccer*?

FIFA The first *FIFA* game appeared in 1994, and since then the series has undergone a succession of facelifts and taken on a battalion of rival titles like *Actua Soccer* and the *International Superstar Soccer/Pro Evolution* dynasty. The rise of the

PC and the PlayStation in the 1990s enabled programmers to take the action game to new levels in terms of graphics and realism, even if *FIFA*'s commentary team of Des, Motty and Andy Gray wasn't quite authentic. **Blur**'s "Song 2" blaring out of *FIFA '98* was pretty cool, mind. In the wake of *FIFA*'s success, there was a scramble to produce official UEFA and Premiership games but pleasingly, they didn't sell, because despite the brands, they weren't much cop. Numerous other FIFA spin-offs continued to emerge including the much advertised street soccer variety, though the core game has always remained the main draw. Graphics apart, *FIFA* for long retained the tag of official but uncool cousin to Pro Evolution with inferior game play and stunning but wooden-looking players until 2009 when the new version received rave reviews for its improvements and it belatedly forged ahead of its rival amongst the few remaining neutrals.

Pro Evolution Soccer A lack of presentational gloss, dodgy names for unlicensed players and clubs and the gaping absence of the entire Bundesliga still haven't quite reversed the loyalty of *PES* die-hards for this other of the big two player focused games. Appearing first in 2001 as *Winning Eleven* from Konami in Japan and thereafter under a variety of names in the US, fans have always valued the game's difficulty and intuitive feel for a hard-fought contest that after days of playing can still yield wholly surprising goal variants. Though if there is one thing that could still turn hard-bitten *PES* addicts to *FIFA* it would have to be Mark Lawrenson's maddening analysis about just about everything. So repetitive. So true to life. So unnecessary.

Championship Manager and **Football Manager** The *CM* series was nothing short of a phenomenon. Devised over five years by brothers Paul and Oliver Collyer, the first edition of "Champo" was released in 1992, with 2003's *CM4* smashing all sales records. Extraordinarily realistic and vast in its scope, it's based around a database of hundreds of thousands of real players from around the world rated by fans themselves. Star devotees included **Ole Gunnar Solskjær** and Rangers' **Michael Ball**, who had to sell himself because he was asking for too much money. Managers have even used it to assess foreign players before signing them, although *CM* superstars like Everton's **Ibrahim Bakayoko** and Derby's **Tonton Zola Kokuoko** sometimes proved less successful in reality. In 2005 the name Championship Manager was retained by publishers Eidos who developed afresh a new competing game to the original that had to be rebranded *Football Manager*. The latter was produced by decamped developers Sports Interactive who retained rights in the underlying computer code thingy and so began a two-horse race in the manager game stakes which has narrowed in recent times, with *Football Manager* just retaining an edge despite numerous *Championship Manager* innovations such as monthly downloadable news updates in addition to the credibility-enhancing inclusion of some of the English lower Leagues. Both games have proved to be time-sinks of a magnitude even Subbuteo never aspired to be.

FASHION

"I was the first man in Britain", declares **Frank Worthington** in his candid autobiography *One Hump Or Two?*, "to own a tank top." The wayward striker's bold claim speaks volumes about the long, shameful relationship between footballers and fashion. Handsomely paid, and with too much time on their hands, players have always had the chance to model the latest threads.

While the results can be impressive, they usually aren't. Serial offenders are numerous, but first into the fashion police's cells would be the likes of **Barry Venison** (leather cowboy ties, chessboard jackets, completely straight face) and **John Barnes**, who has sported a variety of garish monstrosities that even Graham Norton would reject as too outlandish.

It all started, inevitably, in the 1960s. As television made national stars out of local heroes, the more flamboyant footballers found themselves lining up alongside pop groups as fashion icons. George Best led the way, opening a boutique in Manchester and modelling roll-necks, flares and suits with his fifth-Beatle looks. Best's main rival in the fashion stakes was Peter Osgood, the Chelsea forward and Kings Road dandy. The dapper forward always had the latest tailoring, and his style even attracted actress and sex symbol Raquel Welch. "Osgood epitomized swinging London as much as David Bailey or Paul McCartney", reckoned Chelsea chairman Brian Mears.

Mike Summerbee managed to run a high-quality bespoke tailors (with Michael Caine and, later, Sylvester Stallone, as clients), but others had less success, notably Malcolm Macdonald's Newcastle store – called Malcolm Macdonald – and Kenny Dalglish's menswear shop, Dalglish. **Terry Venables** invested, too, but the 1970s and 1980s were pretty much a write-off fashion-wise, summed up by dodgy perms, tracksuits and Kevin Keegan's massive collars (it was perhaps inadvisable for Kev to start his own range, but he did anyway).

You'd have thought a suit would help avoid derision, but even this wardrobe staple (usually kept handy for court appearances) can go wrong. Liverpool's hideous cream Armani '96 Cup final outfit confirmed the side's reputation as the "Spice Boys", a triumph of appearance (though certainly not style) over substance. Several players had modelling as well as football contracts – David James' Armani gig just topping Jason McAteer's work for Head & Shoulders. Even a tie can cause offence – **Wayne Rooney**'s skewwhiff kipper at the BBC *Sports Personality of the Year* awards led to uproar from Middle England.

Then there's the omnipresent **David Beckham**: a one-man ongoing fashion revolution, with triumphs sitting equally alongside terrible disasters. Highlights to date include wearing a sarong, nail varnish and his wife's underwear; endorsing Brylcreem and then immediately shaving his head; and inspiring a generation to get mohican, spiked and plaited haircuts. And that's before you get to his huge contracts with Police sunglasses and Adidas, and his much imitated, ever-growing collection of tattoos. He's even been credited with putting men in touch with their feminine, grooming-friendly sides.

Thierry Henry's "first" fashion collection, launched in 2007 in collaboration with designer Tommy Hilfiger, was an unsurprisingly elegant mixture of classic suit jackets and casual staples, in subdued colours. But the heir to Beckham was undoubtedly **Cristiano Ronaldo**, the new metrosexual man, who indulged his love for flashy leather, hot colours and bling in his CR7 boutique, which he opened with his sisters in Madeira. Ronaldo's darkly handsome Mediterranean sultriness and ripped torso made him the perfect replacement for Becks in his kecks as poster boy for Armani underwear, though his crotch is considerably less prominent than David's much-flaunted protuberance. The days when footballers had simple tastes – for snooker, *Minder* and tank tops – seem long gone, and nobody can predict quite what will be beckoned in next. One thing is for sure, though: it's unlikely to be tasteful.

THE WORST FOOTBALL KITS OF ALL TIME ...

Coventry City, 1978–81 Brown is a colour synonymous with the 1970s, when it principally adorned sofas, lampshades and wallpaper, but was still rarely seen on football shirts. Coventry City broke the mould and committed a double faux pas by including double white stripes which ran up the shorts and onto the shirts.

Brighton & Hove Albion, 1987–90 Brighton's blue-and-white striped kit has always had the overall air of the Tesco carrier bag, as many opposing fans have noted to their amusement. The 1987-era kit was particularly cheap-looking and bag-like, and saw the indignity completed by the inclusion of the sponsors' name – stationery firm NOBO. Some fans took self-deprecation to new heights by actually donning a Tesco bag with holes cut in for arms. Attempting to make amends, the daring 1991–92 away shirt was a memorable red-and-white combo which, as fans pointed out with a by-now weary disdain, resembled a Chewits wrapper.

Arsenal, 1990–91 Accurately compared to a bruised banana, the infamous black splodges on Arsenal's yellow change shirt must have seemed like a novel idea at the time, but it struck about as much fear into the opposition as Everton's salmon pink change shirts a few years later.

Hull City, 1992–93 Hull City are nicknamed the Tigers, and their marketing department – who presumably didn't really understand this new-fangled football thing – decided a tiger-striped shirt was therefore in order. The result was universally mocked – and ultimately disappointing, as touching the shirt revealed it to be made of cotton rather than fur.

Norwich City, 1993–94 The Norfolk side's yellow-and-green ensemble had worked well for decades, but tradition counts for nothing when madmen are let loose with the colours, and the result in the 1993–94 season was a yellow background with loud, random green splodges. So keen were the club to avoid a similar disaster that in 1997 they had designer Bruce Oldfield come up with something a tad more refined.

... AND THE BEST

Peru, 1970 A diagonal red stripe on a white shirt with white shorts, it seemed to symbolize the attacking football played by Teofilo Cubillas and masterminded by their coach, the Brazilian great Didi. It was later adopted, to less effect, by Crystal Palace, when the club, with such alumni as Vince Hilaire on their books, tried to become the Team of the Eighties. There's still the 2080s ...

The Science
DNA, Multiple Regressions and
the Magnus Force

◀◀ Previous page: Applying the Magnus Force. David Beckham (front) celebrates with team-mate Emile Heskey after scoring a curling free-kick equaliser against Greece in the dying seconds of the final group qualifing match at Old Trafford, Manchester, October 2001.

The Science

F = 1.5 x D3 x f x V newtons – where D is the diameter of the ball in metres, f is the spin frequency of the ball, and V its velocity

The mathematical formula behind the perfect David Beckham curling free kick

BORN NOT MADE?

As our most miserable poet laureate Philip Larkin almost said, they really screw you up, your mum and dad. One of the hitherto unremarked-upon ways they foul things up is by not being footballing geniuses. As naïve eight-year-olds kicking the ball around the back garden, we all dreamed of scoring that winning goal in an FA Cup final but, sadly, for many of us it was already too late. There is a growing body of statistical and scientific evidence to suggest that, as the Finnish sports scientist Per-Olof Astrand says, if you want to be a sporting legend, you have to pick your parents wisely.

This is not to say that you should give up just because your mum didn't play for Doncaster Belles and your dad's idea of fancy footwork is kicking the cat. It's just that if your family could put the gene into footballing genius, the odds are slightly more likely to be in your favour.

It's at this point that you're probably stifling a yawn thinking that the clichéd story of the **Charlton** dynasty is about to rear its head once again. The Charlton/Milburn story is probably the most conspicuous example of family footballing talent (nine league players in the same branch of the family, three of whom became full England internationals and one an England B international) but the point is perhaps as convincingly illustrated by looking at the beautiful game's most beautiful team: **Felix**, **Carlos Alberto**, **Brito**, **Piazza**, **Everaldo**, **Gerson**, **Clodoaldo**, **Rivelino**, **Jairzinho**, **Tostao** and **Pelé**.

The Brazilian team of 1970 was so ludicrously talented, it seems impertinent to try and trace the roots of their footballing genius. Pelé, particularly, seemed one of a kind. But he only became a footballer despite his mother's opposition; she regarded his chosen profession as "somewhere beneath bank robbery". She didn't want him to fail like his father, Dodinho. After starring in the local football team in the town of Tres Coracoes, Dodinho signed for the Belo Horizonte club Atlético Mineiro only to tear his knee ligaments on his debut. He returned to his hometown club and extended his playing career by the dangerous expedient of packing his knee with ice between matches. His son still loyally says of him: "He was my first coach. He taught me how to trap the ball with either foot. He would have been a great player but for the injury." It is doubtful if even paternal pride would enable Pelé to say the same about his own son **Edinho**, jailed for manslaughter in 1999, who kept goal for Santos for two years.

Although Tostao, aka the White Pelé, came from a comfortable middle-class background, his father played amateur football for a Belo Horizonte club so it was no great surprise when Tostao and his four brothers all played for local youth sides. Roberto Rivelino's father, Nicolino Rivelino was, in his son's loving words, "full of shit. He says he was a great player, but they called him The Horse." Rivelino Snr insists this nickname was a compliment and that he turned down a deal with a big club because the money they offered wasn't as good as his salary at the telephone company. Gerson, the side's playmaker (who even in the Mexican heat always lit a fag at half-time), had a father and an uncle who played professionally for clubs in Rio, while two of Carlos Alberto's brothers struggled in the lower echelons of the Brazilian game.

The more biographies of famous players you examine, the more family ties to the game you find. **Michel Platini** was a second-generation footballing genius (his dad Aldo was captain of the local side AS Jouef in which junior made his debut), **Uwe Seeler**'s father played for Hamburg, as did his elder brother Dieter, **Mathias Sammer**'s dad Klaus won 21 caps for the GDR and **Ruud Gullit**'s dad George played international football for Surinam. You can add to this vaguely contemporary pan-European list the **Cruyffs**, the **Maldinis**, the **Inzaghis**, the **de Boers** and the **Laudrups**.

Michael and Brian Laudrup are of particular note because their childhood was dominated by spherical objects. Father Finn was a Danish international in the 1970s and their mum Lone was a professional handball player, while Michael's son Andreas joined Amsterdam side AFC a few years back. (Among the other players whose family history includes other sporting skills are **Ryan Giggs**, whose father Danny Wilson played rugby league for Wales and **Gustavo Poyet**, whose dad was a basketball professional.)

But is there anything beyond a pile of anecdotal evidence? The obvious way to solve this argument – compulsory DNA tests for all PFA members – seems a tad unrealistic. But an analysis of the professional footballers in a recent PFA handbook found 37 famous sons, 40 famous brothers, 6 famous cousins and 1 famous great-grandson. The pick of the bunch is not **Gary** and **Phil Neville** (even if they were the twentieth set of brothers to play for England) but Derby County's goalkeeper **Stephen Bywater**. Signed as a teenager for up to £2.3 million from Rochdale, young Steve is the fourth generation of Bywaters to keep goal. His great-grandfather plied his trade for Aston Villa, his grandfather Leslie for Huddersfield and Rochdale and his dad, David, for Halifax. Yet taken together, these dynasties only represent about 4 percent of the talent registered to the PFA and besides, scientists will say, even if 72 Charltons had played for England this wouldn't prove footballing skill was inherited.

It wouldn't because geneticists still argue how much of what we are is down to nature or nurture. There is also the undeniable fact that having, say, **Frank Lampard** as your dad gives you a head start. "By the time Frank and **Jamie** [**Redknapp**, Frank's cousin] were six or seven, you could see they had good touch on the ball and the fact they came from a football environment meant they picked up things quickly", said Lampard Snr. "As a father you want them to improve and as a coach you're more aware of what they should be doing." Shaun Wright-Phillips, the stepson of Ian Wright, has undoubtedly benefited from Ian's tutelage, even if he has not inherited his footballing genes. Ian's biological son, Bradley Wright-Phillips, has not been as successful as his step-brother. Gavin Strachan, Kaspar Schmeichel and Alex Bruce are just some of the sons whose famous fathers have promoted their careers as well as passing on their skills. Darren Ferguson not only followed his famous father's footsteps into playing football, but into management, as has Nigel Clough.

The state of the current debate is summed up by Professor Dave Collins, head of sport at Edinburgh University, who says: "All of these things only mean that people have the potential to go on. You also have to consider opportunity and tradition." Scientists have begun to identify specific genes which may influence sporting behaviour but each new study needs to be treated with caution as many headline claims for various genes have soon been rubbished. A growing band of psychologists are also redefining human intelligence in ways that might lead them to trace skills like spatial awareness to certain parts of the brain.

If football is a game of gene rummy, not everyone gets a winning hand. Imagine how poor old Joel Cantona feels looking at brother Eric's career and thinking: "Hey, there but for a tiny bit of genetic code go I." Other famous sons have ended up looking as if they're a few links down the football evolutionary chain from their dad. The saddest case (yes, sadder even than Sam Shilton) is probably **Stefan Beckenbauer**. When Stefan was a kid, his dad's mate Helmut Schoen came around one day and watched him kick the ball around. "You see Franz", said the German national coach, "the boy is football crazy. What a pity you weren't that crazy about football when you were a boy." Unfortunately, Stefan's rare combination of football craziness and the most famous surname in German football couldn't hide the fact that his career never really got any better after he'd signed on for Bayern Munich as a trainee. Father Franz did the decent thing and paid for his boy to join newly promoted Saarbrucken in 1992, but after two years which saw the club relegated again, Stefan rode off into German football's equivalent of a Western movie sunset.

THE MAGNUS FORCE

No doubt about it: **David Beckham** is a master of non-linear differential equations. Just think about that curling free kick he sent past the Greek defence from thirty yards out in the World Cup qualifying match in June 2001. While the rest of

On Their Knees

The next time you hear of a star player being sidelined by unspecified "knee problems", a call to the *News of the World* may be in order. A London medical student identified sexually acquired reactive arthritis (SARA) as being widespread among footballers – and because diagnosis is difficult, it often ends careers. The virus which causes the condition is sexually transmitted and is far more prevalent among sportsmen than ordinary members of the public, with footballers the worst culprits. This isn't particularly surprising – one club doctor reports that when asked if they have had sex recently, most players take this to mean "in the past couple of hours".

us were making paper darts and playing hangman in maths class, Beckham, D. was getting to grips with the finer points of Reynolds Numbers, Magnus Forces and drag coefficients (and no, before you ask, that's got nothing to do with being persuaded to wear your wife's underwear).

Of course, like all geniuses, Beckham didn't do his swotting in something as conventional as a classroom. He picked up his equation-solving tricks by booting a ball a few million times. For while any smart-aleck physicist can write down the equations governing the dynamics of the Curling Kick, actually getting them to work during a real match is another matter. Like all the great dead-ball players of our time – Carlos, Figo, Zola, Zidane – Beckham wisely eschewed hours in theoretical physics classes in favour of years of trial and error on the pitch.

For those of us who'd be glad just to get a ball to travel in a straight line, there's still some advantage in mugging up on the physics behind such amazing shots, as it gives an even greater appreciation of the skill of these players. What they're doing is little short of miraculous, optimizing three different forces, two of which change constantly while the ball is in flight.

The first force is the most familiar: gravity. Nothing too complicated there, as it stays constant. The second is much trickier to deal with. Known as the Magnus Force (after H.G. Magnus, a German physicist who first investigated its properties about 150 years ago), this is the force directly responsible for curling the ball off its normal trajectory. Unless a ball is kicked dead-centre, it always spins slightly as it flies through the air. As one side of the spinning ball is thus moving in the direction of flight while the other side turns away, there's a difference in the relative speed of the air on either side of the ball. That, in turn, creates a pressure difference which forces the ball to curl as it flies. The rule is: kick right-of-centre to give the ball an anticlockwise spin, and it will curl to the left.

It sounds simple, except that getting the ball to curl isn't enough: it must curl by precisely the right amount, and that depends not only on the spin-rate, but also on

Roberto Carlos takes a freekick, Le Tournoi de France, 1997 – Brazil v. France.

the speed of the ball through the air. The force of the kick has to be perfectly judged, so that it optimizes both speed and spin-rate.

With a bit of practice, even your average Sunday clogger has some chance of getting a ball to curl past a keeper every now and again. The real skill comes when there's a defensive wall to beat as well. Then the maestros show their mastery of the third force involved in the curling kick: aerodynamic drag. Like the Magnus Force, the drag force changes with the speed of travel. The trouble is, it does so in a much more complex way, making it harder to control. Worse still, its strength critically affects the size of the Magnus Force, and thus the way the ball curls.

The obvious way to cut through all this is just to hit the ball with the same force every time, and focus on getting the spin-rate right. But to a dead-ball genius confronted by a defensive wall, the drag force offers a handy way of fooling both the defenders and the goalkeeper at the same time.

Struck off-centre and hard – say, over 70mph – the ball starts off flying wide of the wall, with little drag and no obvious hope of going in the net. The defenders relax and the keeper rolls his eyes in contempt. But as the ball slows, the drag increases rapidly, which in turn boosts the Magnus Force, making the ball curl ever more swiftly. All of a sudden the keeper finds the ball curling in towards him, then towards the far post; and before he can get anywhere near it, it's gone in.

Back-of-the-envelope calculations show that the swing from 25 yards out can exceed five yards, well over half the width of the goal-mouth. It has to be seen to be believed, and Beckham's impressive effort was far from the most extraordinary demonstration of the effect. That accolade belongs to **Roberto Carlos** of Brazil in the pre-World Cup Tournoi match against France in June 1997.

Slicing the ball with the outside of his left foot from 35 yards out, Carlos sent the ball spinning at 85mph to the right of the defensive wall. It seemed so far off target that the ball-boy standing to the side of the goal ducked. But as the ball slowed, the magic of the Magnus Force revealed itself. Spinning anticlockwise, the ball curled left at an ever-faster rate and shot into the net.

Cristiano Ronaldo's "dipper" free kick, which he has nicknamed "the tomahawk", has added a new twist. The Madeiran peacock has shown he is more than just a pretty face with his manipulation of the laws of physics. Rather than altering the ball's axis of spin to bend it like Beckham, his technique aims to eliminate as much spin as possible. Modern footballs lose up to forty percent of their speed after impact. By hitting the ball slightly to one side with his instep, possibly exploiting the seam pattern and the laces of his own boot, the ball suddenly dips, while losing none of its speed.

THE OFFSIDE CONUNDRUM

You can always spot real football aficionados: they're the ones who can identify a dodgy offside decision faster than Motty. For while even maiden aunts can tell the difference between a foul and a dive, only true fans get into a lather over the geometrical relationship between three blokes and a ball.

They have much to get into a lather about: recent research suggests that assistant referees make errors in as many as one in five offside decisions. That's a pretty high failure rate for something that can affect the outcome of a multi-million pound event like a Premiership fixture. But before you fire off a note to the FA querying its policy of hiring the illegitimate and visually impaired to act as assistant referees, grab a couple of pens and try the following little experiment.

Hold a pen upright in each hand, and line the pens up at arm's length, so that one is hidden behind the other. Now, imagine that hidden pen is **Wayne Rooney** on a run from left to right, and the pen closer to you is **John Terry**, playing the offside trap. Clearly, from where you're looking at them now, they're right in line, and so Rooney is onside. But keeping the two pens dead still, just move your head slightly to the right. As you now see it, Rooney appears to be to the right of Terry – that is, closer to the goal-line. Of course, he's really still in line with Terry, yet he appears to be just offside. In other words, only an assistant referee who's exactly in line with the players involved in an offside decision can call it reliably. If he's closer to the goal-line and therefore looking backwards at the action, he's more likely to get it wrong.

In a study published in 2000 in the prestigious science journal *Nature*, Raoul Oudejans and his colleagues at the Free University of Amsterdam showed that assistant referees were indeed slightly ahead and looking backwards at the key players in ninety percent of offside decisions. They weren't out of line with the players by very much – just a yard or so – but experiments proved it was still enough to lead to the flag being raised far too often.

There's more. Using video analysis of real matches, the researchers also found that when the action was taking place close to the assistant referee, a striker attempting an outside run against a defender was more likely to get the benefit of the doubt. Again, the pen experiment shows why. Line the pens up close to your eyes, this time with the defender hidden behind the striker. Keeping the pens still, move your head right, towards the goal-line. The defender now appears to the right of the striker and thus closer to the goal-line. That means the striker can be quite a way forward of the defender before he'll seem obviously offside.

This shows quite clearly that strikers should try to make their runs along paths that put them closer to the assistant referee than the defenders. That way, they'll be able to exploit the optical effect found by the scientists, and, in theory at least, get the benefit of the doubt from the assistant referee.

THE DISMAL SCIENCE

Back pages used to be covered with stories about football. You know the game: not the stuff about salary bills as percentage of club turnover, debt ratios, administration orders and dodgy oligarchs rumoured to be licking their lips at the prospect of a piece of Notts County. No doubt about it, football economics has made it centre stage.

It was Scottish writer **Thomas Carlyle** came up with the phrase "dismal science" for economics and though he wasn't probably thinking about non payment of player's wages or Setanta defaulting on payments to the SPL, the word dismal in relation to football and economics isn't altogether inappropriate. In the past soccer has not featured high on the agenda of economics but that seems to be changing. In 2009 journalist Simon Kuper and economist Stefan Szymanski in *Why England Lose and Other Curious Phenomena Explained* (*Soccernomics* in the US) came out with the first mainstream tome applying lots of "multiple regression" analysis to all sorts of issues. Lots of statistics in other words.

What were their conclusions? They prove for instance that the England does "just fine" in relation to population and other factors like income and the team's results in World Cups are no different from what you'd expect with a flip of the coin. Just indifferent luck in other words. At club level they prove that football is one of the worst businesses in the world. Because? Clubs cannot convert more than a fraction of fans love of soccer –the passion, the gossip –into profits, and most of the money they do accumulate goes into player wages the scale of which prove to be *the* key factor in a team's success. (Not as it turns out the total transfer fee spending, though the two aren't unrelated of course).

The news isn't all bad. Because clubs have a monopoly of local fans loyalty, so the survival rate of clubs – despite all the losses and recent collapses – remains very high compared to nearly any other type of enterprise. Indeed the very idea that such a low-turnover business can make money is probably over-ambitious. The sensible model should not be FTSE 100 companies but "museums" – community organizations that serve the public whilst operating around breakeven. Neither should countries expect to acquire great riches from hosting a football tournament. Study after study has proved that the much-touted economic bounce is illusory. Politicians know not what they do, but may still be right to lobby for the big competitions. Why? For the fact that during tournaments, host-nation populations get happy – even if the anticipation of one tends to trigger a slight downturn in national mood. Similarly heartening is the authors' conclusion that football in general makes you happy. Suicide rates for men a*nd* women fall whenever their is a big tournament on – when everyone, they speculate, is brought into the national conversation and there is a tad more togetherness. Even winning proves not to be so crucial as this general increase in social cohesion.

And what of the game itself? Penalty takers should follow a "randomized mixed strategy" which means hitting them well to both sides in no particular order. England players take note. And that means *under* the bar and *between* the two posts. Unsung Norway is apparently the most football-mad nation in the World based on enthusiasm and numbers of supporters for population. Likeliest new winners of the World Cup outside Europe? Not as **Pelé** predicted an African team, but China, Japan or the USA. Turkey and Australia aren't bad outside bets for the big prize. either.

Now you know!

FOOTBALLERS' DIETS

"It's not good if they've had two vindaloos and a kebab"
Iain Dowie.

"Grilled broccoli?"
Ian Wright takes exception to Arsène Wenger's diet revolution at Highbury.

The importance of diet in ensuring peak performance has always been recognized, although exactly what constitutes ideal nutrition for footballers has varied dramatically. **Stanley Matthews** in the 1930s and 1940s was considered eccentric for his insistence on light meals with little red meat, which he regularly vomited up anyway before games – even though he played until he was 55. Raich Carter swallowed six sugar lumps for energy before taking the field. Most footballers went for bulk. Newcastle's 1950s hero **Jackie Milburn** stoked up on "the miners' favourite", steak and kidney pie, and enjoyed a few cigs at half-time to settle his nerves. Bobby Charlton, along with others, knocked back a small sherry or whisky to help his breathing. Without restaurants or cooks at football grounds, players usually made for the local greasy spoon café. Until the late 1960s, in those innocent pre-cholesterol-count days, "official" pre-match meals consisted of steak and chips, until nutritionists warned that it took 24 hours to digest.

Although the influx of foreign coaches into British football is credited with revolutionizing attitudes to diet, Alex Ferguson had already banned steak when he arrived at Old Trafford in 1986 and employed dieticians. Pasta became the new religion, carbs and vitamins the new commandments. The ascetic **Arsène Wenger**, fresh from Japan, and "the best diet in the world", advocated "boiled vegetables, fish and rice. No fat, no sugar", shuddering with distaste at dressing rooms awash with tea and fatty cakes and biscuits. Not all professionals have embraced the new creed wholeheartedly. According to Gerard Piqué, at Manchester United:

> Everyone ate what they wanted and when you take into account the English diet you can imagine what I am talking about. Every 15 days they would put us on what we called the "spare-tyre machine" to measure our body fat. You would be amazed at how many top players practically broke the machine because their diet was based on beer and burgers.

Junk food devotee Wayne Rooney's shopping basket once famously contained 28 bags of crisps.

The Twilight Zone

Where Adolf Hitler rubs shoulders with Maradona as Lord Nelson looks on

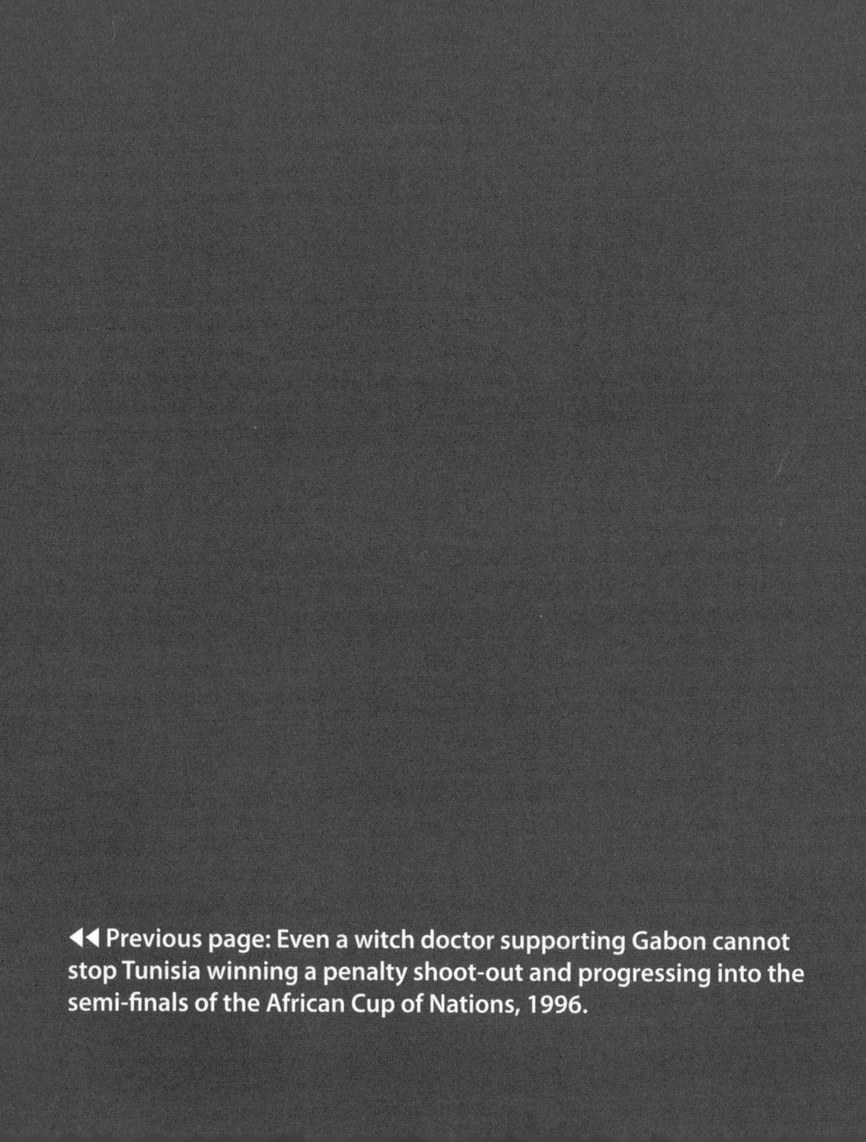

◀◀ Previous page: Even a witch doctor supporting Gabon cannot stop Tunisia winning a penalty shoot-out and progressing into the semi-finals of the African Cup of Nations, 1996.

The Twilight Zone

"Football – it's an old, funny game"

Gianluca Vialli reinvents the cliché

TOP FOOTBALLING GHOSTS

Ghost Lady Elizabeth Hoby
Ground haunted England's HQ, Bisham Abbey
This lass is said to slip out of her portrait (which hangs in the great hall) and go off for a walk whenever it takes her fancy. She died in 1609 and her ghost is believed to be constantly washing her hands, perhaps in **David Beckham**'s bathroom – well, if you had a choice of basins … Anyway, many of the England squad say they have seen her or felt her presence. The Sunday tabloids have yet to run a kiss-a-ghost-and-tell so maybe she's keeping a few stories up her medieval sleeves for when she needs some quick cash. She's permanently sorrowful, which some say is because one of her six children died after she locked him in a tiny room and forgot about him.

Ghost Fred
Ground haunted Boundary Park, Oldham
Legend, or at least word, has it that a loyal fan, perhaps called Fred, who always stood in the same place and died during the 1960s, does stuff that freaks people out. Or maybe he just gets in the way – after all, there's not much room between seats in the stands these days and he must wonder where he's meant to go.

Ghost John Thomson
Ground haunted Celtic Park
Thomson was a goalie who died in a collision with a Rangers forward in 1931. He may be a figurative rather than a literal ghost, but he is celebrated for his bravery by the Celtic faithful in his own song – "Between your posts there stands a ghost".

Ghosts The White Horse & Herbert Chapman
Ground once haunted Highbury
Supernatural sounds abounded at the former Arsenal Stadium. A horse died during the construction of Arsenal's North Bank – builders these days, they're all cowboys – and apparently he neighed during crucial games. He must have been loud. Apparently the great manager's footsteps could be heard walking through the marble halls. How anybody knew they were his footsteps remains undisclosed.

Ghost Lord Nelson
Ground haunted Bloomfield Road, Blackpool
The admiral haunts Blackpool's boardroom. Not because he was a Blackpool fan who was aggrieved at a transfer, but because the panels in the room were apparently constructed from wood from one of his flagships. The club labrador occasionally goes all funny and barks at the walls, a sure sign that England's greatest one-eyed war hero is looking for his bunk.

Ghost Unknown
Ground haunted The Old Show Ground, Scunthorpe
The ground vacated by Scunthorpe United in 1988, in favour of their new purpose-built accommodation at Glanford Park, is said to reverberate at night to the sound of the thud of leather on leather and rustling goal nets. Anyone know any of the Iron squad of 1988 who haven't been seen for a while …?

Ghost The Bee Hole Boggart
Ground haunted Turf Moor
Nasty goings on in Burnley where a malevolent goblin or boggart lurked close to the Clarets' home. It once kidnapped an old woman, "Old Bet", leaving her skin on a rose bush. Boggarts are hairy, squat and smelly so they'd blend in perfectly in the average football crowd.

FOOTBALL AND RELIGION

"God's footballer hears the voices of angels above the choir at Molineux", sings folk-rocker Billy Bragg in "God's Footballer", about the career change of footballer-cum-Jehovah's Witness **Peter Knowles**. In 1970, Knowles, aged 24 and on the verge of an England call-up, swapped scoring goals for Wolves for door-to-door soul-saving. Apparently he feared his temper would get the better of him and he'd put someone out of the game. Truly the Lord works in mysterious ways. Knowles is not alone in embracing religion having previously been fully immersed in the world of professional football (a fact that maybe says something about football's inherent insignificance in the great scheme of things).

For one there was **David Icke**. Former Coventry and Hereford keeper Icke worked as a journalist, TV presenter and a Green Party parliamentary candidate before famously appearing on the Terry Wogan chat show in 1991 to proclaim he was the Son of God and cataclysmic flooding and earthquakes were imminent. Icke seemed surprised that nobody took him seriously. His turquoise shellsuit didn't help. Nowadays he tours the globe, lecturing and selling books, the focal point of his theory being that the world is run by a shape-shifting reptilian elite.

Danish European Championship winner (1992) and Luton Town record signing (1989) **Lars Elstrup** quit football to join the Wild Goose Buddhist sect in 1993, changing his name to Darando (which translates as "the river that streams into the sea"). A little while afterwards he was arrested in Copenhagen for flashing. Elstrup attempted a football comeback and still plays in Danish amateur leagues, though "finding inner truths and to get more contact with Self and God", still takes up a serious amount of his time.

In 1999, **Carlos Roa** stunned Real Mallorca by announcing that, at thirty, he was quitting football for God. He had become a Seventh Day Adventist Church pastor and the former Argentinian international retreated to a mountain farm to await the Apocalypse, scheduled for the new millennium. When the end of the world discourteously declined to show up, however, Roa reappeared on the football scene and went looking for a new club.

Brazilian superstar **Kaka** frequently advertises his faith on the pitch, stripping off his shirt to reveal a T-shirt emblazoned with the message, "I Belong to Jesus". He may have been inspired by his fellow countryman, Junior, who, during a brief, but electrifying spell at Walsall FC, unveiled his own version, "Jesus Lives in Walsall". Shirt-lifting of this type at the 2009 Confederations Cup brought the Brazilian squad into conflict with FIFA, who reminded them that the display of religious, political and personal slogans is banned. **David Beckham** has found a neat way to get round the prohibition, with a 2010 tattoo of Christ sitting on a cross on his chest, along with the two "religious" tattoos on his back.

Football is full of people who believe in various gods – but not many players can boast that they are a religion. Step forward **Diego Maradona**, who has inspired a hundred-member-strong church of "Diegorian Brothers" who hold his autobiography as their bible, celebrate Christmas on his birthday and have rewritten the calendar – AD (After Diego) begins in 1960, the year he was born.

DICTATORS

Football is said to be the opiate of the masses – and, as such, a pretty useful way to exert mass control over the proles. Throughout history, dictators have recognized the dark power of the beautiful game, though their forays into the sport haven't always entirely gone to plan.

Witch Doctors

"We are no more willing", announced the Confederation of African Football (CAF) in early 2002, "to see witch doctors on the pitch than to see cannibals at the concession stands. "With that bold statement, issued at the African Cup of Nations finals in Mali, did the continent´s governing body seek to draw a line under a topic that had, said CAF, contributed to a "third-world image" for the African game.

Superstition exists throughout football, everywhere. In Africa, you just hear the best stories about it. Call it "juju", "muti", "voodoo", "wak", "gris-gris", or whatever, it has been a contentious issue since well before colonial officials in pre-World War II Nigeria outlawed, at the local army games, "any team or individual displaying a juju or anything purporting to be a juju or charm". Twenty years later, American academics were devoting research to the "inyanga", or spirit medium, who in Zululand, South Africa, "serves the dual purpose of strengthening his own team by magic ritual and of forestalling the sorcery directed at his team by rival inyangas." Fast forward another decade or so, and the Australian national team reported that their play-off matches for the 1970 World Cup finals against what was then Rhodesia were overshadowed by all sorts of fearful hocus-pocus, apparently applied by Southern African mystics. In the former Zaïre, a human skull was dug up from beneath the centre circle of Kinshasa's 20 May stadium in 1969, encouraging rivals of the club, Tout Puissant Mazembe, to mutter darkly about why TP Mazembe were unbeaten at that

Adolf Hitler The Führer was a fan of opera and film, but football held little allure because, some suggest, it was very difficult for him to control. This view is borne out by the only recorded instance of Hitler watching a game, the Germany v. Norway clash in Berlin in 1936. The VIP box was a fearsome sight, with Goebbels, Goering and Hess accompanying the dictator. After six minutes, Norway took the lead and Goebbels noted: "The Führer is very agitated. I'm almost unable to control myself." Hitler upped and left when the fatherland went 2–0 down.

Franco The Spanish dictator abandoned his home-town club to seek glory as Real Madrid's number one fan. Franco is frequently accused of bribing referees and opposition to ensure Real won, but in fact the only charge that really sticks is of using his influence to ensure the club had the pick of the best players available. Franco was also a pool obsessive, playing twice a week until his death.

Mobutu Though a former sports journalist, the Congolese big man mostly saw football as a way of coralling the masses. So it was that some of the country's vast ground. As for the Zaïre national side, the huge delegation that accompanied the so-called Leopards to their disastrous World Cup finals in West Germany in 1974 included a number of mysterious seers and fetishists.

In the early 1980s, the Nigerian Football Association employed a Dr Godwin Okunzua, a "parapsychologist", to solve the enigma of why Africa's most populous country consistently failed to reach a World Cup finals. This after several visiting teams had encountered wildly dressed men chanting and dancing behind the goals at Lagos's Surulere stadium, and strange objects, made of ribbons, planted in visiting dressing rooms. Ivory Coast's footballers were even in the 1990s being woken in the early hours, not by rowdy opponents, but by their own mystics, one of whom would insist they completed their weird rituals by whispering secrets into the ear of a live pigeon.

Into the new millennium, these mind games were still going on. Cameroon's Samuel Eto'o recalls that immediately ahead of the 2000 African Cup of Nations final against the hosts in Nigeria, a mystic was summoned to "purify both dressing rooms", after a curious incident in the quarter-finals, when a senior Nigerian official had theatrically removed "a fetish" from behind a goal successfully defended by the Senegal goalkeeper. With the object gone, Nigeria won.

These sorts of tales led to CAF's "no-witchdoctors-on-the-pitch" ban on sorcery. Within days of their issuing it, the Cameroon assistant coach and former star Thomas Nkono was arrested, brutally, by Malian police, for allegedly placing mysterious, and powerful, amulets near the goal before a high-profile African Cup of Nations semi-final. Nkono was later banned from Africa's touchlines for a year.

and largely squandered resources found their way into football with a 1968 African Cup of Nations victory the most notable result of this support. Even in victory, the signs were already sadly visible that Mobutu's affection was, let's say *conditional*, when the team were welcomed back to Kinshasa. They were paraded like the nation's property with flowers aplenty but also with their names on large white boards strung around their necks. After a 9–0 drubbing in West Germany at the 1974 World Cup, the national team were disowned – abandoned to find their own way from the airport, before a personally-administered dressing-down at Mobutu's private office the following day. Thereafter (forbidden to play abroad) they were left to eke out a living in Zaire's impoverished provincial cities.

Mussolini Glory-hunting wasn't in the Italian dictator's vocabulary. Mussolini shunned his country's bigger sides to pledge his allegiance to Lazio, then a small, underachieving suburban side from Rome. Though they won nothing during his lifetime, Mussolini's legacy can be seen in the Olympic Stadium he left behind for them, and the other grounds he funded as part of his bid to stage the 1934 World Cup. The well-known story about Il Duce's telegram to national coach

They Do Ron, John, Don ...

Between 1971 and 1988, West Bromwich Albion undertook the most bizarre sequence of managerial names in history – Don, Johnny, Ronnie, Ron, Ronnie, Ron, Johnny, Ron, Ron. Here's how:

Don Howe (1971–75) If there was a world populated with great football coaches/not-so-good football managers, Don Howe would rule the continents. As coach he helped orchestrate Arsenal's march to the 1971 League and Cup double. As manager, he confused everybody with his revolutionary idea: drop the "West Bromwich", keep the "Albion" and thereby ensure the club would be top of the League between May and August. Howe's ultra-defensive football went hand in hand with relegation in 1973 and the failure to bounce back left him waving his P45 like a limp, white flag.

Johnny Giles (1975–77) Having gone down the tried and tested route, Albion's board opted for the great unknown when they appointed the untried Johnny Giles. In doing so they helped to mould one of the first successful player-managers, clinching promotion in his first season. Giles then took the well-trodden path of Albion successes by creating a summer of discontent and resigning, citing board power and a lack of influence in club affairs. But supporter and player power changed his mind: he stayed on and the club finished seventh in 1977 – when he quit again.

Ronnie Allen (1977) Blink and you may have missed him. Allen, a goalscoring hero for Albion and England in the 1950s, barely had time to warm the hot seat vacated by his predecessor before leaving it himself. The lure of sun, sand and silver was too much for Allen, who (presumably inspired by Don Revie) decided to quit the glamour of the Black Country to take charge of the Saudi Arabian national team.

Ron Atkinson (1978–81) Had Graham Taylor accepted Bert Millichip's offer to manage the club, you wouldn't be reading this now. But he didn't and Atkinson said yes. Having guided Albion to the FA Cup semi-final within three months of his arrival, the sun-tanned one made the first of many TV gaffes by allowing the BBC to film him walking out at Wembley on the morning of the clash against

Vittorio Pozzo on the eve of the 1938 World Cup final ("win or die") is probably apocryphal.

Joseph Stalin Stalin, it's fair to say, was not a football fan, but he tolerated the game to keep the crowds happy. In the 1936 gymnasts' parade, he arranged for the

Ipswich. Albion lost 3–1 with Ipswich boss Bobby Robson later claiming no team-talk was needed.

Ronnie Allen (1981–82) For those of you who dozed off for a few weeks of 1978, Allen was back. Bereft of Old Trafford-bound midfielders Remi Moses and Bryan Robson, Allen struggled to recapture Atkinson's exciting era. Semi-final defeats in the FA Cup and League Cup were followed by a flirtation with relegation. Amid reports of dressing room bust-ups, Allen was eventually asked to "go upstairs" to become general manager.

Ron Wylie (1982–84) With Albion chairmen slowly working their way through the Rons, along came Mr Wylie. Or, "that bloke from Coventry" as he was known on the Birmingham Road End. His inglorious and largely anonymous spell at The Hawthorns was punctuated by the retirement of Brendon Batson, as well as poor defeats on the pitch.

Johnny Giles (1984–85) Johnny Giles, Nobby Stiles and Norman Hunter arrived in 1984 as Albion's three musketeers, but were more *Z Cars* than *A-Team*. Giles upset the fans by growing an unnecessary perm, sending hero Cyrille Regis to Coventry City and guiding Albion to an astonishing nine defeats in the opening ten games of 1985–86.

Ron Saunders (1986–87) Replacing caretaker-boss Nobby Stiles and having already more or less relegated Birmingham, Saunders was brought in to trim the club of its high-earners. Sam Fox couldn't have done a better job of stripping. Asset after asset was flung out of The Hawthorns' exit door, with future England cap Steve Bull being sold to Wolves for supposedly not being good enough.

Ron Atkinson (1987–88) The saviour returns. Actually, Jesus was involved, but only as the man who ended up whisking Atkinson away after just fourteen months of a stumbling second reign at The Hawthorns. This time he had to make do with journeymen players and those at the wrong end of their careers to keep Albion in Division Two. The big man lasted just twelve games of the 1988-89 season before Atlético Madrid's eccentric chairman Jesús Gil offered him an exciting (but ultimately short-lived) exit route to Spain, thus bringing Albion's "glorious" seventeen-year era to an end. It was to be followed by the less-thrilling Life of Brian (Talbot).

Spartak Moscow side to display their skills, but if he waved a white handkerchief they were to be removed from his sight. As one biographer recalled: "Stalin did not wave his handkerchief and the footballers interpreted this to mean they found favour. They were mistaken. The Boss was simply allowing these pathetic, puny creatures to amuse themselves. For the last time."

WE BURIED THEM!

Superstition is rubbish? Try tell that to the fans of Buenos Aires Racing Club from the Avellaneda district of the city. As the team were celebrating a World Club Championship victory over Celtic in 1967 supporters of bitter rivals Independiente were busy burying the remains of seven dead cats on Racing stadium premises. The result? Thirty Five years of hurt without a championship victory – a lean run broken only when, after finding six of the cats, the seventh was located after a huge search instigated by a new manager Reinaldo "Mustard" Merlo. The sorry creature's bones were in a moat that had been filled in with concrete. That 2001 victory has not however been repeated. So the rumour mill started again. Was there actually an eighth cat? The story only loses a little gloss if you note that long-suffering Racing *did* win a trophy in the feline-jinxed years, two in fact: the South American Supercup and the Inter-American Supercup in 1988. Too bad that their Avellaneda neighbours Independiente have won both those trophies more times. Still superstitious English fans can rest assured. There can't be many dead cats left under the new Wembley playing surface which since first unveiled has been undergoing almost weekly relaying.

The Gadaffis When Colonel Gadaffi, apparently a big Burnley fan, discussed investing in the Clarets, owner Brendan Flood mused: "The BNP on the council and Gadaffi at the football club. That's an eclectic mix for any town." Gadaffi's family owns a 7.5 per cent stake in Juventus, which is looked after by his football-mad son Al-Saadi. Saadi is widely regarded as one of the best players in his homeland, although owning the club he played for until summer 2003 (Al Ittihad in Tripoli) gave him quite an advantage. Saadi then surprised the football world by signing for Serie A team Perugia, the club vehemently denying that this was a publicity stunt. He managed to make his debut, before being suspended for steroid use. The Italian League had one more all-too-brief opportunity to glimpse his talents, when he played for ten minutes during his next club Udinese's final match of the 2005–06 season. This was obviously enough for Sampdoria to snap him up. Saadi, who is president of the Libyan Football Federation, has also been busy showing interest in buying a stake in several English football clubs, including Crystal Palace, Manchester United (baulked, according to Saadi, because it would be like Libya "buying the Church of England") and Portsmouth.

The Husseins Saddam himself wasn't fussed about football, but eldest son Uday certainly took an interest – much to the disgust of the players. Named head of the Iraqi Football Federation at the age of 21, Uday picked the team, screamed at players down a walkie-talkie and, it's alleged, beat the side savagely when they lost a

World Cup qualifier to Kazakhstan in 1997. The allegations weren't proved when FIFA went to Baghdad to ask questions, although as one anti-Saddam campaigner pointed out: "That's like going to the streets of Chicago in the 1930s and asking the shop owners, 'Do you like Al Capone?'" The players' one consolation was Uday's own lack of talent in the game, although that didn't stop him summoning the country's best footballers to his palace at 2.00am because he fancied a kickaround.

SUPERSTITION

Every team boasts at least one superstitious character – the sort who needs to be last out, first out or wearing the same boots they first put on in 1984. Some players, however, have taken the concept of the pre-match ritual to extremes. Alan Rough, the former Scotland goalkeeper, who carried half a dozen lucky items around with

Scotland v. Northern Ireland, May 1981: Scotland's superstitious goalkeeper Alan Rough chats to the Band's drummer.

him (including an old tennis ball and a keyring), wore a number eleven shirt underneath his own, bounced the ball on the wall of the tunnel on the way out and blew his nose during games for good luck. Quite what all this did for Rough, who was widely regarded as one of the dodgiest of the suspect custodians from north of the border, is unclear. Like Rough, Ronnie Whelan only shaved on a match day, while Gary Lineker refused to shoot in the warm-up. At the height of his managerial power, Don Revie wore the same blue suit on match day for ten years. King of superstition, however, was Argentinian keeper Sergio Goycochea, who relieved himself on the pitch prior to the penalty shoot-out with Italy in the semi-final of the 1990 World Cup; having won, the urination became a pre-penalty ritual. Barry Fry, as Birmingham boss, urinated in all four corners of St Andrews, in an unsuccessful attempt to lift an ancient Gypsy curse.

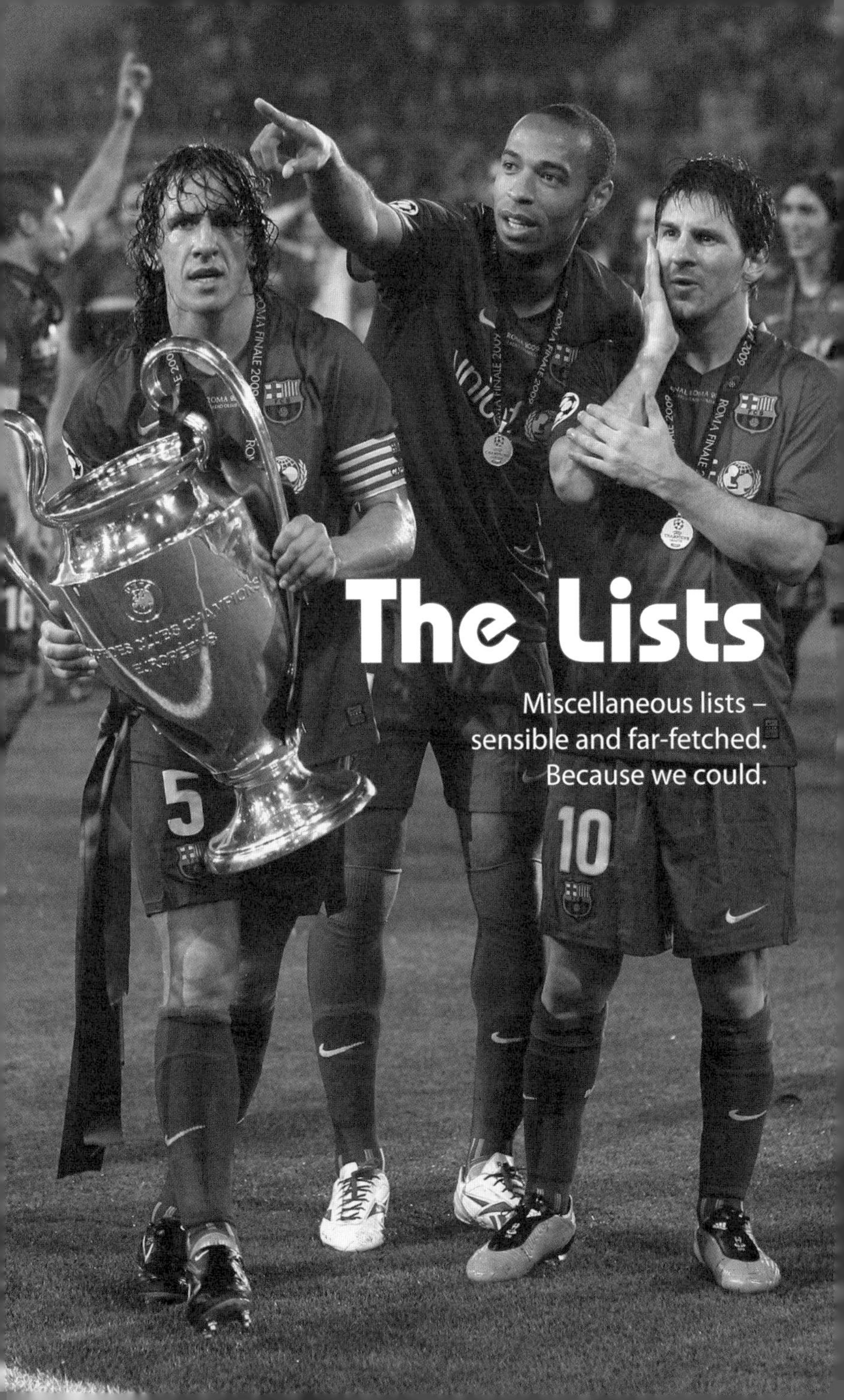

The Lists

Miscellaneous lists –
sensible and far-fetched.
Because we could.

◀◀ Previous page: Barça (l. to r. Carles Puyol, Thierry Henry and Lionel Messi) on their way to the sextuple – European champions after beating Manchester United, May 2009.

The Lists

"They're the second best team in the world and there's no higher praise than that"

Kevin Keegan

The only list that really counts in football is, of course, the league table, that unyielding final report on a team's performance. They say the table doesn't lie (although **Rafa Benitez** is just the latest in a long line of managers to suggest that it maybe does distort the position a tad), but for Minerul Aninoasa of Romania's Divizia C in the early 1980s, the truth was hard to bear: they finished last in their sexteen-team league despite amassing just three points fewer than the second-placed team (see p.269).

There are other reasons, of course, why lists are important:

1. They enable us to forget the team nature of the game by ranking players and coaches on an unashamedly subjective basis. On such a basis, **Dave Bassett** is a finer manager than **Busby**, **Shankly** and **Ferguson** combined.
2. Some lists are finite, but others are endless: such as the list of reasons why **Graham Taylor** should never have been appointed England manager, Scottish World Cup disappointments or inexplicable refereeing decisions that went against your team.
3. You can always think of lists, as football magazines and broadsheet newspaper sports sections know only too well. Already done the World's Greatest Players or Ten Great FA Cup Upsets? No problem – how about Twenty Great Players Who Aren't in the Premiership at the Moment but Were at One Point (playing fewer than Twenty games)?
4. People like lists, and writers like making them. If you space them out nicely like

   this, then you can take up lots of space with very few words, thus exerting less effort in the process. Not for nothing does the word "journalists" end as it does.

TOP TEN TEAMS IN THE HISTORY OF THE ENGLISH FOOTBALL LEAGUE

1.	Liverpool	99 seasons	5157 points
2.	Manchester United	100 seasons	5127 points
3.	Arsenal	99 seasons	4923 points
4.	Wolverhampton Wanderers	104 seasons	4792 points

5.	Aston Villa	104 seasons	4742 points
6.	Preston North End	104 seasons	4743 points
7.	Sunderland	102 seasons	4716 points
8.	Burnley	104 seasons	4681 points
9.	Everton	104 seasons	4669 points
10.	Blackburn Rovers	104 seasons	4647 points

THE FIVE ENGLISH LEAGUE CLUBS WHOSE NAMES START AND END WITH THE SAME LETTER

Aston Villa
Charlton Athletic
Liverpool
Northampton Town
York City

PLAYERS WHO'VE APPEARED FOR MORE THAN ONE NATIONAL TEAM

John Hawley Edwards started the phenomenon in 1876, when he appeared for Wales despite having already played for England against Scotland two years previously. **Stan Mortensen** made his international debut for Wales against England at Wembley in 1943, despite being English; a half-time injury left the visitors short of players, so Mortensen turned out for them in the second half.

Ferenc Puskás and **Alfredo di Stéfano** are the two most famous dual-country players. Both ended up playing for Spain at Franco's insistence, having begun their international careers with Hungary and Argentina respectively before moving to Real Madrid. Franco also persuaded **Ladislao Kubala** to turn out for Spain from 1953-56 after he'd already played for Czechoslovakia and Hungary.

Kubala aside, three other players are known to have performed for three different countries. Both **Yury Nikiforov** and **Akhrik Tsveiba** made their debuts for the CIS before playing for both the Ukraine and Russia during the 1990s. **Josef Bican**, meanwhile, played for Austria and Czechoslovakia but also won one cap for Moravia, a Czech state "liberated" by the Germans in 1939.

The most-capped two-country player to date is **Victor Onopko**, the Real Oviedo defender who won 107 caps for Russia. Onopko also won four caps at the start of his career for the CIS, but after the break-up of the Soviet Union he chose to play for Russia ahead of his native Ukraine.

Political changes have seen a huge rise in the number of dual-country caps: former East Germans to play for the German national team include **Ulf Kirsten** and **Mattias Sammer**; among former Yugoslavians to wear Croatian colours are **Robert Jarni** and **Robert Prosinečki**; and **Lubomir Moravcik** and **Dusan Tittel** switched from Czechoslovakia to Slovakia.

The only player to appear in two World Cup finals for different sides is **Luis Felipe Monti**, a loser with Argentina in 1930 who turned up again four years later as a 33-year-old with Italy, finally gaining himself a winner's medal as they beat Czechoslovakia 2–1.

MOST FREQUENT CHAMPIONS OF THE CHAMPIONSHIP/ DIVISION ONE (FORMERLY DIVISION TWO)

1.	Manchester City	7
2.	Leicester City	6
3.	Sheffield Wednesday/The Wednesday	5
	= Sunderland	5
5.	Small Heath/Birmingham City	4
	= Liverpool	4
	= Derby County	4
	= Middlesbrough	4
9.	Notts County	3
	= Preston North End	3
	= Ipswich Town	3
	= Leeds United	3
	= Bolton Wanderers	3
	= Nottingham Forest	3

THE EIGHT DOUBLE GOLDEN BOOT WINNERS

1.	Eusebio	1967–68	Benfica, 42 goals
		1972–73	Benfica, 40 goals
2.	Gerd Müller	1969–70	Bayern Munich, 38 goals
		1971–72	Bayern Munich, 40 goals
3.	Dudu Georgescu	1974–75	Dinamo Bucuresti, 33 goals
		1976–77	Dinamo Bucuresti, 47 goals

4.	Fernando Gomez	1982–83	Porto, 36 goals
		1984–85	Porto, 39 goals
5.	Ally McCoist	1991–92	Rangers, 34 goals
		1992–93	Rangers, 34 goals
6.	Mario Jardel	1998–99	Porto, 36 goals
		2001–02	Sporting Lisbon, 42 goals
7.	Thierry Henry	2003–04	Arsenal, 30 goals (joint winner with Diego Forlan),
		2004–05	Arsenal, 25 goals
8.	Diego Forlan	2004–05	Villareal, 25 goals
		2008–09	Atlético Madrid, 32 goals

MOST ENGLISH CHAMPIONSHIP WINS

1.	Liverpool	18
	= Manchester United	18
3.	Arsenal	13
4.	Everton	9
5.	Aston Villa	7
6.	Sunderland	6
7.	Newcastle United	4
	= Sheffield Wednesday/The Wednesday	4
	= Chelsea	4
10.	= Huddersfield Town	3
	=Wolverhampton Wanderers	3
	= Leeds United	3
	= Blackburn Rovers	3

BRITISH TEAMS WHO HAVE GONE AN ENTIRE SEASON UNBEATEN

1.	Linfield	1892–93	10 games
		1894–95	6 games
		1903–04	14 games
		1917–18	10 games
		1921–22	10 games
2.	Belfast Celtic	1926–27	22 games
		1928–29	26 games
3.	Shamrock Rovers	1924–25	18 games
		1926–27	18 games

4.	Glentoran	1916–17	10 games
		1980–81	22 games
5.	Preston North End	1888–89	22 games
6.	Celtic	1897–98	18 games
7.	Rangers	1898–99	18 games
8.	Arsenal	2003–04	38 games

BIGGEST TITLE-WINNING MARGINS (ENGLAND)

1.	Manchester United, Premiership, 2000	18 points
	= Bolton Wanderers, Division One, 1997	18 points
	= Sunderland, Division One, 1999	18 points
	= Swindon Town, (old) Division Four, 1986	18 points
5.	Notts County, Division Three, 1998	17 points
6.	York City, (old) Division Four, 1984	16 points
7.	Middlesbrough, (old) Division Two, 1974	15 points
8.	Fulham, Division Two, 1999	14 points
	= Wigan Athletic, Division Two, 2003	14 points
10.	Everton, (old) Division One, 1985	13 points

STARS WHO WERE TURNED DOWN BY CLUBS

Paul Gascoigne was turned down as a fourteen-year-old by Ipswich boss Bobby Robson after the youngster came down to Portman Road for a trial; apparently Robson was wary of taking a chance on the overweight teenager.

David Johnson, who made his name at Nottingham Forest, was released by Manchester United because he was regarded as too short to make the grade.

Kevin Phillips only turned pro at 21, but having moved to Watford from non-league Baldock Town proved his goalscoring prowess and was soon on his way to Sunderland… and an England cap.

Alan Ball was turned down by Blackpool, who told him "you'd make a good little jockey".

Kevin Keegan, who grew up in Armthorpe, was a massive Doncaster Rovers fan but was rejected by the club for being too small – not something that seemed a problem as he took Liverpool (and then Newcastle) by storm, and was twice named European Footballer of the Year.

Roy Keane wrote to English clubs for a trial as a youngster, but didn't write to Manchester United. He didn't think he was good enough and was also led to believe he was too small – a problem he addressed by getting a job lifting beer barrels to increase his strength. He was eighteen when Brian Clough invited him over from Ireland for a trial with Nottingham Forest.

TEAMS WHO TOOK THE TITLE THE YEAR AFTER WINNING PROMOTION TO THE TOP FLIGHT

1.	Liverpool	Promoted 1905	Champions 1906
2.	Everton	Promoted 1931	Champions 1932
3.	Tottenham Hotspur	Promoted 1950	Champions 1951
4.	Ipswich Town	Promoted 1961	Champions 1962
5.	Nottingham Forest	Promoted 1977	Champions 1978

LOWEST LEAGUE POINTS TALLIES (POST-WAR)

1.	Derby County†	Premiership, 2007–08	38 games	11pts
2.	Sunderland†	Premiership, 2005–06	38 games	15pts
3.	Stoke City†	Division One, 1984–85	42 games	17pts
4.	Leeds United	Division One, 1946–47	42 games	18pts
	= Barnsley	Division Two, 1952–53	42 games	18pts
	= Queens Park Rangers	Division One, 1968–69	42 games	18pts
7.	Sunderland†	Premiership, 2002–03	38 games	19pts
	= Portsmouth‡	Premiership, 2009-10	42 games	19pts
	= Crystal Palace	Division One, 1980–81	42 games	19pts
	= Watford	Division Two, 1971–72	42 games	19pts
	= Workington	Division Four, 1976–77	46 games	19pts
12.	Doncaster Rovers†	Division Three, 1997–98	46 games	20pts
	= Chelsea	Division One, 1978–79	42 games	20pts

† Three points for a win ‡ Nine points deducted for going into administration

PLAYERS WHO'VE PLAYED FOR ENGLAND WHILE WITH OVERSEAS CLUBS

David Beckham	Real Madrid, LA Galaxy, AC Milan
Luther Blissett	AC Milan
Gordon Cowans	Bari
Laurie Cunningham	Real Madrid
Trevor Francis	Sampdoria
Paul Gascoigne	Lazio
Owen Hargreaves	Bayern Munich
Mark Hateley	AC Milan and Monaco
Gerry Hitchens	Inter Milan
Glenn Hoddle	Monaco

Paul Ince	Inter Milan
Kevin Keegan	Hamburg
Gary Lineker	Barcelona
Steve McManaman	Real Madrid
Michael Owen	Real Madrid
David Platt	Bari, Juventus and Sampdoria
Trevor Steven	Marseille
Chris Waddle	Marseille
Des Walker	Sampdoria
Dave Watson	Werder Bremen
Ray Wilkins	AC Milan
Tony Woodcock	Cologne

FOOTBALLERS WHO'VE BEEN TO JAIL

George Best – drink-driving, assaulting a policeman and jumping bail (1982)
Jamie Lawrence (Walsall) – armed robbery (1988)
Jan Molby – reckless driving (1988)
Tony Adams – drink-driving (1990)
Peter Storey – attempting to import pornography (1990)
Terry Fenwick – drink-driving (1991)
Mickey Thomas – passing forged bank notes (1993)
Duncan Ferguson – head-butting Raith Rovers' John McStay (1995)
Simon Garner – contempt of court during divorce proceedings (1996)
Stig Tofting – assault (2002)
Lee Hughes – causing death by dangerous driving (2005)

Diego Maradona has yet to serve the two-year sentence he received for shooting journalists with an air-powered pellet rifle in 1998.

TEAMS RELEGATED AFTER MAKING IT TO BOTH THE LEAGUE AND FA CUP FINALS

1.	Chelsea	1915†
2.	Manchester City	1926
3.	Leicester City	1969
4.	Brighton & Hove Albion	1983
5.	Middlesbrough	1997

† Were re-elected to the top division after the war without having to play in the Second Division

TOP TEN FA CUP-WINNING TEAMS

1.	Manchester United	11
2.	Arsenal	10
3.	Tottenham Hotspur	8
4.	Aston Villa	7
	= Liverpool	7
6.	Blackburn Rovers	6
	= Newcastle United	6
	= Chelsea	6
9.	The Wanderers	5
	= West Bromwich Albion	5
	= Everton	5

BOXING DAY GOAL BONANZA – THE EXTRAORDINARY FINAL SCORES IN THE FIRST DIVISION ON 26 DECEMBER 1963

Blackpool	1–5	Chelsea
Burnley	6–1	Manchester United
Fulham	10–1	Ipswich Town
Leicester City	2–0	Everton
Liverpool	6–1	Stoke City
Nottingham Forest	3–3	Sheffield United
WBA	4–4	Tottenham Hotspur
Sheffield Wednesday	3–0	Bolton Wanderers
Wolves	3–3	Aston Villa
West Ham United	2–8	Blackburn Rovers

THE GOLDEN BOOT WINNERS WHO SCORED MORE THAN FORTY GOALS

1.	Dudu Georgescu	Dinamo Bucuresti (Romania)	47 goals	1976–77
2.	Hector Yazalde	Sporting Lisbon (Portugal)	46 goals	1973–74
3.	Josip Skoblar	Marseille (France)	44 goals	1970–71
	= Rodion Camataru	Dinamo Bucuresti (Romania)	44 goals	1986–87
5.	Dorin Mateut	Dinamo Bucuresti (Romania)	43 goals	1988–89
	= David Taylor	Porthmadog FC (Wales)	43 goals	1993–94
7.	Mario Jardel	Sporting Lisbon (Portugal)	42 goals	2001–02
	= Eusebio	Benfica (Portugal)	42 goals	1967–68
9.	Hans Krankl	Rapid Vienna (Austria)	41 goals	1977–78

CLUBS NAMED AFTER PEOPLE

Newell's Old Boys Much-travelled Professor Don Isaac Newell, born in Kent, made such an impression on his ex-pupils that they decided to name the Argentinian town of Rosario's football club after him in 1903. Diego Maradona would later pull on the Newell's shirt.

Vasco da Gama This Rio-based club, founded in 1898, were named after the Portuguese explorer who discovered the sea route from Europe to the East Indies. The city's Portuguese community still makes up the club's core support.

Deportivo Colo Colo Based in Santiago, Chile's most successful side are named after the Mapuche native Indian chief, Colo Colo, who fought against European influence and the Chilean army for the freedom of his people.

Willem II Founded in 1896, Tilberg's "royal" club adopted the name of the Netherlands' former ruler, who reigned from 1840–49 and had his military headquarters in the city.

FC Prince Louis Burundi's 1981 League champions' moniker is a tribute to their former Tutsi prince and prime minister Louis Rwagasore, who made major political reforms before being assassinated in 1961 – an act remembered annually on "Murder of the Hero Day".

Velez Sarsfield Sarsfield (1801–75) was the Argentinian patriot, lawyer, author and historian who helped write the constitution for the State of Buenos Aires and the Argentine Code of Commerce. The Buenos Aires team named in his honour are one of the most successful in South America.

ENGLAND'S PENALTY SHOOT-OUT HISTORY

England v. West Germany	1990	World Cup finals	Lost 4–3
England v. Spain	1996	European Championships finals	Won 4–2
England v. Germany	1996	European Championships finals	Lost 6–5
England v. Belgium	1998	International Tournament	Lost 4–3
England v. Argentina	1998	World Cup finals	Lost 4–3
England v. Portugal	2004	European Championship finals	Lost 6–5
England v. Portugal	2006	World Cup finals	Lost 3–1

ENGLAND'S BIGGEST VICTORIES

1.	England v. Ireland	(away)	1882	13–0
2.	England v. Ireland	(home)	1899	13–2
3.	England v. Austria	(away)	1908	11–1
4.	England v. Portugal	(away)	1947	10–0
	England v. USA	(away)	1964	10–0

6.	England v. Ireland	(home)	1895	9–0
	England v. Luxembourg	(away)	1960	9–0
	England v. Luxembourg	(home)	1982	9–0
9.	England v. Ireland	(away)	1890	9–1
	England v. Wales	(away)	1896	9–1
	England v. Belgium	(away)	1927	9–1

FOOTBALLERS WITH STAYING POWER

Stanley Matthews	Oldest player in English top flight at 50 years 3 months
Roger Milla	Oldest player in World Cup history at 42
Jim Ryan	Oldest player to play for a senior professional club at 52
Dino Zoff	Oldest player to win the World Cup at 40
Leslie Compton	Oldest player to make his debut for England at 38
John Burridge	Oldest Premiership player at 43 years 5 months

TEN FORMER PROFESSIONALS WHOSE NAMES ALONE SHOULD HAVE MADE THEM FAMOUS

Frank Shufflebottom Ipswich, Nottingham Forest, Bradford
Roy Proverbs Coventry City, Gillingham
Tunji Banjo Leyton Orient
Patrick Quartermain Oxford United
Thomas Vansittart Crystal Palace, Wrexham
Odysseus (Seth) Vafiadis QPR, Millwall
Richard (Flip) Le Flem Nottingham Forest, Wolves, Middlesbrough, Leyton Orient
Anthony Geidmintis Workington, Watford, Northampton, Halifax
Rudolph Kaiser Coventry City
David Hockaday Blackpool, Swindon, Hull, Stoke, Shrewsbury

SIX PLAYERS WHO'VE SCORED FOR FIVE DIFFERENT PREMIERSHIP CLUBS

Stan Collymore Nottingham Forest, Liverpool, Aston Villa, Leicester, Bradford
Ashley Ward Norwich, Derby, Barnsley, Blackburn, Bradford
Mark Hughes Manchester United, Chelsea, Southampton, Everton, Blackburn
Benito Carbone Sheffield Wednesday, Aston Villa, Bradford, Derby, Middlesbrough
Nick Barmby Tottenham, Middlesbrough, Liverpool, Everton, Leeds
Teddy Sheringham Nottingham Forest, Tottenham Hotspur, Manchester United, West Ham, Portsmouth

TOP FREAK INJURIES SUSTAINED BY FOOTBALLERS

1. **Santiago Canizares, Valencia** The Spanish Number One was ruled out of the 2002 World Cup after a shard of glass from a broken aftershave bottle severed a tendon in his foot.
2. **Alan Mullery, Tottenham** Was ruled out of England's 1964 tour of South Africa after cricking his back while shaving.
3. **Dave Beasant, Southampton** Damaged his foot trying to trap a bottle of salad cream that fell from a cupboard and was out for a couple of months.
4. **Richard Wright, Everton** On the sick list for a couple of months after falling out of the loft at his Suffolk home and damaging his shoulder, ruining his 2003 summer holidays.
5. **Celestine Babayaro, Chelsea** Launched into a somersault to celebrate someone else's goal in a pre-season match at Stevenage, and couldn't make his debut for the Blues until October.
6. **Alan McLoughlin, Portsmouth** Picked up his baby daughter and tore tendons in his arm; he was out for a month.
7. **Michael Stensgaard, Liverpool** Out for six months with a dislocated shoulder sustained trying to stop an ironing board from falling over.
8. **Alex Stepney, Manchester United** Dislocated his jaw shouting at his defence.
9. **Darren Barnard, Barnsley** Slipped on a puddle left by a puppy and was sidelined for several months with knee ligament damage.
10. **Kevin Keegan, Liverpool** Got a toe stuck in a bath tap; the injury ruled him out of several games.
11. **Rio Ferdinand, Leeds** Watching TV with his feet up on a coffee table left him with a damaged tendon.
12. **Steve Morrow, Arsenal** One of the most bizarre ends to a big match: Arsenal matchwinner Morrow left the Wembley pitch with a dislocated shoulder after being thrown backwards over skipper Tony Adams' shoulders during the over-exuberant celebrations that followed the 1993 League Cup final.
13. **Svein Grondalen, Norway** Had to withdraw from an international match after colliding with a moose while out jogging.
14. **Allan Nielsen, Tottenham** Missed several matches after his daughter prodded him in the eye.
15. **Charlie George, Southampton** Cut off his finger in a freak lawnmower accident.
16. **Kirk Broadfoot, Rangers** Sustained a burnt face when an egg he was trying to cook in a microwave exploded.
17. **Darius Vassell, Aston Villa** Had to have his toenail removed after a DIY treatment on a blood blister with an electric drill became infected.

FIVE SCOTTISH CLUBS BEGINNING AND ENDING WITH THE SAME LETTER

Celtic
Dundee United
East Fife
East Stirlingshire
Kilmarnock

PLAYERS WHO WENT INTO POLITICS

Henry McLeish On schoolboy forms at Leeds United, then played 108 times for East Fife. His political career peaked when he was made Scotland's (second) first minister but resigned after just 378 days.

Lavrenty Beria Left-back for a club in Georgia and head of KGB under Stalin.

Pelé The world's best ever player became the Brazilian sports minister.

Zico Another great Brazilian who had a brief foray into politics after retiring (he headed the Brazilian bid to host the 2006 World Cup, which was abandoned three days before the vote).

Biren Nongthombam Played for Manipur, in eastern India, in the National Football Championship and took part in club tournaments in the late 1970s and early 1980s for the BSF, before becoming a member of the Manipur Legislative Assembly representing the Democratic People's Party.

Jamal Nasir The former Malaysian footballer once made it as a Pahang assemblyman.

Willi Lemke (coach) Coached Werder Bremen to the 1993 Bundesliga championship and is now a Social Democrat minister in the city-state government of Bremen.

H'Angus the Monkey (mascot) Successfully elected mayor of Hartlepool … then took off his club mascot monkey suit and tried to be a serious politician.

George Weah Stood for election as president of Liberia in 2005.

Roman Pavyluchenko Won a seat on the Russian regional council of Stavropol in 2008 for Putin's United Russian Party.

ENGLAND'S MOST-CAPPED PLAYERS

1.	Peter Shilton	125
2.	David Beckham	115
3.	Bobby Moore	108
4.	Bobby Charlton	105

5.	Billy Wright	104
6.	Bryan Robson	90
7.	Michael Owen	89
8.	Kenny Sansom	86
9.	Gary Neville	85
10.	Ray Wilkins	84

NOT VERY LOCAL "LOCAL" DERBIES

1.	Perth Glory v. Adelaide City Force	Australia	1700 miles (2700km)
2.	Baltika Kaliningrad v. Zenit	Russia	600 miles (964km)
3.	Bodo Glimt v. Tromso	Norway	254 miles (410km)
4.	Marseille v. Bastia ("Med ports derby")	France	205 miles (331km)
5.	Bordeaux v. Toulouse ("Southwest derby")	France	132 miles (212km)
6.	Marseille v. Nice ("Med derby")	France	97 miles (156km)

FOOTBALLERS UNDER ASSUMED NAMES

Kaká Ricardo Izecson dos Santos Leite
Pelé Edson Arantes do Nascimento†
Pirri Jose Martinez Sanchez
Zico Artur Antunes Coimbra
Didi Waldyr Pereira
Garrincha Manoel Francisco dos Santos
Jairzhino Jair Ventura Filho
Zizinho Thomaz Soares da Silva
Ronaldinho Ronaldo de Assis Moreira
A.H. Chequer Morton Peto Betts (scored only goal in the first FA Cup final, 1872)
Juninho Oswaldo Giroldo Junior
Hamilton Colin Veitch, Newcastle United 1899–1915††

† Pelé explains that at school, a boy called him Pelé for no apparent reason; he started a fight with him and received two days' suspension, but soon even his parents were using the new moniker

†† As a trainee schoolteacher, he played under an assumed name due to the prejudice against professionalism at the time

THE MOST SUCCESSFUL MANAGERS TO GET THE BOOT

Vicente Del Bosque, Real Madrid Delivered Real Madrid's 29th League title and was rewarded with a sharp exit from the Bernabeu in 2003 when his contract was not renewed, presumably for failing to deliver a tenth European Cup.

Fabio Capello, Real Madrid Spotted a pattern emerging yet? Del Bosque should have seen it coming given Real's disposal of Capello, now the England boss, despite him winning them La Liga. It was a decision that led to some serious backtracking by Real Madrid who, having dismissed Guus Hiddink, tried to woo Capello back – unsuccessfully.

Bobby Robson, Barcelona In ten months in charge of the Catalan giants, Bobby Robson reeled in the Cup Winners' Cup, the Super Cup and the Spanish Cup. With all those distractions surely he could be forgiven for only steering Barça to second in La Liga? Well, no he couldn't.

Micky Adams, Fulham Two words: Kevin Keegan. Impatient new Fulham owner Mohammed al Fayed was after a big-name gaffer. Keegan was his chosen one and Micky Adams never stood a chance, despite having saved the Cottagers from dropping into the Conference and subsequently building a side that played its way into Division Two.

Ruud Gullit, Chelsea Ruud Gullit was brought in to steady the Chelsea ship after the departure of Glenn Hoddle to the England hot seat, and the Dutch legend took the Blues to the quarter-finals of the Cup Winners' Cup and second in the table (and picked up the FA Cup along the way). He forgot to keep in with Ken Bates though, and in February 1998 was on his way.

Mike Newell, Hartlepool United In six months at the Hartlepool helm, Mike Newell got the club promoted automatically to Division Two. But chairman Ken Hodcroft had wanted the 2002–03 Third Division title too; a late-season slump saw Rushden & Diamonds pip 'Pool to top slot and Newell's hopes of a new contract evaporated.

Ron Atkinson, Sheffield Wednesday In November 1997 Sheffield Wednesday appealed to Big Ron to get them out of trouble. Ron duly obliged but come the following May, with Premiership status secured, he was out on his ear.

THE WORST TEAM EVER?

The 2000–01 results for Burton Brewers of the West Midland Regional Women's Football League, Division One North (fifth level):

Burton Brewers	0–6	Bescot
Burton Brewers	0–17	Shrewsbury Town Youth
Burton Brewers	0–18	Wolverhampton United
Burton Brewers	2–13	Crewe Vagrants

Burton Brewers	0–21	Darlaston
Burton Brewers	0–27	North Staffs
Burton Brewers	0–23	Willenhall Town
Crewe Vagrants	22–0	**Burton Brewers**
Burton Brewers	1–14	City of Stoke
Burton Brewers	0–16	Wem Raiders
Burton Brewers	0–57	Willenhall Town†

† Possibly a world record

HARD TO BELIEVE CELEBRITY FANS

"When I asked him, what does he know about football he said, 'absolutely nothing, but I love Exeter City'"

Uri Geller sums up the late Michael Jackson's acquaintance with English football after making him an honorary director of the Grecians following a visit to St James Park in 2002

Barack Obama West Ham United (family connections)
Hillary & Bill Clinton, Brad Pitt Manchester United
Justin Timberlake Manchester United – snapped wearing a United beanie hat when invited to Old Trafford by his big mate and then United player, Alan Smith
Usain Bolt Manchester United, Real Madrid, any team Cristiano Ronaldo plays for
David Cameron Aston Villa (his uncle was former Villa chairman, Sir William Dugdale)
Tom Hanks Aston Villa (he thinks the name is romantic)
Prince William Aston Villa
Sylvester Stallone Everton (on the basis that he appeared on the pitch at Goodison wearing an Everton scarf when he had a film to promote)

BROTHERS WHO HAVE PLAYED FOR ENGLAND

1. Arthur, Edward and Ernest Bambridge (the only instance of three brothers)
2. Jack and Bobby Charlton
3. John and William Clegg
4. Bertie and Reginald Corbett
5. Arthur and Henry Cursham
6. Alfred and Charles Dobson
7. Frank and Frederick Forman
8. Frederick and John Hargreaves
9. Charles and George Heron
10. Alfred and Edward Lyttelton
11. Gary and Philip Neville

12. Frank and Reginald Osbourne
13. Charles and Thomas Perry
14. Herbert and William Rawson
15. Alfred and Charles Shelton
16. John and Septimus Smith
17. Clement and George Stephenson
18. Arthur and Robert Topham
19. Arthur and Percy Walters
20. Charles and Geoffrey Wilson

FOOTBALL CLUBS' ORIGINAL NAMES

Dial Square	Arsenal
Small Heath Alliance	Birmingham
South Shore	Blackpool
Christ Church FC	Bolton
Boscombe St John's	Bournemouth
Black Arabs	Bristol Rovers
Abbey United	Cambridge United
Riverside	Cardiff City
Shaddongate United	Carlisle United
Singers FC	Coventry City
St Domingo FC	Everton
New Brompton	Gillingham
Glyn Cricket & Football Club	Leyton Orient
Ardwick FC	Manchester City
Newton Heath	Manchester United
Stanley	Newcastle United
Pine Villa	Oldham Athletic
Headington	Oxford United
St Jude's	Queens Park Rangers
Heaton Norris Rovers	Stockport County
Belmont AFC	Tranmere Rovers
Thames Iron Works	West Ham United
St Luke's	Wolverhampton Wanderers

THE MOST RADICAL CHANGES TO CLUB COLOURS

Leeds United Changed from blue and gold to all-white by Don Revie when he took over as manager at Elland Road in 1961, to make the team seem as slick and modern as the all-white Real Madrid.

Albion Rovers Changed from blue and white to the current yellow and red in 1961.

Newton Heath Changed colours from green and gold to white shirts and blue shorts in 1895, then to red shirts and white shorts in 1901-02 (the year they became Manchester United).

Burnley Played in green until 1911 when they were persuaded that it was unlucky.

Newcastle United Originally played in red-and-white stripes – the same as Sunderland; the switch to black and white came in 1904.

Everton Early colours included black with a red sash, and salmon pink.

Gillingham Changed their home shirts (which were originally black-and-white stripes) to blue to white.

Juventus Played in pink shirts for the first six years before adopting the black and white stripes of Notts County.

Crystal Palace Switched to red and blue from claret and blue (a result of initial kits being borrowed from Aston Villa) for the 1973 season, a change instigated by then-manager Malcolm Allison.

Arbroath Now playing in predominantly maroon shirts and white shorts, Arbroath's original shirts were white with "black and spider stripes".

Tottenham The White Hart Lane club's original colours were navy blue.

THE SEVENTEEN LAST NAMES OF SCOTTISH LEAGUE CLUBS

Academical
Albion
Athletic
City
County
Fife
Johnstone
Midlothian
Mirren
Morton
Park
Rangers
Rovers
South
Stirlingshire
Thistle
United

THE 21 LAST NAMES OF ENGLISH LEAGUE CLUBS

Albion
Alexandra
Argyle
Athletic
City
County
Diamonds
End
Forest
Harriers
Hotspur
Orient
Palace
Rangers
Rovers
Town
United
Vale
Villa
Wanderers
Wednesday

TEN MOST UNLIKELY ENGLAND INTERNATIONALS

Chris Powell	Charlton Athletic
Mel Sterland	Leeds United
Paul Walsh	Luton Town
Steve Guppy	Leicester City
Mike Phelan	Manchester United
Michael Ricketts	Bolton
Eric Gates	Ipswich Town
Paul Stewart	Tottenham Hotspur
Seth Johnson	Derby County
Francis Jeffers	Arsenal

THE ALTERNATIVE MARADONAS

Gheorge Hagi	Romania	Maradona of the Carpathians
Aḥmed Al Kass	Egypt	Maradona of the Nile
Saeed Owairan	Saudi Arabia	Maradona of the Desert
Emre Belozogle	Turkey	Maradona of the Bosphorus
Edvin Murati	Albania	Maradona of the Balkans
Georgi Kinkladze	Georgia	Maradona of the Caucasus
Gianfranco Zola	Italy	The Italian Maradona
Paul Gascoigne	England	The English Maradona
Joe Cole	England	The Maradona of the East End

TEN MOST PROLIFIC GOALSCORERS IN INTERNATIONAL FOOTBALL

Ali Daei	Iran	1993–2006	109
Ferenc Puskás	Hungary/Spain	1945–56	84
Pelé	Brazil	1957–71	77
Bashar Abdullah	Kuwait	1996–2007	75
Sandor Kocsis	Hungary	1948–56	75
Hossam Hassan	Egypt	1985–2006	69
Stern John	Trinidad and Tobago	1995–	69
Gerd Müller	West Germany	1966–74	68
Majed Abdullah	Saudi Arabia	1977–93	67
Kiatisuk Senamuang	Thailand	1993–2007	65

PLAYERS WHO'VE SCORED IN THE WORLD CUP FINAL – AND WON

1930	Dorado, Cea, Iriarte, Castro (Uruguay)
1934	Orsi, Schiavio (Italy)
1938	Colaussi 2, Piola 2 (Italy)
1950	Schiaffino, Ghiggia (Uruguay)
1954	Morlock, Rahn 2 (West Germany)
1958	Vavá 2, Pelé 2, Zagalo (Brazil)
1962	Amarildo, Zito, Vavá (Brazil)
1966	Hurst 3, Peters (England)
1970	Pelé, Gerson, Jairzinho, Carlos Alberto (Brazil)
1974	Breitner, Müller (West Germany)
1978	Kempes 2, Bertoni (Argentina)
1982	Rossi, Tardelli, Altobelli (Italy)
1986	Brown, Valdano, Burruchaga (Argentina)
1990	Brehme (West Germany)
1998	Zidane 2, Petit (France)
2002	Ronaldo (Brazil)
2006	Materazzi (Italy)

FIVE TEAMS WHO MANAGED TO DEFEND THE DOUBLE AT LEAST FOUR TIMES IN A ROW

Dinamo Tbilisi (Georgia)	1992–97	6
Djoliba AC (Mali)	1973–76, 1979	5†
Dinamo Tirane (Albania)	1950–53	4
Etoile Filante (Burkina Faso)	1990–93	4
Muharraq (Bahrain)	1961–64	4

† There was no League competition in Mali in 1977 and 1978.

Nissan in Japan, and South China in Hong Kong are the only clubs in the world to defend their domestic trebles. South China were the first side in world football to manage this feat in 1988 and Nissan followed suit in 1990.

TEN PLAYERS LABELLED "THE NEW PELÉ"

Jason Euell (or so claimed Sam Hammam)
Abedi Pele
Ronaldinho
Michael Owen
Ronaldo
Nii Lamptey
Shaun Wright-Phillips
Wayne Rooney
Eusebio
Nicolas Anelka

CLUBS WHO HAVE GONE BEYOND TREBLES

Achievement	Club	Country	Season	Honours won
Sextuple	Linfield	N. Ireland	1921–22	League Champions, Irish Cup, County Antrim Shield, Intermediate Cup, New Charity Cup, Gold Cup
Sextuple	Valletta	Malta	2000–01	League Champions, Rothmans Trophy, Super Cup, Lowenbrau Cup, Air Malta Centenary Cup, Super 5 Cup
Sextuple	Barcelona	Spain	2008–09	Primera Liga, UEFA Champions League, UEFA Super Cup, Copa Del Rey, FIFA Club World Cup Championship
Quintuple	Celtic	Scotland	1966–67	League Champions, European Cup, Scottish Cup, Scottish League Cup, Glasgow Cup
Quintuple	Ajax	Holland	1971–72	League Champions, European Cup, Dutch Cup, Intercontinental Cup, European Super Cup
Quintuple	Liverpool	England	2000–01	FA Cup, League Cup, UEFA Cup, UEFA Super Cup, FA Community Shield

FOURTEEN SCANDINAVIAN TEAMS WHO WERE RELEGATED THE SEASON AFTER WINNING THE LEAGUE

B 71	Faroe Islands	1989 – champions; 1990 – relegated
Djurgårdens	Sweden	1959 – champions; 1960 – relegated
Fram	Norway	1950 – champions; 1951 – relegated

Freidrig	Norway	1948 – champions; 1949 – relegated
GAIS	Sweden	1954 – champions; 1955 – relegated
Haka Valkeakoski	Finland	1995 – champions; 1996 – relegated
Helsingborgs	Sweden	1934 – champions; 1935 – relegated
Herfølge BK	Denmark	2000 – champions; 2001 – relegated
Hvidovre	Denmark	1973 – champions; 1974 – relegated
IFK Goteborg	Sweden	1969 – champions; 1970 – relegated
Ilves-Kissat	Finland	1950 – champions; 1951 – relegated
KB	Denmark	1950 – champions; 1951 – relegated
SK Brann	Norway	1963 – champions; 1964 – relegated
TPV	Finland	1994 – champions; 1995 – relegated

THE TIGHTEST-EVER LEAGUE

Romania 1983–84, Divizia C, Seria a VIII-a

		P	W	D	L	F–A	Pts	
1.	Muresul Deva	30	16	6	8	53–33	38	Promoted to Div. B
2.	UMT Timisoara	30	14	3	13	57–37	31	
3.	Mecanica Orastie	30	15	1	14	49–53	31	
4.	Minerul Paroseni	30	13	5	12	41–46	31	
5.	Minerul Moldova-Noua	30	14	2	14	41–39	30	
6.	Minerul Stiinta Vulcan	30	13	4	13	38–47	30	
7.	Metalul Bocsa	30	13	3	14	40–32	29	
8.	Dacia Orastie	30	11	7	12	58–50	29	
9.	Minerul Certej	30	13	3	14	48–47	29	
10.	Metalul Otelu-Rosu	30	14	1	15	38–40	29	
11.	Minerul Anina	30	13	3	14	46–48	29	
12.	Victoria Calan	30	13	3	14	35–37	29	
13.	Constructorul Timisoara	30	13	3	14	57–62	29	
14.	Minerul Oravita	30	13	3	14	39–45	29	
15.	Minerul Ghelar	30	12	5	13	35–52	29	Relegated
16.	Minerul Aninoasa	30	11	6	13	32–39	28	Relegated

This remarkable league table speaks for itself but it's worth noting that nine out of sixteen teams in this division ended the season level on points. This is the only known case of an end-of-season table where two points separate the runners-up from the team which finished second-from-bottom. Fortunately, Divizia C didn't get much TV coverage – otherwise, the commentators could have come to grief as eight of the teams' names begin with "Minerul" and two begin with "Metalul".

SK BRANN'S CRAZY YO-YO 1980S

1979	Relegated to second division
1980	Promoted to first division
1981	Relegated to second division
1982	Promoted to first division
1983	Relegated to second division
1984	Promoted to first division
1985	Relegated to second division
1986	Promoted to first division

If you thought Leicester City were forever bouncing between the top divisions, you haven't been to Bergen. Norway's second biggest city is home to SK Brann, who hold the unusual record of having spent more seasons than any other club being relegated and promoted between two leagues.